VOTESCAM

THE
STEALING
OF
AMERICA

JAMES M. COLLIER
KENNETH F. COLLIER

Votescam: The Stealing Of America

ISBN: 0-9634163-0-8

Library of Congress Catalogue Number 93-093814
Cover Design & Illustration: Steve Gordon

**To our daughters
Amy, Unity and Victoria**

CONTENTS

BOOK ONE
1970-1989

*"Who shall stand guard
to the guards themselves?"*

—Juvenal

THE PREMISE

Votescam asserts the unthinkable.

It is a strange and frightening true detective story. It contains fact, film, documents and visions seldom seen by the public. It is a troubling look at the corruption of the American vote that most Americans cannot bear to believe is even partly true.

The authors assert, and back it up with daring reporting, that your vote and mine may now be a meaningless bit of energy directed by pre-programmed computers — which can be fixed to select certain pre-ordained candidates and leave no footprints or paper trail.

In short, computers are covertly stealing your vote.

• For almost three decades the American vote has been subject to government-sponsored electronic theft.

• The vote has been stolen from you by a cartel of federal "national security" bureaucrats, who include higher-ups in the Central Intelligence Agency, political party leaders, Congressmen, co-opted journalists — and the owners and managers of the major Establishment news media, who have decided in concert that how America's votes are counted, by whom they are counted and how the results are verified and delivered to the public is, as one of them put it, *"Not a proper area of inquiry."*

• By means of an unofficial private corporation named News Election Service (NES), the Establishment press has actual physical control of the counting and dissemination of the vote, and it refuses to let the public know how it is done.

This book also contends that the theft of your vote or *Votescam*, is part of a supposedly patriotic "collaboration" between federal officials and the news media that began shortly after the assassination of John F. Kennedy in 1963, when the "responsible" American press was persuaded by American intelligence services to hide from the American people the actual implications of the Kennedy murder.

My brothers, Jim and Ken Collier, report this story as if the "hounds of hell," as Ken used to put it, were snapping at their journalistic heels.

I, too, am a journalist and editor by profession, and a skeptic by training. Yet, as hard as I have tried *not* to, I now believe they were actually holding the tail of an elephantine conspiracy that they uncovered, inch by heart-rending inch.

After reading *Votescam*, the impatient

citizen may well ask: "Why, if there is truth in the charges, are there no indictments?"

That question is one of many provoked by *Votescam's* reporting, and if Americans actually value their vote then there will be indictments based on this book's data and documentation.

My brothers peeked behind Oz's curtain and into a voting booth where people of power had secret hold of all the levers — as well as all the keys on the computer keyboard.

Yes, that's one hell of a conspiracy, and it — as Jim and Ken uncorked it — doesn't stop there. You may be shocked, annoyed, angry, astounded or alarmed to find out where and how deep my brothers feel it penetrates.

Votescam is one of the weirdest trips 1990s Americans may take. My hope is that you will suspend disbelief for a while and read it with an open mind. If it raises questions you will demand answers.

Answers to *"improper inquiries"* is what this book is about. It's what excellent journalism, in its best days, is also about.

Barnard L. Collier
New York City, 1992

1

ELECTRONIC HOODWINK

*"We can now speak the most majestic
words a democracy can offer:
'The people have spoken'…"*

First words spoken by
President-elect, George Bush,
November 8, 1988 victory speech
in Houston, Texas, 11:30 PM EST.

*"Once, during the time when days were
darker, I made a promise. Thanks,
New Hampshire!"*

Same speech, final words.

It was not "the People" of the United States of
America who did "the speaking" on that election
day, although most of them believed it was, and
still believe so.

In fact, the People did not speak at all, and
George Bush may have known it or, at least,
strongly suspected it.

The voices most of us really heard that day were the voices of computers – strong, loud, authoritative, unquestioned in their electronic finality. The computers counted more than 55 million American votes in 1988 – more than enough to swing election after election across the nation. In that election, a difference of just 535,000 or so votes would have put Dukakis into the White House.

The computers that spoke in November 1988 held in their inner workings small boxes that contained secret codes that only the sellers of the computers could read. The programs, or "source codes," were regarded as "trade secrets." The sellers of the vote-counting software zealously guarded their programs from the public, from election officials, from everyone – on the dubious grounds that competitors could steal their ideas if the source codes were open to inspection.

You may ask: What "ideas" does it require to count something as simple as ballots?

Can the "ideas" be much more complex than, let's say, a supermarket computerized cash register or an automatic bank teller machine?

The computer voting machines do not have to do anything complicated at all; they simply must be able to register votes for the correct candidate or party or proposal, tabulate them, count them up, and deliver arithmetically correct additions. People with no formal training, even children, used to do it all the time.

So why can't the public know what those secret source codes instruct the computers to do? It only makes common sense that every gear, every mechanism, every nook and cranny of every part of the voting process ought to be in the sunlight, wide open to public view.

How else can the public be reasonably assured that they are participating in an unrigged election where their vote actually means something?

Yet one of the most mysterious, low-profile, covert, shadowy, questionable mechanisms of American democracy is the American vote count.

There is so profound a public despair about keeping the vote system honest that a man with immaculate academic credentials can sound the alarm on Dan Rather's CBS Evening News – charging that America's elections are being compromised by computer felons – and still get only three calls about it.

Dr. Howard Strauss, a Princeton computer sciences professor and a member of a tiny nationwide group of worried citizens who call themselves "Election Watch," says:

"The presidential election of 1992, without too much difficulty and with little chance of the felons getting caught, could be stolen by computers for one candidate or another. The candidate who can win by computer has worked far enough ahead to rig the election by getting his 'consultants' to write the software that

runs thousands of vote-counting computers from coast to coast. There are so many computers that use the same software now that a presidential election can be tampered with – in fact, may already be tampered with. Because of the trade secrecy, nobody can be the wiser."

Computers in voting machines are effectively immune from checking and rechecking. If they are fixed, you cannot know it, and you cannot be at all sure of an honest tally.

In the 1988 Republican primary in New Hampshire, there was no panel of computer experts who worked for the people and thoroughly examined the source codes before and after the voting. It is likely that a notoriously riggable collection of "Shouptronic" computers "preordained" voting results to give George Bush his "Hail Mary" victory in New Hampshire.

Nobody save a small group of computer engineers, like John Sununu, the state's Republican governor, would be the wiser.

If you think back carefully to November 8, 1988, it may strike you that your belief in who won at the polls was *not* formed as the result of openly voiced "ayes" or "nays" in a public forum.

Nor was your perception of who won or lost based on the honest and visible marks on paper ballots that were checked and rechecked by all concerned parties or their chosen representatives.

The truth, if you recall it clearly, is that you

learned about George Bush's astounding victory in New Hampshire from a television program or newspaper, which supposedly learned about it from a computer center into which other computers fed information.

You learned the "predicted outcome" within minutes after the polls in New Hampshire closed, and by and large you believed what you heard because you had no cause, it seemed, to be skeptical or suspicious.

If you had any doubts about how the vote was counted, you probably dismissed them after asking yourself questions like:

1) *Why would the computer people lie?*
2) *How could they lie? There must be public checks and balances.*
3) *If they lie, how can they get away with it? The losers will surely raise hell.*

Because you, and most of us, dismiss the possibility that the American vote is routinely stolen, distorted or otherwise monkeyed with by corrupt computer wizards, you resist questioning further and dismiss as crackpots or fanatics those who do.

Yet, not long ago, Robert Flaherty, the president of News Election Services (NES), the private company that compiles voting results and feeds them to the major media, was asked to make it clear how the NES system works.

As usual when asked about how NES counts and disseminates the vote, he replied:

"This is not a proper area of inquiry."

Can it be that the methods used to accept, tally and broadcast the results of the American vote are improper areas for questioning?

"Yes," says Mr. Flaherty, "that is a proprietary matter not open to the public."

We will describe the operations of the secretive NES later on, although it is noteworthy here to mention that this corporation, which fanatically guards its people and processes from the public view, is a consortium of the three major television networks: ABC, NBC and CBS, plus the Associated Press wire service, CNN, the New York *Times,* the Washington *Post* and other news-gathering organizations.

These "First Amendment" institutions each raise the cry of "impropriety" and "improper inquiry" when asked about their unspoken role in the American vote count.

Actually, the major news organizations foster the illusion that the American press competes to get the correct vote count to the public, and they imply by omission that "ballots" are counted in the traditional, accountable ways that once fostered confidence and a sense of fairness in the hearts and minds of the American voter.

However, the American voter has grown steadily more apathetic in both presidential and off-year elections, with sometimes less than 25 percent of those eligible taking the opportunity to cast a ballot. The press blames this on the politicians and the public itself, but the public may be aware, if only vaguely, that in some unfathomable way their vote counts for little or nothing.

There have been too many odd coincidences and peculiar results over the past quarter century, and the decline in voter participation in national elections over the past two decades is directly proportional to the rise of computerized voting.

The People are naive about computer voting and somewhat less than entirely computer literate. They do intuit, however, that it is a mistake to put much faith in the integrity of computerized voting systems. Except in matters spiritual, intelligent people tend not to place much faith in what they cannot see. They could see paper ballots marked and placed into a slot in ballot boxes, and except for certain infamous precincts in Chicago, people generally trusted the American voting process. They could see it, touch it, and their vote left a paper trail that could be followed if there was a need for verification. That can no longer be said.

The instant after a voter chooses his or her ballot selection on a computer, the electronic impulse that is triggered either records that vote or it does not. Either way, the computer program immediately erases all record of the transaction except for the result, which is subject to an infinite variety of switching, column jumping, multiplication, division, subtraction, addition and erasure.

All these operations take place in the electronic universe within the computer and are entirely under the direction of the program or "source code." It is impossible to go back to the original event, like you can with a paper ballot, and start over again in case fraud is suspected. With computer voting the results are virtually final, and, in all cases, hatched in the electronic dark. No human eye can watch or protect your vote once it is cast in a computer voting machine.

People who mistrust the voting process cannot, in the traditional American way, accept the defeat of their candidates gracefully and work loyally with the winners. Instead, more and more American voters are feeling "had," "scammed," "hoodwinked" by the voting system. Trust has almost departed. There is the nagging, unproven, yet pervasive feeling that the "experts," the "spin doctors," the "covert operators" and the "private interests" have put their technicians and consultants in absolute control of the national vote count, and that in any selected situation these computer wizards can and will program the vote as their masters wish.

All over the United States of America there are people who listen to the facts about computer voting and then tell horror stories of candidates, who didn't have a prayer before election day, then slip into office by an uncheckable computer vote. Most common is the story of the computer that "breaks down" when one candidate is securely in the lead, and after the computer is "fixed," the losing candidate pulls ahead and wins. The evil feelings left behind by such shenanigans are festering across America.

Among the wickedest recent examples of possible computerized vote fraud, of the sort that has disillusioned millions of Americans, is the 1988 New Hampshire primary that saved George Bush from getting knocked out of the race to the White House.

Was the New Hampshire Primary scenario a modern classic in computerized vote manipulation? Here is the gist of it.

The Bush campaign of 1988, as historians have since recollected it, was filled with CIA-type disinformation operations and deceptions of the sort that America used in Viet Nam, Chile and the Soviet Union. Since George Bush was one of the most admired CIA directors in the history of the organization, this was not so surprising.

Yet George Bush stood to lose the Republican Party nomination if he was beaten by Sen. Robert Dole in the snows of New Hampshire. He had suffered a terrible political wound when Dole won big by a show of hands in an unriggable Iowa caucus. Bush came to New Hampshire with all the earmarks of a loser whom the press had come to identify as a "wimp."

Political observers were downbeat in their observations of Bush's chances in the face of Dole's Iowa momentum. Virtually every television and newspaper poll had Bush losing by up to eight points just hours before the balloting.

Desperate times require desperate measures. Perhaps that's what it required for "steps to be taken," and phone calls to be made. Then came a widely reported promise made by Bush to his campaign manager, Gov. Sununu. It happens that Sununu's computer engineering skills approach "genius" on the tests. If Sununu could "deliver" New Hampshire, and Bush didn't care how and didn't want to know how – then Sununu would become his chief of staff in the White House.

When election day was over the following headline appeared in the Washington *Post:*

NEW HAMPSHIRE CONFOUNDED MOST POLLSTERS

Voters Were a Step Ahead of Tracking Measurements

By Lloyd Grove
Washington Post Staff Writer

For Vice President Bush and his supporters, Tuesday's 9-percentage-point victory over Sen. Robert J. Dole (R-Kan.) in New Hampshire was a delightful surprise; for Andrew Kohut, it was a horror story.

Kohut is president of the Gallup poll, whose final New Hampshire survey was wrong by 17 points: it had put

Dole ahead by 8; Bush won by 9. "I was dismayed," Kohut acknowledged yesterday.

This New Hampshire primary was perhaps the most polled primary election in American history, and in the end, the Republican voters in the state confounded the predictions of nearly every published survey of voter opinion.

Gallup's glaring error and the miscalls of other polling organizations once again raise questions about the accuracy of polls, their use by the media and the impact they have on voters' choices and the public perception of elections. In New Hampshire this year, news organizations' use of "tracking polls" to try to follow the movement of public opinion night after night came to dominate news accounts of the campaigning and the thinking of the campaigns themselves.

Tracking polls usually survey a relatively small number of voters every night: 150 to 400 in each party, in the case of The Post-ABC poll. The results are averaged over several days. See POLLS, A11, Col. 1

Had the terms of Bush's "promise" to Sununu been met?

Whatever magic Sununu was able to conjure up during those final hours preceding the overnight resurrection of the Bush campaign, it worked.

There are those who believe that such a wild reversal of form would have been subject to an immediate inquiry by the stewards if it had happened in the Kentucky Derby. Any horseplayer would have nodded sagely, put a finger up to his eye, pulled down the lower lid, and signaled: "Fix."

Yet in New Hampshire, there was some wonderment expressed in the press, and little

more. There was no rechecking of the
computerized voting machines, no inquiry into
the path of the vote from the voting machines to
the central tallying place, no public scrutiny of
the mechanisms of the mighty peculiar vote that
saved George Bush's career and leapfrogged the
relatively obscure Sununu into the White House.

Nothing was said in the press about the
secretly programmed computer chips inside the
"Shouptronic" Direct Recording Electronic (DRE)
voting machines in Manchester, the state's largest
city.

These 200-pound systems were so easily
tampered with that the integrity of the results
they gave – and George Bush *was* the
beneficiary of their tallies – will forever be in
doubt. Consider these points:

1. The "Shouptronic" was purchased directly
   from a company whose owner, Ransom
   Shoup, had been twice convicted of vote
   fraud in Philadelphia.
2. It bristled with telephone lines that made it
   possible for instructions from the outside to
   be telephoned into the machine without
   anyone's clear knowledge.
3. It completely lacked an "audit trail," an
   independent record that could be checked in
   case the machine "broke down" or its results
   were challenged.
4. Roy G. Saltman, of the federal Institute for
   Computer Sciences and Technology, called

the Shouptronic "much more risky" than any other computerized tabulation system because "You are fundamentally required to accept the logical operation of the machine, there is no way to do an independent check."

A year later, in June of 1989, Robert J. Naegele, who had investigated all computerized voting systems for New York State, warned: "The DRE (which the Shouptronic was) is still at least a year and possibly two away from what I would consider a marketable product. The hardware problems are relatively minor, but the software problems are conceptual and really major."

A source close to Gov. Sununu insists that Sununu knew from his perspective as a politician, and his expertise as a computer engineer, that the Shouptronic was prime for tampering.

How could such an offense against the United States electoral process have been carried out under the gaze of professionals from the nation's TV networks, newspapers and wire services?

There are lawyers who will argue that the party primary election is essentially an intra-party matter over which "outsiders" have no legal rights. That, in fact, if a political party wants to rig its elections, it can do so without violation of federal, state or local laws.

As long as men and women in charge of the vote count are on the take, or can be persuaded that tampering is "good for the party," that one candidate should win no matter what the vote count is – then wholesale vote rigging throughout America can be accomplished quite easily. It is a sick and vicious way to operate within the two-party system, and there is reason to believe that it is epidemic on a national scale.

The concept is clear, simple and it works. Computerized voting gives the power of selection, without fear of discovery, to whomever controls the computer.

Of course, there are problems about getting control of more and more computers, and that problem has been brilliantly solved with the help, and in some cases the unwitting collaboration, of the major news-gathering organizations.

Over the past generation, when television news became an unstoppable force in America's political life, competition grew between the major networks to be "first" with the voting results – proving they had better reporters, better contacts, better organizations than the opposition.

At first, the race to call the winners was sportsmanlike and played much like print journalism played "scoops." Then, almost imperceptibly, the networks' urge to "give the public timely results" crossed over the line into territory more sinister.

The early position taken by network

spokesmen was that slow vote counts increased the likelihood of vote fraud, and besides, the American people had a "right" to know as soon as possible how their candidates fared.

You may ask: *Why all the rush?*

In a fair election, how does the passage of a reasonable amount of time, less than a day or two, say, negatively affect the outcome of the election or the people's perception of it? In the early days of the nation it required months to find out who was elected president, since the electoral college met in January to cast their votes.

Clearly, democracy can survive without immediate election results.

Yet the media's clamor for speed went on, encouraged by inventors who had early knowledge of computers and knew how to use them to accelerate the processes of ordinary life. It became possible, with fast counters developed by International Business Machine Corporation, to use punch cards, with rows of small, rectangular holes, as ballots. These old cards could be counted at the rate of thousands per minute by an IBM sorting machine hooked up with a photoelectric cell and a computerized tabulator. It seemed like progress at the time. Vote counting got a lot faster in a big hurry.

But after several years, IBM realized that the Vote-amatic voting machine, the patents on which IBM had bought from its inventor, T.K. Harris, was actually a Pandora's box. IBM, following several disturbing public relations problems brought about by both incompetent and malicious "mishaps" during elections, took its name off the product. IBM eventually sold its rights in the company after IBM's president, Thomas Watson, read an article that implied he might be trying to install IBM voting machines in enough precincts to win him the first electronically rigged election for President of the United States. Watson had no ambitions to become a U.S. president and was mortified that his computers would be implicated in anti-democratic functions.

With the crusty, impeccable IBM out of the business, the scramble to produce new, improved, less scrupulous voting hardware and software began in earnest. Entrepreneurs made fortunes peddling the early computerized counters to towns and cities across America. They sold the machines as the "patriotic," "progressive" thing to do for American voters.

Newspaper and broadcast media seldom bothered to look into the voting machine industry and, in fact, took advantage of the speed the new machines offered in counting. The press did not investigate the accuracy, or lack of it, of the final tallies.

All of the computerized machines, from the earliest versions on, were peculiarly susceptible to vote fraud despite the ingenuous claims made by the manufacturers. The issue of "speed" in counting actually meant little or nothing to the voting public, except as it was staged as a competition by the press. Yes, the computers offered speed on the one hand, but on the other hand they all, *without exception*, did their operations in the electronic dark where ordinary citizens, who had previously taken the responsibility for a fair and accurate vote, could never venture.

Most Americans did not realize that such an anti-democratic virus had infected their vote. Most do not realize it today. If you ask your friends to describe how their vote (if they cast a vote) is counted, they are unlikely to get much further than the polling booth and the rudimentary requirements to operate the machine. Beyond that they are probably ignorant. Most people expect that the Democrat and Republican poll watchers will watch out for their interests, and if not them, the Board of Elections or some federal elections commission will keep the fraud down to manageable proportions

Naturally, in the vacuum of ethics and in the depths of ignorance about computerized voting, the opportunists arrived on the scene. It was already clear that IBM considered the business too dirty to mess with. Yet salesmen had placed the machines, along with service contracts and consulting fees, in thousands of America's precincts.

All over the nation the local election boards

were taking delivery of Trojan horses that could be programmed to bide their time and then, when the proper moment came, to mistabulate election results on command. Computer experts with even the most vestigial imaginations figured out dozens of ways to compromise a vote, many of them so elegant that getting caught was almost impossible.

During a little-publicized court trial in West Virginia, it was revealed that there were ways to stop the computers during a count, while everyone watched. Simply fiddle with a few switches, turn the computer back on again, and thereby alter the entire vote, or parts of it. If anyone asked questions, the fixers could make any number of plausible excuses. Mostly all they had to say was "just checking that everything's running okay," and that was satisfactory.

With voting machines attached to telephone lines it was possible to meddle with the actual vote from a telephone miles away. Getting caught was not possible. "Deniability" and "untrackability" were built into the secret source codes that animated the machines.

It was possible to rig elections electronically in separate communities across the country, but until 1964 it was not considered possible to rig a national election. Then, in August 1964, News Election Service was created.

Perhaps the most important piece of history uncovered during the *Votescam* probe is a potently candid study of the U.S. electoral system conducted in 1980 by the CIA-linked Air Command and Staff College in cooperation with the University of New Mexico. It establishes the TV corporate networks' interest in NES. The study was commissioned by the CIA and published in the International Journal of Public Administration that was distributed to selected government agencies. We discovered a copy in the Library of Congress.

It is safe to say that almost nobody in America is aware of the activities of NES on election night. The on-air scripts of each TV network during the years since the founding of NES have seldom, if ever, mentioned its existence. The silence smacks of collusion among press "competitors" to keep NES away from public scrutiny. A portion of the study read:

"The United States government has no elections office and does not attempt to administer congressional elections. The responsibility for the administration of elections and certification of winners in the United States national election rests with a consortium of private entities, including 111,000 members of the national League of Women Voters. The formal structure of election administration in the United States is not capable of providing the major TV networks with timely results of the presidential and congressional elections. In the case of counting actual ballots on national election night, public

officials have abdicated responsibility of aggregation of election night vote totals to a private organization, News Election Service of New York (NES). NES is a wholly-owned subsidiary joint-venture of national television networks ABC, CBS and NBC and the press wire-services AP and UPI. <u>This private organization performs without a contract; without supervision by public officials. It makes decisions concerning its duties according to its own criteria. The question and accountability of News Election Service has not arisen in the nation's press because the responsibility NES now has in counting the nation's votes was assumed gradually over a lengthy period without ever being evaluated as an item on the public agenda.</u> (Underlined for emphasis. Ed.)

This privately owned vote counting cartel (NES) uses the vast membership of the network-subsidized League of Women Voters as field personnel whose exclusive job is to phone in *unofficial* vote totals to NES on election night. NES also operates a "master computer" in New York City, located on 34th Street. (Because the *League of Women Voters* has about it a perfume of volunteerism and do-goodism, the fact that it is actually a political club with a political agenda and a hungry treasury is shrouded by the false myth that it is a reliable election-day watchdog.)

The NES mainframe computer has the capability, via telephone lines, of "talking" back and forth with county and state government mainframes. During the important 60-day certification period after an election, the counts in the county and state mainframes can still be manipulated by outsiders to conform to earlier TV "projections."

Without this capability of using the NES mainframe to "balance the books " between initial network projections of Bush as "winner" and the final official totals published two months later, Bush may have lost the election to Dukakis.

It is the prescription for the covert stealing of America.

2

BALLOTS NOT BULLETS

"Ballots are the rightful and peaceful successors to bullets"

—Abraham Lincoln

Accept the idea for a few hours that your vote is, in fact, being stolen before your eyes. Put aside your beliefs or disbeliefs in the rectitude of the federal, state and local governments. Journey back to a time just a year after "Woodstock," when today's new grandfathers were in their twenties and both Jimi Hendrix and Jim Morrison were still alive.

We are two brothers from Michigan at play in Miami in 1970. The Cuban refugees have not yet taken political control. We have shared professions as rock and roll empresarios, drug store owners, suntan lotion manufacturers and journalists.

When Jim Morrison of "The Doors" executed his notorious simulated jerk-off jump from the stage into the crowd, and set in motion the chain of events that plagued him until his death in Paris, it was us, Jim and Ken Collier, who promoted that historic show. We also swallowed the financial consequences after Morrison and "The Doors" left town.

It is after "The Doors" hysteria that we are in Miami trying to decide what to do next. We want to do something that just might raise eyebrows and blood pressure in a Richard Nixon world. We decide to write a book. We could write two books about rock and roll and the actual life backstage, but we have a lot of friends in the music business, and if we tell the truth we alienate most of them. The idea of combining a book with running for public office comes up.

"It seems like a good idea," Ken says.

"It's a great idea. You going to run, or me?"

We went to Dell Publishing in New York and sold the idea that Tom Hayden, Jerry Rubin, Abbie Hoffman and all the hippies against the system had all overlooked an intriguing possibility – to use the system and see if things that needed to get done actually could get done without revolution. Ken would run for Congress and scrupulously work *within the system* to find out. We titled the book: *Running Through the*

System: Ballots Not Bullets. The editors agreed that it was a good idea and paid us $3,500 as an advance.

Winning the congressional seat was not a requirement of Dell. They also agreed that we would not ask for contributions. The campaign would be as "grass roots" as possible, based on the theory that even the poorest person in America can run for office by merely knocking on every door, shaking every hand and giving speeches at every political club or church. Whatever percentage of the vote we managed to get at the end of the campaign trail would depend strictly on whether the people believed in us.

Ken was already the front man at our rock club, *Thee Image*, and he had that Sixties need to see things change. From the time he was a teenager he had a burning desire to be a Congressman, a profession he considered idealistic and romantic. He had been buying ad space on the back page of the University of Miami *Hurricane* student newspaper (Jim had been The *Hurricane* managing editor in 1959) in the name of *Thee Image* to write essays on the political upheavals of the time: against the Viet Nam war, for freedom of speech, against imprisonment of political radicals.

Now Ken closed his eyes and put the possibilities together. His imagination was tweaked by the potential for high drama. At 29 years old, a romantic poet, Ken was brazen, impulsive, Tom Wolfe-like in his stature, over six feet of it, big hands, big head, big shoes, big dreams.

"We can do it," Jim said.

Two years older than Ken, Jim was quiet and private. Nothing intrigued him more than orchestrating scenes from behind the scenes.

"I'll be your campaign manager."

"Who do we run against?" Ken asked.

"Hmmmmmm."

Claude Pepper was a lusty old Harvard man with a face like an overripe tomato. He was known as "The Father of Social Security." He was also the incumbent in the House of Representatives. Pepper was a cosmopolitan, and he was happy to be in Washington where his talents as a speaker and a storyteller were recognized and appreciated.

Pepper was on the board of the bank that held the lease on the building that housed *Thee Image*. The bank had refused to renew the lease after "The Doors" concert, using the controversy in the press as an excuse. Rock and roll, they said, was an unsavory influence on the community, even though parents, police and prosecutors were invited into the club without charge, at any time, to see that the kids were not subjected to drug dealing.

"Let's run for Congress against Claude Pepper," Jim said.

It was decided that Ken would run as a

Democrat ($2,100 was paid for the filing fee and it came from a Ted Nugent concert we held at the Miami Jai-Alai Fronton). Neither of us were Nixon Republicans and to run as an independent would have been decidedly outside the system.

On July 21, 1970 the grass roots campaign began.

We talked at every possible church. We went into public housing in Liberty City and Overtown, which were black innercity areas. We passed out leaflets and talked some more. In the Jewish sections of Miami Beach there were public meetings held in banks and on South Beach (now the art deco revival section). The old people were charmed by Ken, who swapped stories with World War II vets about his paratrooper jumps.

We campaigned 42 days, 18 hours-a-day, every day.

When the U.S. Congress recessed in August, Claude Pepper returned home to Dade County. Prior to his showing up we had almost convinced leaders of the black community, which included newspaper editors, civic activists and HUD executives, that Ken's ideas were the wave of the future, the hope of the next generation.

In August, with the recess in Congress, Claude Pepper returned to the area and the atmosphere abruptly changed. At a black church in Liberty City, we attended an obligatory political breakfast. Five-minute speeches were scheduled by all the candidates. Pepper, who was nearly 70-years old, gave his speech in his usual mush-mouthed way. He sat down and Ken got up to speak. But the moderator pointedly ignored him. When Ken realized that he wasn't going to get equal time, he asked: "Does anybody care to hear me speak?"

Pepper nodded his head at two very serious guys. They approached Ken from both sides, grabbed his arms, and dragged him out like a fish.

We called the cops on a pay phone. Alcee Hastings, who eventually became the first black federal judge in the area, rushed outside.

"Don't go back in there," he warned. "They'll beat you up next time. It's dangerous."

We called the television stations and told them how a candidate got dragged out of a political breakfast. Only Channel 4's reporter came and took pictures of the purple bruises on Ken's arms. But at the studio, the news director didn't even look at the tape. "This isn't going to air," he told the reporter.

And that was that.

One of the theories of the Dell book *Running Through The System*, was that we use the system whenever possible. So instead of merely going back in and shooting the old bastard, we swore out a warrant for Pepper's arrest for ordering the assault. Not one word in the media. We couldn't get even a *second* on television. We sent a telegram to the Federal Communications Commission and complained, within the system, that we couldn't get any television time. The FCC wrote back to the local stations and said, unspecifically, "Give them time."

One station gave us 18 seconds.

Pepper went to Texas avoiding arrest, while his lawyers visited a judge without our knowledge (*ex parte*) and had the warrant quashed.

They might have been irked by the garbage incident.

We had to make a clear statement about our candidacy. One that would show that Pepper was basically a hypocrite who didn't care about anyone but the richest segment, white or black. Our opportunity came when we walked through the streets of the black areas and saw the results of a political project that black leaders called "Teen Clean."

The idea was to clean up houses, gutters, streets, lawns of all the garbage that had turned the area into a slum. The teens turned out with great enthusiasm and they piled coconuts, palm fronds, broken glass, toilet seats, rusty old refrigerators, and mattresses in heaps on the street, some as high as six feet. The Metro garbage trucks were supposed to pick it all up, but although most of the drivers were black, their white bosses refused to let them go. The reason: "We didn't expect hundreds of piles of Teen Clean garbage and we don't have the budget for it." People in the community were angry, and they felt betrayed. Rats and roaches, however, loved the stuff.

"Look," Jim suggested, "let's rent a pick-up truck, pick a load of that shit up and get some press at the same time."

So one hot August afternoon, we appeared in Liberty City in a half-ton truck and loaded it up. We had the enthusiastic help of about 100 local kids. Then Ken drove east across the 36th Street Causeway to pristine Miami Beach. Had any alert cop seen us heading east with a load of garbage, he would surely have stopped us. Nobody brings garbage *to* Miami Beach.

Once across the bay, we headed for the bank on 17th street, where we backed the truck up to the front door, pulled the hydraulic handle, and watched as a half ton of unsavory objects built a monument to the Pepper campaign. Just before we drove away, Jim grabbed a cardboard sign that read, **"This is a Teen Clean Project"** and jammed it into the top of the heap like the flag at Iwo Jima.

Later we drove by the bank, on whose board Pepper sat, and watched as hired black men scooped up the garbage into a truck and then headed back *west* across the causeway.

We parked the truck in front of our townhouses and waited. Two Miami Beach detectives eventually knocked on Ken's door.

"We not only did it," Jim assured them, "but we're going to do it again tomorrow."

We did go back into Liberty City the next day for a repeat performance, but all the garbage was being picked up by a fleet of Metro trucks. And although there were photographers, police and reporters who saw the garbage pile in front of the bank, not a word was mentioned in the media, not even in the black-owned newspaper.

The remainder of the campaign was waged mainly in the streets. Miami in August can be a sticky mixture of sun, squalls and stifling heat. All day we trudged the streets, putting fliers in doors of houses, talking to people who were home, some giving us a cold drink.

Pepper bought TV time and seldom left his home. Then, in the last two days before the vote, as we made our last up-this-street-down-that-street run, we saw Pepper's face everywhere. He had used county employees to nail his campaign posters on hundreds of telephone poles in the black communities. He put none on the Beach.

"That's illegal," Ken said, ripping one down. "He can't put his posters on public property."

That night we drove the convertible along each street, Jim standing on the trunk, and we ripped every poster down. It took four hours, but that night we slept great.

On election evening we were at Ken's house to watch the returns on television. The numbers were flashed on the screen about every 20 minutes and our percentage of the vote remained consistent at 16 percent. Channels 4 and 7 were giving the election full coverage but Channel 10, for the first time in its history, ran a *movie* instead of voting results. Sometime after 9 p.m. our vote percentage jumped to 31 percent.

"Hey, we just doubled our vote!" Ken was excited.

"If it holds we'll have enough strength to run again in '72," Jim said.

Suddenly the news director came on the air and announced that the election "computer has broken down." Instead of giving official returns from the courthouse, the station would instead broadcast returns based on its "projections."

When the next "projection" was flashed 20 minutes later, Ken's vote had fallen back to 16 percent. No other vote had fluctuated, only ours.

We didn't know it at the time, but across the country in the 1970s and 1980s, that sequence of events was a phenomenon that became rather common. 1) A candidate is ahead, the good guy, the one who wanted the city audit, the one who'll make a difference. 2) Television announcement: "The computer has broken down at the courthouse and official votes will no longer be forthcoming." 3) When the

*computer comes back, your guy is behind again,
and there he or she remains.*

By the 11 p.m. news it was over. We hadn't
expected to win; after all, we spent so little
money, we bought no television time and we
were new at political campaigns. But what was
that 31 percent we got at about 9:30?

The next day we drove to the Board of
Elections in Miami, and after watching a while,
we asked Election Supervisor Martin Braterman
if we could look at the canvass sheets we saw
stored in an open vault. He escorted us to the
vault and Jim started flipping the sheets, trying
to get a quick visual grasp of the entire stack. He
had never seen a canvass sheet before so he had
no idea of what he was looking at, much less
what he was looking for.

"I'm not sure," he said. "but it looks like there
are more votes cast than people who voted."

Ken, who was still surveying the room, moved
in closer. "Where?… show me."

"Get out," Braterman ordered, "you guys are
nuisances."

"This is public information," Ken said. "Are
you telling us that we are not entitled to
examine public information about the electoral
process?"

"This is not the right time. We're certifying the
vote here."

Ken persisted. "We want to see them now

because something looks very wrong with the sheets. Let us look at them before something happens to them. It's evidence."

There was more heated dialogue. Ken sat on the counter and refused to go until he could examine the canvass sheets.

Braterman picked up the phone: "We got a disturbance here. Send a cop."

A few minutes later a young policeman asked Ken what he was doing.

"Just checking out the system," Ken grinned. The policeman laughed, Ken laughed. Then he booked Ken on a misdemeanor. Jim bailed him out.

The next day, with a call to the election division, we got a full explanation of what a canvass sheet was: the official, hand-written record of the voting machine tallies. There are rules written on the flip-side of the sheet. The official rules state: At 7 a.m. the precinct captains must open up the back of the voting machine and certify that all candidate counters are set with zeroes showing. They sign their names to those sheets swearing that they actually saw the zeroes.

Then the machine is closed and locked for the day while voting goes on. At 7 p.m., after the voting ends, the back is again opened with keys, and representatives from each party call out the numbers to the precinct people who fill in the front side of each canvass sheet. Three canvass sheets are filled out per machine. One sheet is to be posted on the wall after the election for the public. One goes to the Elections Department. One is sent to the County Judge's office.

Once we knew what it was we were looking for we returned to the Elections Department where Braterman, still grumpy from the day before, again refused an examination of the records. Not wanting to get busted again we walked over to the County Judge's office where copies of the sheets were already bound in a book. The clerk there permitted closer examination.

"What are we looking for?" Ken asked.

"Look for a pattern."

The sheets were three feet wide and two feet high. On the front there were a lot of squares corresponding to each candidate, and there were numbers in most of the squares in the handwriting, it seemed, of just the one person who filled out each sheet. On the back were from ten to twelve signatures of workers who swore they saw all zeroes in the morning and final numbers at night.

As we turned the pages Jim was puzzled: "There's a kind of uniform grayness about all these sheets. Look here." He flipped the pages like one would do to a cartoon layout. "Except for these few precincts...look." He pointed to a page of scrawly looking numbers. "See?"

Ken could see it immediately. The handwriting on about five of the pages was messy and broken...and real looking. "But the rest of this stack is too neat, isn't it? All of these appear to be written by the same hand!"

"You think these might be forgeries?"

"Let's find a handwriting expert."

The Yellow Pages listed only one handwriting expert, Robert Lynch. We telephoned him and made an appointment to meet at the courthouse the next morning.

Lynch turned out to be a man in his fifties. He wore glasses but he only needed one flip through the bound stack before making his pronouncement.

"These are not forgeries."

We had absolutely no reason to believe that Lynch was anything other than your honest neighborhood handwriting expert. If he said they weren't forgeries, what was the use in chasing rabbits down that hole?

With our forgery suspicion gone, the election investigation appeared to be over. We went back to shooting pool, learning Shori Goju karate, sailing catamarans and racing Pontiac and Chevy 427's. We were also busy selling our local newspaper, *The Daily Planet*, on street corners.

"The question that still bugs me," Jim said, "is how did we get that 31 percent? I mean, why that momentary thrill? Was it an error?"

"Maybe it was real," Ken answered. "Maybe somehow they let the true vote through. When they saw what it was, they cut it off."

"That's a possibility."

Soon after the November election, in which Claude Pepper was confirmed as Congressman, we went to the local television stations to ask them for copies of the on-air computer "readouts" used during the primary election count.

Both TV stations said that they no longer had possession of the readouts. They were now held by Professor Ross Beiler, in the political science department of the University of Miami. We immediately went to Beiler's office on the Coral Gables campus. It was just a 10-foot by 10-foot cubicle off a loggia, and the door was open.

We walked in and there, scattered in disarray on his desk, were the readouts we wanted. They were big, about the same size as the canvass sheets, with the dark and light green lines of IBM standard computer paper.

They showed vote totals and the times the totals were tallied. There were the names of the stations on them: WCKT (4) and WTVJ (7). Plus some notes and signatures.

"Grab those," Ken whispered.

Jim scooped up a handful of the sheets and turned to walk out. At that instant, Professor Beiler walked in the door. He was a tall, hayseedy looking man. He grabbed Jim, who was a black belt in karate, by the back of the neck and said: "Put those back."

"Exactly what were you going to do with these?" Ken asked.

"I'm going to Washington on a sabbatical. I was going to destroy them."

"Destroy them? You can't do that."

"They belong to me."

"We need them for an investigation." Ken picked up a few papers.

"Put those down."

"All right," Ken said, dropping them back on the desk, "let's put them in the safe in the office of the dean of students."

The professor hesitated.

"Professor, it would be the legally proper thing to do."

"Just for six months," he agreed, "and you can't look at them during that time."

"Let's type up an agreement."

As Beiler sat at the typewriter, with his back to the room, Jim seized the moment and stuffed about ten readout pages under his shirt and slipped unnoticed out the door. He ran to the car, where he jammed the papers in the trunk.

A couple of hours later we excitedly spread the contraband on the pool table in Jim's living room.

"Look at this," Jim pointed to one of the columns on the sheet. "The first report is at 7:24 p.m....just 24 minutes after the polls closed." He scanned the sheet...he knew the future was coming. "It shows the first vote totals are based on," he found the column... "returns from Pepper's Congressional district...see?...it called our race so it's gotta be in our district. This column says ACTUAL VOTES. There's a zero here. No actual votes. And…" his finger moved to the next column, "here it says PROJECTED VOTES…7,100 for us and…46,000 for Pepper."

"So?"

"Under 'MACHINES REPORTING'…one machine."

"Lemme see."

We checked the green computer readouts which we arranged in neat piles under the pool table light. In one of the vertical columns labeled "MACHINES REPORTING" the number "1" appeared.

Jim grinned. "They used one machine's totals to predict how many votes 250 candidates would get?"

He scrambled quickly through the papers until he found the 9:21 p.m. readout. There it was, the 31 percent that had flashed on the screen. "We're not crazy," Jim said.

Ken looked at the numbers.

The documents showed that no actual votes were being reported from 7 p.m. until the 11 p.m. news. We had assumed that the computer had broken down at the time they announced it, 9:21 p.m., but these readouts indicated that the TV stations were not getting official votes from the opening bell.

"They must have relied on information from their reporters at the precincts," Ken said.

"Maybe," Jim answered, "but 99 percent of the

vote was counted by 11 p.m. They would have needed at least 340 reporters to cover the 340 precincts."

We checked the sheets closer and found that the on-air reporting times were set at every 20 minutes throughout the evening. The last report was at 11:15 p.m.

"Ninety-nine percent of the precincts were reported by the time people had to go to bed," Ken mused. "That's very neat."

"If they weren't getting actual votes all night, from 7 p.m. on, and they predicted the final outcome in 24 minutes using one voting machine, maybe they knew they were going to have a blackout all along," Jim said.

"So it was a cover story."

"Gotta be."

"Could they have blacked it out on purpose so they could project winners?"

But the most puzzling question, if we were to believe that the election wasn't rigged, was how Channel 7 could have predicted the exact outcome of 40 races with 250 candidates altogether on the basis of information from just one voting machine located somewhere in Claude Pepper's district. And how could they do it in just 24 minutes?

That 24 minutes rang and rerang and re-re-rerang inside our heads. We talked all night trying to make the pieces of the puzzle fit. By morning we still thought that something was rotten in the count.

There are no tests to determine when the last rock on the ledge of life slips and plunges you into the crater of causes. Suddenly police stations become grossly familiar. So do the courtrooms of various judges. The offices of lawyers are not avoided anymore. Organizations like the CIA and the FBI keep their ears open when you come around. Your home may at times become mobile and the sky becomes your roof. Fear that your cause may be lost ceaselessly batters your confidence. Your relationship with others is more or less determined by the extent to which they will tolerate your cause, which for some of your loved ones may be less attractive than maggot soup.

For us, the last rock fell when we discovered that all the predictions made within 24 minutes after the polls closed were based on results called in from *one* single voting machine.

We decided to get mad.

In those days it was easy to become involved in causes. The Sierra Club was just starting then and it was a loud, strident, articulate toddler. The anti-nukers and pro-abortionists were beginning to set up chapters all over the world and get their messages out by means of concerts and LP records. Richard Nixon was taking hold of power in Washington and if he behaved anything like he had when he lived on Key Biscayne with his friend, Bebe Rebozo, then Nixon was destined for historic trouble. Yes, this was before Watergate, before Nixon resigned, when his attention was turned mostly toward China.

So instead of organizing a group called something like "Victims of Tampered Elections" (VOTE), getting members to pay $15 annual dues ($300,000) to join the cause, put out *Votescam* newsletters, get our collective voices heard on Capitol Hill, we took up the pen feather and challenged the sword.

Years later, with bloodied pen feather in hand, we would understand that people with great illusions are destined to die in the desert, sucking on their sneaker, while waiting for the water truck to come.

All we had to do now was track down that one magic machine.

How did they decide in which precinct that machine would be placed? Pepper's district was spread from east to west across the center of Dade County — from the ocean on the east to the Everglades on the west. The neighborhoods were generally segregated into black, Jewish and WASP. During the campaign we walked down every street in those neighborhoods. None of them could possibly be so typical of us all that the votes coming from just one of its machines could be projected to predict exact final vote totals.

Jim asked: "How did channel 7 and 4 get those numbers? Did people call them in from the precincts? Did they have a reporter in each of 340 precincts?"

"And what about the computer program?" Ken added.

"Do they have a formula, or, let's say a multiplier of some sort that they use to project those numbers from the precincts?" Jim wondered.

He scrawled figures on a piece of paper.

"If we figure that everything Beiler knew before 7 p.m. is listed under the letter "A"…," he wrote the letter "A" on the paper. "The letter "A" would have to represent his formula, or his program. I mean, he couldn't just take the votes off that one machine and magically project them to get a final result without some sort of program.

"Now, let's call the vote totals he got from that one machine "B". Jim wrote "B" on the paper. "To make it easy we'll say you got 10 votes on that machine." He wrote "10" under the letter "B" "So what would that mean?"

"Well," Ken answered, "he'd either have to multiply that "10" or he'd have to add someting to the "10" to get a final number."

"Could he do anything else? "

"I don't know anything about computers, but he can't change the laws of mathematics…he can only multiply that "10" to get a final number…or he can add something to that "10"…I don't care how sophisticated a computer is, all it can do is multiply or add, period."

It seemed so simple. An A x B = C formula. A (Multiplier) x B (Actual votes) = C (The total). And it's the only formula possible no matter how bright a programmer you are. If you use an A x B = C formula, you must also always know *two* of the numbers in advance to calculate the third. But if you know two out of three of those numbers in advance, you've rigged the election.

In the green pile of documents we found the Channel 4 readout, the first report showing only vote percentages (not final totals) was broadcast at 7:04 p.m. Channel 4 projected the outcome for 250 candidates in just 4 minutes!

Hell, you can't even boil a three minute egg in four minutes.

We had a 427-horsepower red Pontiac convertible which the Dade County highway patrol had come to know and respect over the years. The next morning it took us to look for answers. We drove up to the state capitol at Tallahassee, a lushly green southern city in the hills of the Florida Panhandle about 400 miles north of Miami. From the Secretary of State's office we got the *final* vote totals for every candidate in the three elections held in Dade County in 1970. We copied them and brought them back home.

The first thing we did was to lay out the Tallahassee sheets on the pool table and divide them into piles. September primary, October runoff and November final election. Then we arranged the television readouts in time sequence in order to compare the numbers that the state eventually registered as official against the projections from the television stations.

We checked the totals in the Governor's race and found that an aggregate of 141,000 votes were cast on September 8th. Then we checked the runoff election held a month later and the exact same figure —141,000 votes were cast again!

"How is that possible?" Ken asked, and then he answered himself, "It *isn't*. The losing candidates dropped out of the race, and whenever that happens the vote drops, too."

So we checked the final election in November and found once again that 141,000 votes were cast in the Governor's race.

In hockey they call that a hat trick. In politics we call it a fix.

"This is the Stepford vote," Jim said, hardly able to contain his glee. "These bastards didn't have time to change the numbers in the 30 days between elections, so they just ran the same numbers even though all but two of the candidates were out of the race."

Ken was already looking for the figures on the Senate race.

"It was a five-person contest in the primary and 122,000 votes were cast in total," he said. "Look at this! There's 122,000 votes cast in the runoff, and…" he flipped the sheets to the finals. "Well, what do you know…122,000."

Jim picked up the cue stick and smashed the white ball into the rack. He was angry and yet he marvelled at the sheer audacity of the scheme. He pointed the cue at Ken.

"Do you think the Secretary of State is involved?"

"Hell, what about the press?" Ken threw back.

"If the press knew these numbers and never questioned them, then they're either stupid or collaborators."

It was an intriguing thought. We knew the press was capable of keeping candidates who didn't spend advertising dollars from getting publicity, but was it possible they would actually protect the people who were pulling this off?

"What do you think would happen if we went to the *Herald* with this story?" Jim asked.

"You think they'd touch it?"

"Let's push it."

Then we compared the Tallahassee final totals with the numbers on the September 8th readouts from Channel 7.

"Holy shit! Look at this." Ken was doing a dance on one foot.

"What?"

"Compare Channel 7's readouts. . . this is their unofficial projections of what the final totals will be At 9:31…the projection in the unofficial vote total column reads 96,499 votes. That's what they predict the final outcome will be." Then he shifted to the Tallahassee official totals. "And in these official returns, read what it says: 96,499.

That's one-hundred percent *perfect!* They called a perfect race. I'd like to see that computer program."

Jim paced around the table. "They took four minutes on Channel 4 to predict percentages for 250 candidates. You can't even read that many numbers off the back of the machines in four minutes, much less read them...run to a phone...call the TV stations...re-read them to an operator who has to punch them onto IBM cards and then run them through a computer for broadcast to the public. You just can't *do* that in four minutes."

"And what about precincts?" Ken asked. "Did both stations use the same precincts? Did they use the same reporters or were 680 people out there, on payrolls from both stations, calling back votes?"

Jim shook his head in disbelief

We sat and contemplated the possibilities.

Ken said: "Maybe this goes on all the time and we were too out of the action to notice, like most people are. Who thinks about how votes are counted anyway? Nobody pays attention. *We didn't.* We just expected a clean, open election like they taught us in Civics 101 at Royal Oak High School."

"So if you find out that there's a rigged vote with the television stations in on it, who do you go to to complain?" Jim asked.

The next move was to get back to Beiler and

find out about his super-amazing computer program. Ken called the University of Miami and got Beiler's telephone number in Washington at the American University. In a taped conversation he went right to the point.

"What kind of program could you have devised where the information from one machine was used to predict the results of all the races within one percent of perfect?"

"I didn't do it," Beiler replied. "It'd be a *million-to-one* odds that anyone could do that. I was just the on-air analyst but I didn't program it. I don't know how to program."

"Who did it, then?"

"It's a fellow named Elton Davis, who works on computers for a land sales company. He's the one who did it for Channel 7."

"Thank you, sir."

A solid lead. We had to pay Mr. Davis a visit where he worked at Cavanaugh Land Sales, which sold West Coast Florida swampland for development. The office was across the 79th Street Causeway from Channel 7's studios. We made an appointment.

The next day we sat across from a chunky, muscular man in a small and cluttered office. There was a chalk board on the wall.

"Professor Beiler says you programmed the Channel 7 computer," Ken began. "What was the formula you used that could predict 100 percent correct final totals with just one machine reporting?"

Davis stood and walked a few feet to the blackboard. He picked up the chalk in the tray, stood on his tip-toes, and reached up as if to begin to write.

Now, Ken thought, we're going to get the magic algorithm.

Then Davis slowly put the chalk back down, turned to us and in an icy voice, said:

"You'll never prove it. Now, get out."

We couldn't believe it. He opened the door and pointed outside. Ken tried to ask another question but Davis was mute. There was nothing more he was going to say.

It was time to call the FBI. We now knew for sure that the man who was supposed to have written the computer vote-count program had something sinister to hide.

The FBI offices were on Biscayne Boulevard just north of the downtown business area. We were escorted into a small office and then asked if we would agree to be photographed. If we said no, maybe they would refuse to listen. So we put our heads in one of those neck-holders, like the old New England stocks, and a clerk snapped a picture. They didn't request fingerprints.

"We want to make a statement, but we want a stenographer to take it down. We'll sign it and take a copy," Jim said.

The agent, in the government-issue blue suit, agreed.

The statement was twelve pages long and all of what we knew was in it, with as little supposition as we were capable of. We told of Beiler's "million-to-one" statement, the virtually impossible accuracy of a one-machine perfect projection, and Davis' warning that we'd "never prove it." We asked that the FBI interview Beiler and Davis about possible vote fraud in a federal election.

Then it was time to track down that one miracle machine.

Ken telephoned the news director at Channel 7 and asked "who had called in the information from the precincts with the raw vote totals from the machines?" He told us that members of the League of Women Voters, not reporters, had been hired to work in precincts selected by Beiler.

"You mean there weren't people in *all* precincts?" Ken asked.

"No," the news director said, "just in some sample precincts."

"Then how could you have shown 99 percent of the vote counted by 11 p.m. if you only had a few people in a few sample precincts…in light of the fact that you weren't getting any actual votes from the courthouse?"

There was a long pause.

"Call Joyce Deiffenderfer. She's the president of the League."

In early December, we kept an appointment at

Joyce Deiffenderfer's home in a section of Coral Gables known for manicured lawns, lush tropical foliage and big-mortgage houses. She answered the door. Deiffenderfer was tall, about six feet, austere, unsmiling, and bordering on uncordial. She had a friend with her, a woman, who looked as if she was there to be a witness.

Jim explained the mystery of the one-machine projection and asked: "Were you told there was a specific machine that was going to be used to extrapolate a projection?"

"No," she answered.

"Can you give me a list of the people from the League who worked that night in the precincts?"

"There is no list." She began to look uncomfortable. "There were no League women in the precincts that night."

That was a puzzling surprise.

"Channel 7 says the League gave them returns."

She saw the drift. "There was no such thing," she repeated. She started to speak again, changed her mind, and then blurted out: "I don't want to get caught in this thing." She began to weep. Her female companion watched without uttering a word.

We were almost sympathetic. She had just admitted that nobody was in the precincts that night, there was no magic machine, ergo, there could not have been any projected reporting by the television stations based on information supplied by the League.

"Will you go to the press and make a statement?" Jim asked quietly.

"Yes, I will," she said.

We shook hands all round and departed.

We were, in a word, ecstatic. Jim rushed over to The *Daily Planet* to file the story.

When the lease had been pulled on *Thee Image*, our "bully pulpit" was dismantled. So we bought half of the Miami *Free Press* from a guy named Jerry Powers and changed its name to The *Daily Planet*.

With the *Planet* as our new bullhorn we could fight for the causes of the Sixties, created mostly by Nixon's miasma, without begging some local whipped newspaper editor for permission.

One of our first *Planet* stories was about Tom Hayden. Hayden was another buddy of our youth in Royal Oak, Michigan, where we edited the high school paper together. Ken was the photographer who miraculously kept getting photos of record-breaking sports events. Jim and Tom edited the paper. The three of us also created a campus humor paper, The *Daily Smirker*, way back then which still survives today.

Tom had ended the Sixties with that Chicago Seven flourish which landed him in jail for the last time.

So when he told us that nobody but Joan Baez had given a nickel to the Seven's defense fund, we headlined it in the *Planet*.

The *Underground Press Service* picked up the story and distributed it to every other underground paper in the nation, including the college press. The Seven's defense fund swelled mightily soon after.

It was winter and the Sixties were over.

But the *Planet* was still there for us to run the story about Joyce Deiffenderfer. It appeared under the headline: "I DON'T WANT TO GET CAUGHT IN THIS THING."

We also went to the FBI, made another statement, and asked them to talk to Joyce Deiffenderfer.

Christmas passed, then came New Year 1971. We had the evidence, but there was no move on the part of the press to give it a milligram of ink or air time. Here was a major story that was being absolutely ignored by the Miami *Herald* , the Miami *News,* and every TV station. The frustration was galling.

"It's like kicking a marshmallow," Jim said.

We called the FBI to see how its investigation was progressing and one agent or another would always say: "Sorry, it's not our job to tell you anything."

Then we called our editor at Dell to tell him what we'd found, the state of the story, the ramifications of what we'd experienced. As we waited on the line, a strong, authoritative woman's voice came on.

"This is Helen Meyer," she said. She was the

outright owner and publisher of Dell in those days, and for a wild moment we expected her to congratulate us on our book idea, maybe even invite us to a publisher's cocktail party. Instead she said: "I'm cancelling your contract as of today. This book will not be printed." *

It was as if we had just fallen out of a Zeppelin. Why the high-level hostility, the lack of explanation? We hadn't been in touch with her or Dell for a year. After that telephone call everybody at Dell was out to lunch or in a meeting. We had the $3,500, but was the investigation we found so intriguing really over?

"Where are we?" Ken asked.

"Dead in the water."

There was some wallowing in self-pity and some crying in our beer. Then, two days later on Ken's thirtieth birthday, a new idea popped up to get *Votescam* off zero. Ken got the brainstorm to send a telegram to Richard Nixon.

The act of composing and sending a telegram to the President of the United States is like dipping a toe into contemporary history. There are advantages and drawbacks, depending on the tenor of the times and the subject matter. It is akin to sending a rocket ship into the void — you don't know what it's going to hit or how far it will go.

But on that day, as we sent the telegram via Western Union, we just thought it was a hell of a way to blow out the birthday candles.

---

*We later discovered that Ms. Meyer was a long time friend of Washington Post publisher Katharine Graham, a fact that will be better understood later in this book.

TELEGRAM

White House, 23 April 1971
Washington, D.C.

Dear Mr. President,

For the past several months we have pieced together documentation and theory regarding a Federal-State-Local election in Dade County September 8, 1970.

Evidence indicates major vote fraud was perpetrated. Television coverage on Channels 4 and 7 (WTVJ, WCKT) featured computer "projections" of voter turnout and final vote totals by 7:24 p.m. Projections made by Channel 7 were based on returns from only one voting machine. We questioned persons involved and believe election results were pre-arranged by all three TV news departments acting to promote the deception that official returns from the Dade County courthouse would be delayed due to a "computer breakdown." We are providing documentation to Miami FBI, and urgently request that your office direct U.S. Attorney General to investigate.

Kenneth Collier
James Collier

3

THE SILENT PRESS

*"For those who govern, the first thing
required is indifference to newspapers."*

—Thiers

The sudden death of our book deal, we
reasoned, was the first sure sign that our efforts
and instigations had made waves outside the
Miami area.

The fourteen months between April 23, 1971,
when we sent the telegram to President Nixon,
and June 17, 1972, when President Nixon's
"plumbers" were captured in the Watergate, was
a period in Miami when a good deal of noise
was made about the vote fraud issue.

The first above-ground story about rigged
elections in Miami appeared on August 29, 1971 in
the Miami Beach *Reporter* under the byline of its
old and respected editor-publisher, Paul M. Bruun.

Bruun was the last independent editor in Dade County. He didn't owe much to anybody. His word was respected and his opinion carried weight among both Jews and Gentiles on Miami Beach. He was tall, elegant, in his seventies, a man with snowy white hair and moustache. He flourished a cane, had a rich, deep, rumbling voice, and a big Basset hound named Caesar led him about on a leash. He was a world-class gossip and a *bon vivant*. Most important, he was wealthy and hard to corrupt. His column titled "Bruun Over Miami" was famous among the postwar settlers, especially on the Beach.

We ghostwrote "The Great Dade Election Rig Continues" story for him as a factual account of the voting controversy, based on the Channel 7 computer readouts. He told us that he would put his byline on the story only if his own independent checking verified every fact and allegation.

As a hedge against libel suits, Bruun sent a copy of the story to all whose names were mentioned. He advised them that they could "exercise veto power over the story" if they could demonstrate a fault in its factual underpinning. When no objections were raised, the following story appeared in the *Reporter* beneath a headline which read:

THE GREAT VOTE-FORECASTING MYSTERY — AND SOME QUESTIONS...
by Paul M. Bruun, Publisher

Introduction

For months I have hoped that some, whom I am willing to admit know far more about such electronic computations than I do, would answer some very pertinent questions.

Nothing has been printed or broadcast by anybody which in any manner answered any of the questions that have been really bugging me. Read this carefully and see whether you agree there are many that bother you.

Though this is basically a story about Channels 4 and 7, I have sought in vain to find out exactly why television station WPLG, Channel 10, did not broadcast this all-important election, though I understand that elaborate plans had been made by the *Post-Newsweek* subsidiary to do so. What happened that two out of three supposedly competing TV news departments had the broadcasting of projected election results all to themselves?

In all fairness, I sent a copy of this story to Channels 4, 7 and 10, to the Miami *News,* to the Miami *Herald,* to Professors Beiler, Shipley and Wood of the University of Miami Political Science Department with a copy to U.M. President, Dr. Henry King Stanford.

In my vault I have the material from which

his story was written. I think it is news. The daily press in Miami obviously doesn't think this is news. Why? Here goes, with all the facts that I can present…"

The story then went on to recount the election night TV coverage on Channels 4 and 7 featuring the "miracle" projections. It asked the question:

"Was the election rigged?"

Bruun also interviewed Dr. Beiler, who said:

"Oh, let's say even at this point I've had very little experience with computers. You see, what I've always done is simply write the specifications and the programmer programs."

When Bruun questioned the computer-programmer employed by Channel 7 to provide computerized "projections based on results phoned in from so-called sample precincts" he was told:

"…ask Dr. Beiler about it. I only put in those machines whatever he tells me."

Paul Bruun expressed his amazement in the article which continues:

"So here we have the two men responsible for the odds-defying feat of projecting with near-perfect accuracy the detailed outcome of a lengthy election ballot on the basis of phoned-in unofficial returns from the solitary voting machine — and yet each man denies any detailed knowledge of how it was done.

"Radio station WKAT revealed that an investigation is now underway, conducted by one of the losing candidates, to determine if the election itself could have been rigged "by a Dade County Machine in absolute control of local establishment mass media." The U.S. Justice Department has been engaged in accepting information pertinent to this case through the Miami field office of the FBI.

"Martin Braterman, Dade County elections supervisor at the time of the election, resigned in November 1970 after serving for five years. His resignation came just after Dr. Beiler provided our investigations with the Channel 7 computer read-outs. Braterman told this newspaper's publisher: 'Whatever happens at the TV stations on election night has nothing to do with the results of the election. How could it?'

Following are some examples of the amazing accuracy of the 7:24 p.m. projections.

TOTAL VOTES CAST Projection		**TOTAL VOTES CAST** Official totals
Governor	141,387	141,866
Sen. #43	45,696	45,881
House #98	97,031	96,499
House #104	67,940	68,491
House #107	81,802	81,539

The Big Three television stations are network affiliates of ABC, CBS and NBC. The ownership of Channels 4 and 7 has been based in Dade

County since the advent of television in 1949. Washington-based *Post-Newsweek* has owned and operated Channel 10 (whose call-letters WPLG stand for the late Phillip L. Graham, husband of Katharine Graham of the Washington *Post* communications empire) for less than two years.

Both Miami-based stations televised continuous coverage from the moment the polls closed. But Washington *Post*-controlled Channel 10, WPLG, suddenly cancelled elaborately planned coverage which was to have featured the polling techniques of Irwin Premack Associates, a Tampa firm which had been paid $27,000 to provide commentary. At the last minute WPLG's rented computer at its location in the First National Bank Building "broke down," according to WPLG news director Carl Zedell. A movie was run instead. The so-called "blackout" on reports to the public of ACTUAL OFFICIAL VOTES from the Dade County Courthouse is evidenced by two documented facts:

1. The computer read-outs used as the on-air script for Dr. Beiler at Channel 7 show that no actual votes had been received by the station until 11:15 p.m., four hours and fifteen minutes after the beginning of televised election coverage.

2. After the supposed computer breakdown, newscasters Ralph Renick, V.P. News Department, Channel 4 and George Crolius, of

Channel 7, repeatedly told the public they would use a high-speed computer analysis to project the outcome based on returns from phoned-in sample precincts. The "condition" of the Dade County computer, however, was at all times contrary to what the public was being told by TV newspeople.

According to an official press release from Dade data processing chief Leonard White, *"The county computer at the courthouse was never down and it was never slow."*

Professor Tom Wood, Beiler's associate on Channel 7 election analysis offered the *Reporter* this comment: "It looks like we hit the lucky machine. I guess it was right in the middle of things."

This newspaper challenges both Miami TV stations (4 and 7) and/or the political science professors at the University of Miami to demonstrate the manner in which all of the foregoing was accomplished.

And where exactly is the single voting machine which served as bellwether for the balance of 1,647 voting machines active that night?

Are we to seriously believe that any relative handful of votes can be "projected" to be "typical" of us all? Would the people who voted on that single machine be Black, White, Hispanic, Jewish, Italian, Irish, Blue collar, White-collar, Upper-Middle-Lower class models of the way an entire county thinks? Or is the existence of that mystery voting machine a myth?

If, as seems indicated by the foregoing, the election should turn out to have been rigged, then this story will be a catalyst in bringing about its ultimate exposure."

Paul was the kind of man who chortled about stories like this. He knew damned well how uncomfortable he was going to make some very pretentious people, and he loved it. They might be able to say that Jim and Ken Collier were something near to crackpots, or dangerous, or full of misinformation, but they did not dare to say that about Paul Bruun, who was the elder statesman, whose paper was second echelon but who could rake them over some very hot coals if he wanted it to.

Paul Bruun was not about to back off any issue he agreed to start, and any press person worth a quarter knew it. So the immediate letters of denial were pained and defensive, but not insulting.

Here is Channel 7's Corporate reply:

Dear Mr. Bruun:

I wish to acknowledge receipt of your letter of August 13, 1971, with a draft of the story that you plan to publish on Sunday, August 29.

It appears to me that your primary contention

is that by 7:24 p.m. on September 8, 1970, the local television stations accurately projected all races based "solely on the returns from one solitary voting machine."

I wish to assure you that the premise is untrue and preposterous.

Further, the implication of wrong doing and conspiracy is ridiculous.

Sincerely,
Edmund N. Ansin,
Executive Vice President and General Manager
Sunbeam Televison Corporation Channel 7
WCKT

Channel 4's Corporate reply:

Dear Paul:

I am happy you have given us the opportunity to comment on the story you planned to run in the Reporter concerning election coverage by the Miami TV stations. From my own knowledge, I know a great deal of the information which has been given to you on this subject is incorrect and I want to put forth the facts as I know them for you to be able to make a responsible journalistic judgement.

…The implication that there was collaboration between the two stations in the projecting of results and the "withholding" of actual information is completely erroneous. I think you know, Paul, that the various Miami TV operations are, on the contrary, quite competitive.

...There is no secrecy with respect to the readouts which our computer produced during the course of the evening or such data which we have retained concerning the actual information transferred from the Courthouse. You are welcome to look at this material, *although anyone not familiar with computers would need some substantial interpretation to understand the data*. (Emphasis added.)

...This station does not claim to have projected perfect percentages on each candidate in every race by 7:04 p.m.; in fact, in several of the races we were unable to "call" a winner by the end of our election coverage because our projections showed the races to be too close to declare one man definitely the winner.

...It is clear that computers employed by television stations do not decide on an election. They merely provide a means by which actual votes cast in selected representative precincts may be projected in order to give an estimate of the winner. The winning candidate obviously is decided by the voter at the ballot box.

...Ralph Renick (v.p. News) and I will be pleased to go over this matter with you in person. The story as presently written, at least as pertains to this station, contains a great deal of erroneous information and presents a totally misleading picture of the procedures which we employ in reporting election results.

...Being in the news business ourselves, we realize that it is sometimes difficult to track down the true facts; I hope that the information I have outlined above goes some distance in providing you with the data concerning the tight standards of WTVJ practices.

...We are quite proud of the competence which we have developed in the projection of election results through the utilization of sample precincts and we have no desire to hide from you or anyone else the care with which we program our computers to achieve reliable estimates at the earliest moment.

Sincerely,
W.R. Brazzil, V.P. in Charge
WTVJ Channel 4
Miami, Florida

Next, one of the University of Miami professors who appeared on Channel 7 the night of the elections:,

Dear Mr. Bruun:

Thank you for your recent letter enclosing a copy of the story you propose to publish. To my mind, there is no need to comment on a tale so preposterous.

Sincerely yours,
Dr. Thomas J. Wood
Department of Politics and Public Affairs
University of Miami

**Also, a letter from the editor of the
Miami News.**

Dear Paul,

I am interested largely by the accuracy of the
computer...The votes had already been cast and
the election decided before the computer results
were broadcast. While the accuracy of the
projections was amazing, I do not see what
effect they had on the outcome of the elections.
Nor do I see what the stations have to gain with
anything other than accuracy. If indeed, they
used only one voting machine to make the
projections, the risk of being wrong was theirs.

I do not know of a "Dade County Machine" in
absolute control of local mass media. Nobody is
in control of me. I don't see any evidence that
anybody but you is in control of you.

Sincerely,
Sylvan Meyer
Editor, The Miami News

Finally, a letter from the chief executive of the University of Miami.

Dear Paul:

Your note and a copy of the article regarding those voting machine projections arrived yesterday. I simply have not had time to read it carefully enough to comment. I will look it over within the next few days and let you have my comments, if any. I have great confidence in these professors.

Sincerely yours,
Henry King Stanford
U. of M. President

We needed more answers to questions like: How was the fraud accomplished in the field where votes were tallied by 4,000 precinct officials countywide? Who was in a position to do it? How many people would have had to be in on the scheme? Why would any plotters go to the trouble? What part, if any, did the League of Women Voters play?

"We've got to keep up the pressure," Jim kept repeating.

And we did.

On September 24, 1971, the University of Miami student newspaper, The *Hurricane*, chose an eye-opening headline to debut its version of the story:

PROFESSORS IMPLICATED IN LOCAL ELECTION RIGGING

We were pleased with the pugnacious tone of the headline, though purists suggested it was libelous. The *Hurricane's* editor-in-chief, Scott Bressler, stood by the story and wrote the following editorial that accompanied it:

ELECTION RIGGING QUESTIONS MUST HAVE ANSWERS

The alleged rigging of last year's Dade County election as presented by the Miami Beach *Reporter*...has been written off by most as totally absurd. Indeed the charges leveled are fantastic by any stretch of the imagination. Charges of countywide election fraud sound like they belong in a Humphrey Bogart movie. The only catch, however, is that too many questions have been left unanswered.

One voting machine (out of 1,648) was used to accurately project the entire election involving some 40 races and more than 250 candidates. Which machine was it?

What was the formula used by the TV stations to accurately project the entire election at 7:24 p.m. before any official votes had been reported?

Why were there no actual votes reported until

11:15? Some say the computer broke down. Others say it didn't. What is the correct answer?

Why have the three television stations and the Miami *Herald* and the Miami *News* completely ignored this story? They may claim that it's not true, but can they deny its news value?

We feel that these questions must be answered. The *Hurricane* certainly does not feel that three of its professors were involved in an election fraud but we do feel the necessity to find the answers and restore the public's faith in Dade County's electoral process.

Within a week, on October 1, 1971, The *Hurricane* revived the issue once again by printing a Letter to the Editor from Miami *News* editor Sylvan Meyer, who steadfastly refused to use his own columns in Miami's second largest daily to air the controversy he was helping to create.

NEWS EDITOR COMMENTS ON ELECTION STORY

To the Editor:

Permit me to make a few comments about your news story and editorial.

I concede the vote projection was remarkably accurate. Unfortunately, computers are reflecting this sort of accuracy all over the country. The question of computer projections is not a new one and has been the subject of national debate for several years.

There is no way to prevent people from projecting, by guess or by computer, the results of elections and I am not sure I would try to prevent them from doing so if it were within my power.

The Miami *News* did not run a story when shown this material because we do not feel it is a story. It was an issue originally raised by the Collier brothers, two men I would not trust under any circumstances. They have their own political thing and that's okay, but their information in this matter is not news, it is a "so what?"

I do not believe the story to be true, in that it certainly does not establish either a motive *nor a result contrary to the public interest.* (Emphasis added.) I do not believe it has news value because it is entirely speculative and maligns the reputation of otherwise honorable men without cause and without justification.

Your editorial implies that there has been a loss of faith in the integrity of Dade County's electoral process. If this is true, I am not aware of it and I certainly do not believe that the information gathered by Paul Bruun, the Colliers, et al, has resulted in such a loss of faith.

On October 29, 1971, Bressler reported:

CONCERNED DEMOCRATS INVESTIGATE ALLEGED DADE ELECTION RIGGING

The story of an alleged election rigging involving three UM professors will be investigated by the Concerned Democrats, a coalition of liberal groups in Dade County and statewide. The group, after listening to the evidence presented by one of its own members in a closed-door session last Tuesday night, voted to go ahead with the inquiry.

Presentation of pertinent evidence in the case was made by Alvin Entin, a lawyer in the Miami area, who told the *Hurricane,* "I'm not saying that any of the charges are true, but there was found to be enough probable cause to look into it further. From what we've seen there are questions which have to be answered. A lot of people are saying the Colliers are crazy, but you cannot dismiss the evidence just by calling names.

Why won't Dr. Beiler clear this up or tell us anything? If he did, I would be willing to believe him since I don't think he's crazy.

The Concerned Democrats plan to send letters to the three professors, the three TV networks, the two Miami daily newspapers and the local TV news departments to help get to the bottom of this. "We have a responsibility to look into this. Personally, I'm scared to death. I believe in the system and all I can say is, God forbid that this is true," Entin said.

In October, this letter appeared in The *Hurricane:*

BEILER SCOLDS 'CANE EDITOR FOR IRRESPONSIBILITY

To the Editor:

To determine whether election results are real or fraudulent is fairly easy. Some 340 precincts returned reports called Canvass Sheets signed by at least ten election officials in each precinct. These and the physical counting-wheels in the voting machines themselves which were available for re-checking within a certain time period prescribed by law, constitute the guarantee that any dishonesty would have to be at the individual polling places themselves. Do you honestly believe that 3,400 election officials were in on the so-called "rigging"?

I am amazed at your ignorance and your lack of investigating enterprise when faced with the products of totally irresponsible journalism. You merely copy it. You are fully as bad at The *Planet* and the *Reporter.* You should learn now, so that you do not get sued if you ever go into journalism on a responsible paper or channel.

Of course, I have no interest in "laying to rest" such hare-brained "journalism," which condemns itself on its face. The Colliers wasted a great deal of my time with this nonsense. I am certainly not going to let you do the same. As little as I think of your behavior in this matter, I don't think you have their problem.

Ross C. Beiler

On November 11, 1971, The *Daily Planet,* Miami's underground newspaper, ran the following treatment by editor Buzz Kilman:

THE SILENT PRESS
(THE ELECTION NOBODY EVER HEARD OF...)

When is a story not a story?

Several weeks ago the Miami Beach *Reporter* broke with a story that the 1970 Dade County election was rigged.

Impossible?

Maybe, but a lot of impossible things happened on the night of September 8, 1970 that either have not or cannot be explained by those who accomplished them.

Since Publisher Bruun printed the story in the Reporter, The *Daily Planet*, the *South Miami News*, the Hialeah *Home News* and the UM *Hurricane* have run followups.

Throughout the local media uproar, not a word of the mess has been printed in Miami's two dailys, the *News* and the *Herald*.

Why?

As time goes on, this question becomes almost as interesting as the original charge that the elections were rigged. Although both of Miami's dailies have privately dismissed the notion that an election rigging took place, they have failed to explain, privately or in their own newspapers, why they are ignoring what is obviously an outrageously intriguing story.

The Colliers devoutly believe that some sort of conspiracy was culminated on the evening of September 8, 1970 — and this is a line of thought too overwhelming for even the most enthusiastic reporter…and yet, it's not inconceivable as it wouldn't be the first election to be rigged.

Privately, however, the Colliers' obsession has been considered more carefully — and has been the object of much off-the-record discussion among area newsmen. I have personally talked with several, among them Bill Byer of Channel 10, the *Post-Newsweek* subsidiary, and Pat Murphy, editor of the Coral Gables *Times*, a *Herald-owned* newspaper, who have expressed at least a degree of bewilderment on the subject, although they have not been moved to inquire further. In a telephone conversation, Byer termed the issue "serious" and added that it was — and I quote — "a sick, sad, sorry situation."

Every newsperson in the city and probably the state knows about the charges. A great many of them, responsible, establishment reporters, have expressed to me concern over the implications for future elections if computers and the media ever do take over the election system. The most chilling aspect of the entire affair is the ominous and unexplainable silence of the Establishment media in the face of undeniable controversy. What is so special about this case?

And that was that.

It wasn't as if the press was entirely a pussycat then. In 1971 there was a maelstrom of "investigative reporting" going on all over the country, to the extent that one investigation (with many dubious and unanswered motives) eventually resulted in the resignation of Richard Nixon and a new balance of power between the government and the press. To recall history:

In the autumn of 1971 President Nixon was enraged by Daniel Ellsberg's activities in the "Pentagon Papers" affair.

To Nixon, the fact that Ellsberg, a low-level, very wealthy civilian in the Defense Department, turned over Pentagon secrets to The New York *Time*s and The Washington *Post* was deeply disturbing: unpatriotic, perhaps traitorous. Worse, was the U.S. Supreme Court's refusal to issue a restraining order preventing the Ellsberg information from becoming public.

The primary revelation Nixon felt ought to be kept secret was the material that proved the "Gulf of Tonkin" incident was a total ruse concocted by the Executive Branch to stampede the U.S. Congress into voting the President unrestricted war powers in Southeast Asia.

Apparently, the 1964 naval encounter in the

Gulf of Tonkin, where a U.S. cruiser was supposedly fired on by North Vietnamese boats, simply never occurred.

Championing Ellsberg, however, was Nixon's harshest critic, Katharine Graham, publisher of The Washington *Post*, whose First Amendment rights to publish the information were upheld by the high court. Smarting from the Ellsberg case, Nixon, through his Attorney General, John Mitchell, started investigating Mrs. Graham and all her holdings in an effort to find evidence that could jeopardize her empire, including her newly-acquired FCC license for television station WPLG, Miami. WPLG was purchased in 1969 for $20 million. (By 1989 it was estimated to be worth just under $900 million).

In the heirarchy of Miami's press barons, "Kate" Graham was a queen and her family held imperial power in Florida, as well as in and around Washington. Her brother-in-law, Robert, was elected to the Florida legislature on September 8, 1970. He went on to serve two elected terms as Florida governor and then rose to fill a U.S. Senate seat.

Whenever the media leaders of Miami called a conference, Mrs. Graham would chair the function. Such meetings took place at the University of Miami. Channel 7 was owned by the university itself. Channel 4 was owned by Wometco Enterprises, an entertainment and vending machine company.

When Katharine Graham took her place at the head of the conference table, she was flanked by Miami *Herald* lawyer Dan Paul and UM president Henry King Stanford. Further along the table in a prescribed order of rank were the president of the local chapter of the League of Women Voters (LWV); the Dade County Manager; the chief circuit court judge; the liaison from the Chamber of Commerce; assorted lawyers representing Channels 4 and 7.

Mrs. Graham, as she was to prove during the Watergate revelations of the Washington *Post*, had the balls of a Picasso goat. If she had to take on Richard Nixon to get his attention and respect, she would risk her realm to do it. In the Miami area, her power over the press and politicians was unchallenged.

Freedom of the press was a battle cry at the time, and Richard Nixon was on one side and Mrs. Graham and occasionally the Sulzbergers of the New York *Times* were on the other.

That was the political atmosphere we were operating in, and it seemed that most things were possible and that corruption was being rooted out by crusading, gutsy publishers and editors even at the highest levels.

Then why, we wondered, was vote fraud such a special case?

In a private conversation with Jim, Henry King Stanford, the University of Miami's president, gave his perspective on the problem.

"It's such an explosive issue," he said, "that your proof must be incontrovertable. Frankly, there are holes in the story that you've got to close before you can demand that the big papers take you seriously. If you don't come up with a plausible way to explain how 4,000 poll workers' signatures could be circumvented in such a conspiracy, then your theory will die of its own weight."

That was a tall, tall order and we knew he was right. But how the hell could we go about explaining those thousands of corroborating signatures?

4

IT TAKES A THIEF

"The major fact about history is that a large part of it appears to be criminal."

—Anonymous

Our quest looked insanely futile but we stubbornly refused to quit until we were as dead as our theories seemed to be. We worried about being too far out, too intuitive, seeing connections where there were none. The word was that we had gotten "too extreme," and that we'd "lost balance."

Yet the story never faded. We would wander the beaches and wonder about the possible ramifications of what we had dug up. Nonetheless, we decided to pursue it. Jim was the hottest after it. As an avid chess player, he was intrigued by the complexity of it all. Ken kept getting married and having children, and his children's mothers were never too thrilled about the quest. That slowed him down, but it never stopped him.

We needed somebody wise and credible with whom we could talk on the local scene, to validate or reject our conclusions. The agents at the FBI said that U.S. Attorney Robert W. Rust was a good listener.

He was, but he was consistently noncommittal about the use, if any, his superiors in the Justice Department were making of our field work. We never saw the man. He was reachable only by telephone, and our phone conversations were probably recorded.

Because Rust would willingly spend twenty minutes at a time on the phone discussing the implications of our theories, we assumed the jury in the Justice Department was still open minded about the case.

We found ourselves in accord with Rust on two points. If the elections in Dade County were being systematically rigged, it had to be accomplished and/or by:

1) Massive tampering with the voting machines;
2) Massive forgery in the certificates attested to by the signature of poll workers.

Both possibilities seemed far fetched, illogical or impossible.

The 1,648 machines would have to have been pre-set with vote totals without poll workers finding out. The poll workers' duties included visually checking the mechanical counters in back of the machines before allowing voting on election morning.

If forgery was the method, it would appear to be a Houdini-like trick. Each of the 1,648 machines' certificates of canvass were signed in triplicate by at least ten poll-workers per precinct, twice a day, adding up to roughly 32,960 separate signatures.

As impossible as either of those two possibilities sounded, we didn't discount them entirely because of Dade County's track record of "polecat" elections. Polecat elections stink to high heaven.

Our skepticism was founded in the lore of Dade County polecat politics, circa 1959, when perhaps the most important election ever held in the region took place. It was a county-wide referendum in which each of the 27 separate municipalities in Dade County were asked to give up their power to govern themselves autonomously. They were being asked instead to turn over self-governing power to the proposed "Metropolitan Government," or Metro, for short.

Opposition to the "power grab" was fierce and the debate dominated the press for months before the balloting. The Miami *Herald* strongly backed the proposition. The Metro Charter, a set of rules defining the powers of Metro-Dade, was written by Miami *Herald* lawyer Dan Paul. The Charter was a product of many consultations with the insiders, who met regularly in the UM boardroom, under the twin chairmanship of *Herald* publisher John S. Knight and U.M. President Henry King Stanford.

The voluntary divestiture of power by Dade's cluster of independent cities would bring about a whole new way of governing, tax collecting, public servicing, public contracting and election administration. Billions of dollars in commercial and property futures were at stake.

The Fifties were drawing to a close. The architects of regional government viewed their new model of governance by "experts" as a new era. No longer would there be dependence on charismatic publicly elected officials, whose credentials to lead often consisted of no more than a willingness to shake every hand in the neighborhood.

Elite planners sought to diminish the power of mayors, chiefs of police and local heroes of one kind or another who influence public policy.

In their place, operating largely behind-the-scenes with no accountability to the public , would be Public Administration Service (PAS) graduates, trained to be loyal to the Charter. More often than not the county manager came from a different part of the country. It was to be government by "grid," so that personnel from

PAS could be nimbly interchanged throughout the United States, without fanfare, to fill advisory "slots," such as county manager.

As the 1959 Metro referendum drew near, citizens who preferred the old-fashioned way of governing banded together with such vigor that a Miami *News* poll conducted by houndstooth-clean editor Bill Baggs showed Metro was headed for a kick in the ass and down to defeat. (The *News* was still independent in those days.) Baggs commented that it would be surprising if the forces for Metro mustered any backing at all beyond the elite, special-interest voters who stood to benefit financially.

Then, on election night, the electoral reality-quake struck.

Metro *won*, according to the votes counted on Dade's carefully tended Automatic Voting Machines. And while there was some head shaking and muttering after the results were in, the discontent was scantily reported and soon forgotten. Talk radio was a mere glitter in Larry King's eyes then.

But as years passed, old-timers began wondering aloud on the early talk radio programs if something fishy hadn't occurred back in 1959 when Metro was voted in. In 1971, a caller mentioned a group known as "the warehouse gang" as the ones most likely to be behind the original Metro election victory.

The caller hinted mysteriously of a cadre of

"good old boys" who had long been in charge of the county's voting machines, which were stored between elections at a warehouse in Opa Locka, Dade's most rural backwater municipality located on the edge of the Everglades.

There, it was rumored, a flourishing criminal enterprise had evolved over the years. The manipulators in county politics came to depend on the voting machine mechanics to guarantee the outcome of multimillion dollar bond issues and other controversial measures. It was common knowledge, one informant told us, that, "Those guys can make a mechanical voting machine whistle Dixie."

The Opa Locka warehouse at the Opa-Locka Airport is a big World War Two-type hangar. The airport is a vast expanse of concrete at the edge of black swamp water. It's flat and the trees are very low and Jim learned to fly Cessna 150s and 172s out there.

Frank Vickery, a big, old, taciturn "cracker," was in charge of the warehouse. He didn't have much to do out in the swamp all day and he was bored. So he was happy to accept the court order we handed him giving us permission to examine documents. He liked to talk and show people around. So he led and we listened.

Inside the hangar were 1,648 gray-green voting machines with levers, plus a lot of extras, all lined up in rows. They were made by

the Automatic Voting Machine Company of
Jamestown, New York.

"Can you show us the candidate counters and
the wheels inside?" Jim asked.

He led us to a nearby machine and opened
up the back with a key. There were a lot of
plastic, wheels, three-digit counters underneath
a black grid. The insides looked pretty simple.

"How can you rig this thing?" Ken asked.

"One of the best ways," Frank chuckled, "is to
put decals over the counters so that when you
see them in the morning it says "000" but
underneath it says maybe "090," which in any
precinct is a pretty good bonus."

"What else?"

"There's such a thing as a predetermined
counter. It's already set up before the
election…by shaving the plastic wheel inside so
that it slips ahead 100 or 200 or 300 votes. Any
good mechanic can do it with a razor blade." He
took us to his office and reached into his desk,
bringing out one of the counter wheels in his
big rough hands.

"This is a shaved predetermined counter," he
said.

"Can we keep one?"

"Sure, take it."

Jim put the wheel in his pocket.

"Who works on these machines?"

"They're worked on by the mechanics for
Wometco. They have vending machines and
movie houses. They can make those suckers sing."

We shook hands with Frank and said goodbye. Ken walked outside whistling the tune to:

"Way down south in the land of cotton,
good times there are not forgotten...
Lookaway! Lookaway! Lookaway
Dixieland."

Within a week the photograph of the shaved wheel on the counter was on the front page of the *Planet.*

Then Jim called Ellis Rubin, a Miami Beach lawyer whose tactic was to get as much publicity as possible for his clients and causes. Rubin was a tall, lanky, good looking guy in his mid thirties. He had run for Congress as a Republican and lost. We didn't know it at the time, but Rubin's campaign manager had been U.S. Attorney Robert Rust. We didn't know, either, that Rubin was thick as cold grits with the CIA and other intelligence-gathering outfits.

We told him the whole story, or as much as we could get into an hour or so. There was a charisma about Rubin, an intellectual intensity that we liked. He might be able to break the silence in the press because he had chutzpah, brains and the ear of a lot of reporters who liked his style.

He said he'd do what he could, *pro bono*, and we believed him. He was one of the few characters we encountered who was always as good as his word.

After that trip to Opa Locka, we figured there must be some documents out at the hangar that we didn't get to see. We had to go back. We decided that we as American citizens had the right to know everything involved with our so-called free and fair vote.

On a bright, sunny January morning we drove back to the Opa-Locka warehouse and parked in front of the door. As soon as we walked in we saw, about fifty feet ahead of us, a set of wooden steps going up to a loft suspended from the ceiling.

"What are you guys doing here?" It was Vickery.

"We want to check that loft over there," Jim said.

"I got a court order here that says you guys aren't allowed back in here."

He showed us a piece of paper signed by circuit court chief judge, Henry Balaban.

"You can tell Balaban what to do with his order," Ken said. Vickery headed for his office.

"He's probably going to call the cops."

We didn't waste any time. We sprinted up the steps and into the loft.

Before us were boxes and boxes of documents that obviously pertained to the 1970 elections.

"I can't believe it!" Jim breathed.

"Falling into shit."

"Where do we start?"

"Just look and grab."

We took as many papers as we thought were significant from different boxes with a millisecond or so to decide, and we stuffed them under our shirts, smoothing them down so they showed as little as possible. Then we headed out of the loft and back to the car.

But as we were coming down the ladder, we saw three men coming toward us, with the ex-supervisor of elections, Martin Braterman, leading the way. He was dressed in a black overcoat and broadbrimmed black fedora. His appearance in the garb of a traditional "bad guy" was almost surrealistic, given the precarious legal position we found ourselves in.

"What are you guys doing here?" he demanded. "This is County property. Get out or I'll have you arrested."

We didn't say a word. We brushed past him and his two associates and walked to the car as fast as we could, with as much dignity as we could muster. Ken theatrically burned rubber getting away.

Every mile we put between ourselves and the warehouse buoyed our spirits. Within a few minutes on the open road we were making plans to return to the loft.

Once more we spread out the contraband on Jim's pool table.

It was a smorgasbord of stuff.

We had:

1) IBM computer cards with the candidate's name typed on each and hand-written numbers on them.

2) What appeared to be crib sheets that had handwritten numbers that included a time of day, and then other numbers, also in pencil, in the same handwriting.

3) Mimeographed, stapled-together sheets that showed the handouts that were given to the press. It was a workup model, handprinted with a red pencil. On the front of it were the words: "Machine Totals Before Correction." (What did *before correction* mean?)

4) A press release from Leonard White, who ran the computer for the courthouse during the primary. His job was to feed the actual votes over the telephone line, called the "A" line, to the *Herald* and the television stations. It said, "Misinformation" had been given out by the news media on September 8th about the courthouse computer's alleged breakdown. It said that due to careful programming the computer "was never slow and never down."

5) A letter to all precinct workers telling them that they had to be at a "schooling" session two weeks in advance of the election, and they all had to sign in and give their true signatures, otherwise they would not be paid.

Then there was a ream or so of other

papers a little less outstanding but certainly fascinating.

"Man, I want to tell you, this is a hell of a haul," Jim said.

"We could have gotten this same stuff, of course, if we had followed the system," Ken said dryly.

"Okay," Jim took a deep breath, "let's see if it makes sense. Old Martin Braterman resigned. Now he turns up at the warehouse to protect this cache of documents."

"Right," Ken said, "and we now have documents that show there was a way to procure the true signatures from the precinct workers two weeks ahead of the election. Plus, the television stations lied about the computer at the courthouse breaking down and the press release is evidence of that."

"They just needed an excuse to go on the air with their projections. We know that a lot of numbers, handwritten before the election, turned out to be final totals after the election was official."

"Back to the FBI? "

"Yup."

We gave the FBI agents originals and copies of the evidence, including the press release, the computer cards, the workup sheets and the letter from Braterman asking for the signatures.

"Does this disappear into the void, too?" Jim asked.

"Yes," the agent smiled.

We sent much of the same material to Richard Gerstein, the State Attorney. He told us we had violated a court order to get the material and he refused to deal with it.

Jim called U.S. Attorney Rust.

"It's time for a meeting with the Justice Department in Washington."

Rust was his usual vague self.

"Goddamit, we deserve it," Jim's anger spilled over. "We've got the evidence and we want somebody to look at it."

Rust scheduled it for the end of March with Craig C. Donsanto, a Justice Department attorney.

Jim drove to Washington, while Ken stayed in Miami with his wife and daughter.

The afternoon of the meeting, Jim walked to the Justice Department on Pennsylvania Avenue and found his way to Donsanto's office. It wasn't a corner office, and it wasn't a cubicle either, but a middle of the corridor mid-sized office. Donsanto was in his late twenties and he had a melon-shaped head.

Jim told his story and handed him the shaved candidate counter and other significant documents in a manila envelope.

"I want an investigation," Jim told him.

"I'll look into it," Donsanto said. "Thanks for coming."

Jim pushed for a more specific deadline, but

Donsanto refused to give it.

"These things take time," he said, smiling woodenly.

And that was that.

Back in Florida, we tried to pinpoint where we were.

We put together packets of "evidence" in manila envelopes and gave them to the local press. We saw Jack Anderson, the columnist, at the Americana Hotel in Bal Harbor. He took a packet and thanked us and we never heard from him again.

Katharine Graham was at a meeting at the University of Miami when Jim handed the packet to her. She took it and didn't say a word.

And that was that.

In May, Jim drove back to Washington. He took a shot and went unannounced to Jack Anderson's red brick townhouse on Vermont Avenue, but Anderson refused to see him.

Then Jim walked through the glass doors into the offices of the Democratic National Committee in the Watergate Office Building. He found the office of Larry O'Brien, the head of the DNC, and left a *Votescam* packet on his desk.*

---

*A few weeks later, on June 17, 1972, a second break-in by "plumbers" at the DNC resulted in their arrest for what Richard Nixon later called "a third-rate burglary." At this stage of the game, we hadn't the slightest inkling that what took place on June 17th could possibly relate to our investigation. Only Justice Department documents we found years later while rummaging through the system would suggest a connection between Watergate and Votescam.

The off-year primary election rolled around in September and we decided to watch it closely on television at Jim's house. As happened two years earlier, Channel 10 wasn't broadcasting returns but instead was running a movie.

It was, in Yogi Berra's words, *deja vu* all over again, only there was an eerie feeling about it this time.

Not long after the polls closed, Channels 7 and 4 put their commentators on the air. After a little while the anchor people came on and announced that the courthouse computer had broken down and instead of official results, the station would broadcast projections.

"Who computed the program this time?" Ken asked.

"Let's find out."

The next day Jim called Channel 7 and asked the news director who programmed the computers.

"Eastern Airlines," he said.

The next call was to Eastern.

"I'd like to talk to the computer programmer who did the election," Jim told the operator.

"Oh, that's John," she said. She put Jim through.

John was not happy about talking on the telephone to a reporter and when Jim asked the first question, "What was the program you used to call it so close?" the man hung up.

At the *Planet* the editor, Buzz, called John, too.

He wrote in the next edition: "Every time I asked the guy a question, the phone fell out of his hands."

Judge Balaban's latest court order, denying us access to public records, was a definite setback. But it also proved to us that we were on the right track.

Public documents relating to elections were singled out by Florida statute as being open to the public "*without exception*." The only recourse was to get a circuit court hearing where we could attempt to get Judge Balaban to reverse himself.

That brought up the problem of whether or not to get a lawyer. We did have the option of petitioning the Court on our own, acting *pro se,* but we figured that we'd get whipped in court.

Finally, it dawned on us that the only sure way to maneuver ourselves into court, without paying any lawyer or being beholden to a partisan organization, was to call upon the American Civil Liberties Union. The ACLU was the perfect way to fight Balaban for denying us unrestricted access to public voting records.

At the ACLU's next executive session in a big law firm's office with a lot of local lawyers around the table, we took turns telling how our constitutional rights had been violated by being kept away from public election documents, and we warned how the American vote was in danger.

"I'll take the case," offered Shya Estrumpsa, a dark, quiet man. He said that he felt he was on solid legal ground in fighting the restraining order, and that he couldn't imagine what the counter argument might be.

He planned to get Judge Balaban to lift his order in circuit court, and if that failed, to go into federal court for relief based on constitutional grounds.

"We've got a lawyer now, and it's certified that we aren't paying him," Ken said.

Our poetic limitation in *Votescam* was never to pay a lawyer. If you pay a lawyer, he's got to be your advocate, right or wrong. Just paying a lawyer doesn't make you right. If a lawyer takes your anti-Establishment case *pro bono publico*, he usually feels he's sticking his neck out but that he has a winnable case.

We also asked Ellis Rubin what he thought, but we didn't ask him to take the case. Rubin assured us that he would help ferret out the truth.

He thought we were doing something worthwhile and important, and we couldn't help liking him for that.

At a hearing a week later in Balaban's chambers, the ACLU lawyer did his best. But instead of allowing us to dig deeper in the warehouse, the judge simply impounded all the evidence and refused to lift his order.

We didn't want to bother with the long

procedure of going through federal court to challenge Balaban's orders. Realizing that Balaban was not a man to be trusted, and that he kept a secret political agenda, we decided to take another tack. Jim left a message at Rubin's office that said: "We are going to ask Balaban to appoint you as Ombudsman for Vote Fraud in Dade County, and you can be the guardian for vote fraud evidence. Will you accept?"

Ken called Judge Balaban's office at the courthouse and through his secretary left a message: "Will you appoint Ellis Rubin ombudsman for vote fraud in Dade County?"

A few hours later, Balaban passed Rubin in the courthouse corridor and cryptically said: "You got it," and strided on.

Rubin, totally puzzled, said to himself: "Got what?"

When he returned to his office, he was able to put it together. Rubin was now an ombudsman.

5

A TANGLED WEB

"The handwriting on the wall may well be a forgery."

—Hodgson

When we found out that all the poll workers in Florida, and probably in other states, as well, submitted their true signatures two weeks in advance of the election to their "teachers" in the election school, it seemed to follow that anybody collecting those signatures would have a leg up on forging them.

On a cold, rainy afternoon in the spring of 1973, Jim opened the door to his townhouse and there on the pool table were two piles of large paper.

Ken was standing over them with a huge grin on his face.

"Wait'll you see these," he said.

"Where'd you get them?"

"I ripped off the Dade County Courthouse."

"You *stole* the canvass sheets?"

"Yeah. I walked into the clerk's office where they keep them, and I saw these sheets here…sheets with blank backs." He grabbed the top sheet off the pile. "Look, there's no ink on it at all," he said, pointing from corner to corner. "No laws written on it. *Blank*."

"Wow!"

"There's no printing on these, nothing to certify."

"This is fantastic," Jim whooped. "What made you take them?"

"I realized once I found these with blank backs, that if I didn't take them they could destroy them, *especially* if we got a court order to look for them. So I took a whole armful of the blank backs and signature ones, and I walked out of the courthouse. Nobody said a word."

"Nobody saw you?"

"Just grab and walk, don't look around guiltily …just move on."

Jim marveled at the gall of it. To go into the courthouse and steal public documents under the clerks' noses was a third degree felony. It was certainly the most radical thing that was done up-to-date in the whole investigation.

Ken felt as if he had finally *carpe'd* the *diem* and made a move.

"We have them by the balls with this," he said.

"What races do they cover?"

"It's the non partisan races in the 1972 election. There's a machine that stands over in the corner in all of the precincts. The election supervisor never tells you about it. They call it the non partisan machine. That's all the judges, the schoolboard and the state attorney."

"What's it doing over on the side?"

"They don't send anybody over there. Most people don't care about anything except the big races. They're satisfied and don't ask where the other little races are. So the non partisan machines don't get voted on unless somebody asks in particular. Nobody's in charge and nobody reads the numbers off after the election."

"Then that means," Jim said, "that the judges and the state attorney are the two groups that prosecute vote fraud, yet *their election is patently rigged* and *uncertified.*"

"Still, they're the ones you have to go to if you claim there's fraud."

"Only in America."

"We're starting to get to the point where there are no benign explanations," Ken said. "This is vote fraud on a massive, arrogant, amazing scale. At least to me."

"Me, too."

"Do we have them now?" Ken asked.

"Yeah. We've got 'em."

"How are they going to get around no certification? It's one thing to confound people with the signatures, it's another to take those signatures away entirely."

"We'll go to Rubin. Rubin can call a press conference, show these uncertified canvass sheets, and we won't be 'crazy' anymore," Jim said.

"Then we'll go to the FBI."

"If they printed one canvass sheet per machine," Ken calculated, "there'd be 1,648 canvass sheets. If we find out they printed more, that means there must be duplicates floating around somewhere. We've got to find out who ordered these canvass sheets printed, and who ordered that no certification be put on them. Right?"

"Right!"

A clerk in the election division told Ken the name of the printer: Franklin Press in Miami, a big, rich printing company with many government contracts.

Jim, who identified himself as a reporter, called Franklin Press' president and asked:

"How many canvass sheets did you print for the election?"

"We printed about 4,000."

"Do they have certification on the back?"

"Yes."

"How about the non partisan race? Is there certification on the back of those, too?"

"Yes."

"We have sheets here that are blank on the

back. Can we come down and show them to you?"

The president left the line for a minute and then returned:

"We didn't print certifications on some of those sheets on the instructions of William Miller, the elections supervisor," he said.

"Thanks, we'll get back to you."

"I want to try my hand at it," Jim said.

"What?"

"Stealing the canvass sheets."

"Let's go."

We drove to Ft. Lauderdale up U.S.1, through Hollywood, past pistachio-green South Broward High School, which looked the same as when Jim was a Broward Bulldog and devoured the sloppy Joes in the cafeteria at lunch. We drove by the Ft. Lauderdale airport and the conch shell vendors and fruit shippers and orange juice sellers in their low white buildings. We passed "Bet-a-Million Gates" million-dollar banyan tree, which was lusciously green and shade-making. Mr. Bet-a-Million was a Detroiter who would bet on almost anything. In the 1930s, he bet a million dollars that nobody could move that particular banyan tree to his club in Chicago. Its roots spread out forty feet and into the pores of the coral substrata. And huge limbs reached out sixty feet, with dozens of roots falling from each limb and back into the soil. Nobody ever collected on the bet, but once they heard the banyan-tree story, people talked about it for days...the possibilities of how you'd move the damned thing anywhere, much less up North, and get it to live. For a million dollars people are willing to get creative.

Into the Broward County courthouse we went, dressed in jeans. We walked into the clerk's office and asked to see the canvass sheets.

"Of course," the clerk agreed. She brought them out in tall stacks.

Jim looked around and saw that none of the clerks were paying them any attention. He took one stack, held it under his arm like laundry, and walked out of the courthouse. Ken, unburdened by purloined documents, was right behind.

We took off in the green Maverick, and headed back to Jim's townhouse where we dumped the load.

Then we got back in the Maverick and drove to West Palm Beach. This time we passed Ft. Lauderdale and got to Deerfield Beach, a sleepy little town, and Boca Raton, small, undiscovered yet by the hoi-polloi. Then came West Palm Beach. This is not Palm Beach. This is middle to lower class folks who live on the wrong side of the Intercoastal Waterway. It's a bunch of squatty, stucco buildings that look like architectural renegades from Los Angeles. They are inhabited by a volatile mixture of black people and rednecks, a lot of whom worked for the rich people on Palm Beach as bartenders, maids, gardeners, garbage collectors, small shopkeepers. The further west you went the swampier it got, until you hit the Everglades.

Into the Palm Beach County courthouse.

We ask for canvass sheets. They bring them. This time clerks were watching us.

"Stare them down," Ken whispered.

We each stared at whoever was looking at us until they looked away. Then Ken grabbed a pile, and we walked out, got in the car and headed home. It was a long day.

At home, we spread our loot out on the green felt. Jim studied the similarities among the different piles.

"They look a lot like the ones in Dade County. These are all sort of gray...the numbers are written in by hand...when you flip them, see...there's a consistent grayness...the handwriting has the same emotional level, it's all neat...no broken or thick pencil marks. Pencils wear down and break off...in a real sheet, you've got to see all those different strokes, but look at these, man...there's none of it. It's uniformly gray with thin lines, in all of the writing."

"So what do you think?" Ken asked.

"This is getting too big to handle. Nobody's going to believe this. We've got this huge fucker by the tail and nobody's going to believe it."

"Is it possible that the people who fill out canvass sheets all over the state have identical handwriting?"

Jim laughed as he walked over to the refrigerator and pulled out his frozen glass mug from the freezer. "Yeah, right. There must be some kind of kindred spirit that precinct workers share, they all got the same handwriting." He snapped the top off a can of root beer and poured it into the icy mug. "Now we've got three counties and all of the signatures look almost exactly the same in emotional content from morning until night, twelve hours later."

"Yeah, I know. From morning when they signed them, while they were fresh, to night when the signatures all look just like they did in the morning," Ken counted off points: " no alteration of mood, no emotional content, no different slant, no extra pressure."

Jim nodded. "And too much exactness as to where they sign on the line. If a signature is indented in the morning, it's indented almost exactly the same way at night. That's not the way it would be if something is human about it."

"Remember those five messy canvass sheets we saw with Lynch?"

"Yes."

"They looked real, sloppy enough. There was a certain illiteracy about them. Some of the writing was heavy and black, and obviously made by pencils that were nubs. Not all crisp and sharp like these."

Jim flipped through the stack.

"This is forged, it's the same Stepford effect that we saw in Dade County."

"But how the hell could Lynch, our friendly handwriting expert, say they weren't forged?"

"It's a conundrum."

About nine o'clock the next morning, Ken called the sheriff of Broward County.

"I stole all the canvass sheets from the courthouse," Ken said in his coolest, matter-of-fact way. "Arrest me."

The sheriff laughed.

"Keep me out of this," he said. "I don't want any part of it."

Then he called the sheriff of Palm Beach County and told him the same thing.

"Good luck," the sheriff said.

Not only couldn't we garner any publicity, we literally couldn't get arrested.

Next day we visited the FBI.

We met with agent Ed Putz, a very Gary Cooperish guy. We showed him the canvass sheets. He spread them out on a table, shuffled them, looked at them from a standing position, and said:

"These are forgeries."

He gave them a dismissive push and disappeared behind a door. We made our statement to someone else, and left some canvass sheets as evidence.

"How did Putz know they were forged?" Ken asked that night, while he racked the fifteen balls for a game of eight ball. We were at the Bingo Bar – headquarters on the Beach for some of the nation's brightest pool shooters.

"I don't know. He disappeared too fast to find out."

The next day we took sample sheets over to the Organized Crime Bureau of Dade County. Sgt. Walter Blue, a crime lab technician, took us into a room lit by red lights. There were five or six different types of microscopes and lots of chemicals.

He told us that he would put the canvass sheets under the microscope to examine the fibers and ink.

"I'm going to look for broken fibers…" he explained. "All paper, when you magnify it, is made up of what appears to be thick threads, or fibers, criss-crossing each other. So when you write on it, you have to eventually break one of those fibers – especially with all those signatures. Also, the pencils used by the county are those little hard sharp things, you know…"

"The ones they use at race tracks?" Ken offered.

He nodded. "And when most people press down on the paper they make pin point holes. They also indent the paper…so I'll be looking for ridge lines on the backside of the writing.

You should be able to feel them with your finger, in some cases, but under a microscope, they'll look like the Grand Tetons."

"How long is this going to take?" Jim asked.

"I'll call you when I'm done."

When we were in the suntan business everybody advised us as to the best way to promote Sunscrene. They always asked the same thing: "Have you ever thought of those little packages they give away when you fly to Florida? Get it on airplanes!"

And in our *Votescam* investigation, the question almost everybody asked was: "Aren't you guys afraid of getting killed?"

The second question was invariably: "Have you guys gone to '60 Minutes'?"

No, "60 Minutes" came to us.

One day we got a call from Florida State Senator Alan Becker. Becker was a lawyer known as "The Mink Cub." He wore exquisite European-styled vested suits, hankerchief in the pocket. He was perfect. But the "Mink Cub" moniker was due to his hair – slicked back and jet black.

"Mike Wallace is coming over to do a story on me being a condominium advocate," Becker told Jim. "You want to meet him?"

An hour later we were in his office. Wallace was interviewing Becker, and when he finished he turned his attention to us.

"What have you got?" he asked.

We laid out four years of evidence for Wallace and his crew. Wallace appeared flabbergasted, but he put nothing on tape. However, he said that he was headed right back to New York to get approval from his bosses to do our story. In fact, freelance investigative reporter Gaeton Fonzi, wrote a piece about Wallace having the *Votescam* story in his pocket.

MIAMI MAGAZINE

JULY, 1974   MIAMI, FLORIDA

THE GREAT DADE ELECTION RIG CONTINUES

by Gaeton Fonzi

Just recently, Channel 7 television reporter Brian Ross happened to be returning to Miami from New York on the same plane as CBS-TV newsman Mike Wallace. With his number one network show, "60 Minutes", Wallace has earned a reputation as a top investigative journalist who goes after the big stories. Chatting with Ross, Wallace told him that he was coming back to Miami for two specific reasons: one of which was to film an interview with a show business personality appearing on Miami Beach. The other reason, he said, was much more important: to look into what he had been told might be the most shocking vote fraud scandal ever to rock the nation. And, confided Wallace, it involved a conspiracy between major local media and key figures in Miami's power structure.

The Great Dade Election Rig continues.

After four years. Four years! In spite of numerous interments, the amazing story has surfaced anew. Finally it appears to be in the sight of network television. It is the "Loch Ness Monster" of Miami journalism.

For whatever reasons, what Mike Wallace did in Miami on that return trip, we never found out what it was. Most likely, he shot tape and interviewed some people. It appeared obvious from Fonzi's lead sentence that Wallace had gone back to New York, had discussions with associates, and was returning to Miami to follow up on the story. Nothing appeared on the air.*

Meanwhile, while waiting for the handwriting analysis, life in the tropics returned to a steady hum. It was relieved only by trying to figure out our next strategy in the investigation.

Rock was dying and disco was coming in. Disc jockeys played plastic records for people who shook their booty. These booty-shakers grew up to be yuppies. There were still some

---

*Within a month of Fonzi's article appearing in *Miami Magazine*, Miami *News* editor, Sylvan Meyer, purchased that magazine and permanently stopped any followup articles from being written on the *Votescam* story.

good drugs out there, mostly derivitives of nutmeg. They started with the initials DM, like DMA. It was a form of speed, with all the euphoria of cocaine but without the valley. It was the beginning of the designer drugs, and they were called "nice," because everybody who ever took them would say, "Oh, this is *nice*, man."

"Hello."

"Jim, this is Sgt. Walter Blue."

Jim immediately motioned Ken to pick up the other phone.

"These canvass sheets you brought me are forgeries. Why isn't anyone doing anything about this?"

"I don't know, I'm doing my damndest to get somebody to do something." Jim said.

"This is what I found. There are no fibers broken. That means that none of the people who wrote those signatures pressed hard enough to indent the paper or break the fiber. There's not a number big enough to tell you the odds against no breaks with hundreds of signatures involved. Plus the pencil lines all have a uniform flow without breaks in the flow. That's impossible if the signatures are genuine."

"How can that be accomplished?" Jim asked, amazed.

"I don't know, but it bothers me that this is going on. I'm concerned."

"We're doing our best," Jim said.

Now we were pissed. *Lynch!*

Lynch was the handwriting expert who told us the canvass sheet signatures were genuine. We took him at his word. Now we had an FBI agent and a police specialist who swore they were forgeries.

We called Lynch and told him that we had to see him immediately, and that we'd explain when we got there. He lived in Plantation, which is near the Everglades west of Ft. Lauderdale. It was open cattle and citrus land, with thick black soil, cockleburrs, coral snakes and canals planted with mile-long borders of pine trees.

Lynch lived in a stucco subdivision house with a Florida grass lawn, a palm tree, a carport. He met us at the door and led us into a well-equipped home laboratory in the back.

"Let's see these under the microscope." Jim handed Lynch a single canvass sheet.

"Okay."

We waited.

Lynch was peering into the eyepiece and seemed very calm.

"These are not forgeries," he repeated.

Jim took a look. Now he knew what to look for. He saw the letters "floating" on top of the paper fibers. There were no breaks, penpoints, smudges, nothing dissimilar.

"Look," Jim stepped aside so that Ken could see, "not a fiber is broken."

Ken looked, then erupted.

"Hey, what are you saying?" he asked Lynch. 'The ink floats on the surface, there's no breaks, and we've been told twice now that these are forgeries."

While Ken was talking, Jim walked out into the anteroom and examined the books on the shelves. He wanted an idea of who this man was. He saw that he had a technical book selection consistent with all that equipment.

Then, on the coffee table, he spotted an opened magazine. It was on display the same way anyone would leave a "vanity piece" to be admired. Jim walked over and picked it up. It was turned to a page that had the headline: *"How to Forge Documents with a Bank Rapidograph."*

Jim read it twice.

He read it again and it said the same thing.

He looked at who wrote it. It was by *Robert Lynch!*

For the first time in this investigation, the hair on the back of Jim's neck stood up.

He took the magazine to Ken and stuffed it in his hand.

"Look, this guy's got a story in *Police Magazine*, May '72 about forging documents with a bank Rapidograph."

Lynch stood quietly.

Jim heard a rustling in the hall. A flash of paranoia swept over him.

The scene rang through his mind of Lynch's

wife, with a shotgun, shooting them as
intruders. Nobody would have doubted it or
cared less.

"Let's get the fuck out of here," Jim said.

In the car heading back home, Jim explained to
Ken that he had only glanced at the article.

"So what did you see?"

"It's a thing called a bank Rapidograph.
Apparently it's an instrument that you can trace
a signature with. It copies the signature with
one pencil and another pencil or pen is
attached on some kind of a swing arm — it
traces the exact movement on another piece of
paper."

"So if Lynch used a Rapidograph on these
canvass sheets he could trace it off the
signatures he got at the schooling session two
weeks in advance, and repeat them on
unsigned canvass sheets."

"Right."

"Then there would be a set of canvass sheets
that could be substituted for the originals and
nobody would know the difference. Unless they
happened, like we did, to stumble across those
five, where the handwriting was real."

Jim watched the heavy rain as it hammered
the hood. "Well, I think that answers Henry
King Stanford's question," he smiled.

"We can't *prove* Lynch did it."

"But we know how it's done, he wrote the
article on how to do it, and now he denies that

what he saw under the microscope was forgery when two experts say it is," Jim reasoned. "If the fucker quacks like a duck, shoot it."

We headed for Rubin's office on Miami Beach.

The office was in a wing of a baronial mansion from the 1930s with stained glass windows and exotic woods. It felt expensively medieval.

Rubin listened to the story and read the material.

He laughed. He loved this kind of intrigue, especially if it gave him a shot at the Democratic war lords who controlled the county.

"Will you call a press conference?" Ken asked.

"Yes."

The next day all the media showed up at Rubin's office, as they always did, and still do. There was a lot of excitement in the air. Rubin had prepared himself for this conference with a singular focus. His plan was to follow up with a visit to the state attorney's office, to present the evidence and demand an investigation.

At the appointed time, Rubin strode into the scene.

"Ladies and Gentlemen of the press," his voice was compelling, "I've called you here today to offer you what I consider shocking and sickening, but undeniable, admissable and conclusive proof, that elections in this county have been massively tampered with for at least the last six years – and probably well before that."

Rubin held up the blank-backed canvass sheets and the forged certifications and told the press what it all meant. With that opener, he then began exhibiting examples of forgery on canvass sheets from Dade County to Palm Beach. He told the media that the Organized Crime Bureau had confirmed that signatures on every sample were not those of poll workers, but had been affixed by other means.

"Desperate measures by desperate men," hissed a Channel 7 representative. He stalked out.

The Miami *News* ran the story on the front page, with a photograph of Rubin holding up a forged canvass sheet. The Miami *Herald* ran a front-page photograph and a story inside.

A few days later, William Miller, who took over when Braterman quit, also resigned as election supervisor.

Two down.

Joyce Deiffenderfer, the woman from the League of Women Voters who wept and cried that she did not want to "get caught in this thing," was named election supervisor.

There was no followup in the press.

And that was that.

One day Jim got a call at The *Planet* from somebody at the Dade County election division. The hushed female voice said:

"The Metro commission has voted millions of dollars to send all the voting machines up to the

Carolinas to get them retrofitted with Printomatic devices. Meanwhile, they'll gut the machines and crush all the old parts. That gets rid of any evidence of shaved wheels."

What's a Printomatic device?

In early September 1974 the primaries arrived again. At 7 a.m. we drove to a precinct on Biscayne Boulevard in North Miami. It was in Howard's Trailer Camp, four square blocks of mobile homes. What we found shocked and elated us at the same time.

First, the keys to the backs of the new Printomatic-equipped voting machines, for the first time ever, had *not* been issued to the precinct captains. They could no longer open the backs and see the numbers inside. Instead, they were told to crank a handle that had been implanted into the back of the machine up there in Carolina. They were assured it would make a roller run across the paper, which had been treated so that numbers would appear when impressed by the raised counters. After the roller rumbled across the paper from left to right, one of two pieces of paper would slide out of a slot at the bottom. On it would be numbers. For a virgin, un-voted-on machine, it was supposed to show all zeroes. But none of the captains nor anyone else in the precinct actually got to look at the counters themselves.

Jim called Joyce Dieffenderfer from a pay phone.

"Where are the keys to these machines?" he asked.

"They're locked in Jack Wert's desk. He's my assistant."

"Okay."

A call to Wert:

"Yeah, they're locked in my desk because they've got the Printomatic, they don't need keys anymore."

Jim hurried back to the precinct just in time to see two stocky men in dark suits opening the back of a machine.

Ken motioned to Jim: "The roller system isn't working. It's jammed up. They called these guys the troubleshooters." Then he pointed outside to a white Cadillac with Kentucky plates. "That's theirs."

"These guys are decidedly strangers," Jim said.

We watched.

They opened the back door of the machine with a key and took out the Printomatic paper. It was about two feet by three feet, as big as the back of the machine. When they pulled it out, you could see the piece of paper was bunched up in the middle where the roller had wrinkled it. Apparently, that's what had hung it up. The two guys tried to hustle the paper away quickly. One grabbed it to his chest and turned to walk out, calling over his shoulder:

"The machine's out of order until further notice."

In a flash Ken grabbed the paper and yanked it out of the guy's arms. The stranger was momentarily stunned. Then Ken whipped around and spread the paper on the nearest table, smoothing it out. At least ten precinct workers were bug-eyed as they watched.

What we all saw was a wrinkled piece of paper with zeroes corresponding to the candidate counters filling the entire sheet – *even where the roller hadn't touched.*

"Hey, these have been preprinted." Jim said loudly. "The pressure roller only went half-way across before it wrinkled the paper."

A loud barnyard hubub went up from the workers.

"It's fixed!"

"We're not going to sign anything."

The surprised troubleshooter lunged over to grab the paper off the table and walked quickly back to the Cadillac.

The precinct workers were clearly angry. The newfangled crankhandle was actually a vote scam, a decoy. The Printomatic didn't do anything but make people think it imprinted true counter numbers.

"I quit." A worker walked out.

"They want us to certify *that!*" Another followed him.

One by one, every worker walked out of the precinct until in ten minutes it was empty.

The new crank handles and rollers didn't work in most of the other precincts across the county that day either, and the scam was also revealed to precinct workers when troubleshooters came to unstick the rollers. Many of the workers walked out.

The next day The Miami *Herald* carried a story about the poll workers' walkout which said that, due to some "snafu," thousands of precinct workers throughout the county left their jobs and were replaced by Metro police and firemen.

The story neglected to say what the snafu was, or why the workers had walked off.

And that was that.

A day later, in the black-soil "redlands" area south of Miami where they truck-farmed celery, tomatoes, strawberries, limes and Ponderosa lemons, about 200 citizens from all over the county met near the settlement of Perrine on a moonless night.

It was at Clark and Dotty Merrill's place. They were well-known civic activists. Clark worked for the City of Miami as an engineer, and he had a kind of tenure that made it difficult to fire him for voicing his opinions or making waves. Dotty was from Boston, and she was loud and funny, with a marked Bahston accent. They'd gotten the word out on radio and through fliers about the Printomatic fraud. A lot of precinct workers had called them when they realized nothing was going to be said about it in the newspapers. We called them, too.

We parked among a lot of cars and went into the Merrill's lived-in stucco house. The house was filled to the gunwhales with people, mostly in their thirties and up, a lot of municipal employees, merchants and workers. Everybody but lawyers. You couldn't buy a lawyer in that house. Dotty led the town meeting. Clark was a big man who'd rather listen than talk.

"We've seen it with our own eyes, now," a precinct worker said. "And it's a fraud. But the election came off on schedule."

"You should have seen the hysteria when everyone left our precinct and people kept coming in to vote, but there was nobody to sign them in."

"It took Joyce a couple of hours to round up the cops to fill in."

"Why did the *Herald* lie that it was just a snafu? It was a downright rigging and they know it."

Dottie motioned for them to quiet down.

"According to the Colliers here," she said, "the media is involved in all this up to its *cajones*. We've got to put pressure on the *Herald* to print the truth."

The group debated all night, and finally decided to send a mission to The Miami *Herald* and The Miami *News* to get them to do vote fraud stories.

A delegation was also sent to the State Attorney.

By the time the third meeting at the Merrill's house came around, there were reports that nobody was going to do anything. No exposes were going to appear in the *News* or the *Herald*. Editors told the delegation that it was a "non story." A "non issue." The charges were "impossible to prove," and so on. Editors routinely dismissed the messengers as crackpots.

The State Attorney refused to investigate.

And that was that.

On September 9, Ellis Rubin held a standing-room-only press conference.

He had gone to the trouble of having a blackboard set up in the conference room, and now he used it to describe in detail the "Missing Keys Scam." Then he walked over to a Printomatic voting machine set up in the corner. He showed how the device denied poll workers their mandate to visually eyeball the zeroes in the backs of the machines by not giving them the keys to look inside and see the alignment of the counter wheels.

Reporters took notes and video cameras hummed away.

"What are you going to do about it, Ellis?" a reporter asked.

"I intend to present this and other supporting evidence to the State Attorney's office."

"Do you expect any prosecutions…and, if so, who would be the targets?"

"It would be improper for me to speculate," Ellis replied calmly, "but I certainly expect the State Attorney's office to do its duty."

The next day the major newspapers were awash in material about the press conference. Front page headline in the Miami *News* boomed:

MASSIVE VOTE FRAUD CHARGED IN DADE ELECTIONS

That afternoon Rubin went with Ken to the office of Janet Reno, the tall, rawboned daughter of big, rawboned Hank Reno, the best police reporter in Miami, bar none. Janet Reno was an assistant State Attorney.

Rubin intended to ask Reno to accept the blank-backed canvass sheets, make a full investigation and go to the grand jury to have them indict somebody for tampering with the 1972 election. Ken and Rubin signed a waiver of immunity in order to make a statement about vote fraud for the record. The waiver meant they were entirely responsible for their testimony, even if it meant a lot of personal trouble. If they hadn't signed the waiver it would have looked suspicious.

The press was waiting by the score outside Reno's office.

We were sure that Rubin would come out and announce that Reno was going to take the evidence to the grand jury, or appoint a special prosecutor.

Instead, when Rubin finally emerged from behind the closed doors of that inner sanctum, he was literally ashen-faced, downcast, and crestfallen all in one. We had never seen him like this.

The lights and cameras all came on.

Rubin walked to the bank of microphones. "Miss Reno has asked me to inform you that she has examined the evidence and as far as any prosecutions are concerned, the statute of limitations has expired."

With that barebones statement still hanging in the air, Rubin bolted to a nearby escalator and charged down its stairs to avoid any questions from the press, or from us.

We didn't let it go at that.

In the extreme tension of the moment we saw four years of research trashed by Reno. We took the stairs three at a time and chased our former paladin out of the Metro Justice Building. We caught up with him just as his antique red convertible was pulling away from the curb.

Ken jumped on the running board and leaned over. He looked into Rubin's eyes for a split second. Then he jumped off as Rubin gunned the motor and sped away.

"What did he say?" Jim asked.

"Nothing, he just stared straight ahead."

"What was his expression?"

"Fear."

"No." Jim was dumbfounded. "Not Ellis Rubin...lawyer for the Watergate burglars... the man who visits Richard Nixon at his home ...asshole buddies with the CIA and the FBI and and Naval Intelligence and probably the Mossad! So what the hell could Janet Reno have said to scare him?"

We wouldn't know that answer until we met up with him in the future, eight years later.

6

HOUNDS OF HELL

"The humblest citizen...when clad in
the armour of a righteous cause, is
stronger than all the hosts of Error."

—William Jennings Bryan

As long as the Warren Report stays on the
books as the officially recognized "truth"
about the JFK case, there will be an open
wound in the body politic that defies
healing. Assassination researchers are so
virulent in scavenging the field in search of
any shred of evidence, they have come to be
known as "The Hounds of Hell."

But there's another public cause that has
captured the imagination of the Hound
mentality. Vote fraud. Consider the strong
emotional values that we Americans attach
to the sanctity of the U.S. ballot. The ballot

is America's number one export. It is the hallowed ground and shed blood of ten generations of "those who made the supreme sacrifice."

As with the JFK breed of Hound, vote fraud trackers have the gut feeling that some fundamental outrage has occurred and is being covered up in the highest levels of government.

One never knows the exact moment of transition from common citizen to Hound.

After the the Reno-Rubin confrontation, the investigation seemed pretty much over. Rubin wouldn't take our calls and there was no point in pursuing him any further. We figured that whatever Reno told him in her private chambers that day must have scared the hell out of him.

Jim said: "I can't imagine him acting like that unless she had something on him."

"Well, I doubt that it's political," Ken reflected. "Maybe she painted a really frightening scenario, possibly threatening to expose him somehow, to embarrass his kids and family, you know what I mean? After all, we're not dealing in torts here. If Reno called for a full investigation the lid could blow off the Establishment. That's why Gerstein didn't want this case, so he gave it to Reno and she wasn't about to bite the hand that feeds her."

"She must have torn into him something fierce," Jim speculated, "like 'Ellis, if you pursue this it could take down the entire structure, not only of the city, but possibly the state. Do you want to do this for the Collier brothers?'"

"Sure," Ken nodded, "but that look on his face, that stark blank stare...it was eerie...I don't think just politics would do it. It had to be a personal threat."

We were both in the midst of divorce proceedings. It seemed like something in the stars was breaking everything apart. The *Daily Planet* was going out of business. The public was more interested in the Bee Gees than in revolution. *DC Comics* was threatening to sue over what they claimed was the use of their Superman trademark, and *The Underground Press Service* was turning into *High Times* magazine. During the Sixties the suntan lotion business was the engine that drove our small financial empire, but it required a full time effort and we just didn't have it in us anymore. Politics is a strong drug and anger was replacing the drive we had to make money.

Back when we started *Sunscrene*, Kennedy was in his second year as President, and the world seemed bright. Now it was the Nixon-Ford era; we were growing older and there wasn't much challenge left in selling suntan lotion to beach boys.

The five-year renewable leases on our beach stores were coming due and without wives or kids to support, they just didn't seem important anymore. Ken's wife was a millionairess who didn't want child support, and she didn't want Ken around either, at least not as long as he was willing to pursue *Votescam*. Jim's wife was twelve years his junior, and after five years of a childless marriage and listening to *Votescam*, she wanted some fresh air in California.

"If we give up *Votescam*," Jim told Ken, "when we're old men we're going to look back and ask why didn't we fight the bastards. We're going to add up the plus and minus columns and all we'll have is money. I don't want to spend the rest of my life with this seething anger because I know I let them get away with it without going the last fucking inch."

"How are we going to live?"

"Let's do a Siddhartha – lets give it all up: the pool table, the cars, the townhouses, the business."

Ken took a long toke on the pipe Jimi Hendrix had given him that night his concert got rained out at Gulfstream Race Track.

It wasn't our concert, but the promoters, Michael Lang and Marshall Brevitz (Lang was a co-producer of Woodstock) had no way to refund the ticket money. So we invited Hendrix to *Thee Image*, where we would throw open the doors to anybody who wanted to walk in. Jim went on stage at Gulfstream and invited everybody to come to the club.

It was now about 8 o'clock on a stormy tropical night.

We called all of our concession people, the ice

cream vendors, the chocolate cake sellers, hot dog guys, the body painters, and asked them to come right down.

The body painters gave away Day-Glo paint that lit up under black light, which was the big deal in concert lighting at the time. *Thee Image* boasted a hundred blacklight bulbs.

Hendrix and his roadies and his band turned up, as promised, for free, and started to set up on the stage. The club already had a wall of Ampeg speakers with enough amps to blow out a window. There were also the two giant strobe lights with a slow to fast speed dialer that made people look like they were moving very fast or very slow, like a haywire silent film.

Word had gotten out. Kids started calling kids. By nine o'clock the parking lot was packed. So was Collins Avenue, and there was a traffic jam down to Haulover Beach.

Jimi started playing about nine. He began by using all of *Thee Image's* speakers and his own to produce wild feedback wailing.

That got people's attention. Then he jammed with the house band, The *Blues Image*, (*Ride, Captain, Ride)* in a set that never stopped until after midnight. The audience, full of painted bodies, mostly sat on the floor and listened, in various states of high, higher and highest, while Jimi played rock guitar that was more dramatic than anything most of the audience had ever heard. His guitar solos melted down and re-formed, turned into vivid images and then into smoke.

It was a wild night of cheering. Then the ice cream battle began.

Somebody brought Jimi an ice cream cone with a ball of chocolate on it. Jimi threw the ice cream ball to somebody in the crowd. That somebody threw it back at Jimi.

"Get me ten cones," Hendrix called.

He passed them out to everyone in the band, and they began to throw ice cream balls at each other. Pretty soon hundreds of members of the audience raced to the concession stand to buy scoops of ice cream, forget the cone. In 15 minutes the air in the club, under the Day-Glo lights, was filled with flying ice cream balls. They hit the walls, the speakers, people's heads, hair and clothes. Then, when the ice cream ran out, they all began throwing chocolate cake.

Meanwhile, Jimi and the band kept on jamming.

Then Jimi says: "Let's go swimming."

He left the stage without his guitar, walked through the crowd and out the front door. Like a Pied Piper he walked past the International House of Pancakes up to Collins Avenue, three to four thousand kids dancing insanely behind him.

This was a few months before Jimi played his irreverant Star-Spangled Banner at Woodstock.

All those memories were attached to Ken's pipe as he thought of leaving the security he'd always known.

For a couple of guys who were raised middle class in the Middle West, giving up the easy life was truly radical. We'd seen Tom Hayden live out of a sleeping bag as he fought his battles for social equality in the Sixties, and we even housed him when he was worn out and bedraggled.

One time Tom came to New York with his first wife Casey, and an old station wagon. He had the key to a friend's empty apartment, so Tom and Casey took an old mattress off the street and spread it on the floor. The next night they knocked on Jim's door on East 88th Street.

"We got bedbugs," Tom said, lifting his pant leg and showing a track of bug bites.

Jim paid for a hotel room on 86th Street.

Now Ken pondered the idea of living out of sleeping bags on Miami Beach.

"Where do we put the sleeping bags and how do we eat? And do we *really* want to do this?"

"Well, it's that or give it all up and just be merchants. What's money gotten us but divorces and abject comfort?"

"But what about *Sunscrene*, we can't just drop it."

"Why not?"

So we gave it all away to our top salesman in Daytona Beach, named Ron Rice, and he changed the name to *Hawaiian Tropic*.

In the fall of 1974 we were living in the sea

grapes near 86th and Collins Avenue on Miami Beach. It was less than two blocks from the Holiday Inn, but it was tropical and secluded. Sea grapes are trees that grow about 15 feet high with leaves like large green pancakes. The leaves formed a cathedral ceiling, screened the sun and provided some privacy from the public on the beach. Foreign tourists had heard about this wild stretch and although it was against the law to camp there, they had found the sea grape patch as inviting as we had. We often had to roust a sleeping German, Frenchman or Italian out of our favorite spot.

There were freshwater showers nearby and a public bathroom. There was no place to cook, so we subsisted on fruit and cheese. A high grassy jungle-like area hid the sleeping bags. When it rained, which wasn't that often, we rolled up our bags, hid them, and ran for motel cover.

From our refuge in the sea grapes, we wrote, with pen and pencil, a rock opera entitled "*Year One.*" The title was based on John Lennon's concept, conceived at John and Yoko's bed-in in Toronto in 1970. John said that we should label all our correspondence *Year One A.P.* (After Peace), and that there should be a new beginning. So the story was about the Children-at-Arms, a rock group from the Center of the Galaxy, ordered to earth to reunite Sgt. Pepper's team.

We wrote the basic book and lyrics and

Gregory Scott Kimple wrote the music. Although the studio album wasn't bad (Lou O'Neil, Jr. of *Circus Magazine* called it "one of the top ten albums of the year"), we decided to re-record the album live and videotape the *Year One* band at the Grand Canyon.

On 7/7/77 we produced the first free rock concert ever performed live in the Grand Canyon. *Rolling Stone Magazine* wrote ahead of time that six million people would turn up for the concert (to hear "*The Year One Band*"). The Interior Department, concerned for the ecosystem and crowd control, cancelled the event. Now for the first time in our lives we had no mama, no papa, no businesses, no money — but we did have George.

By the grace of George, our friend and chess master, Ken flew out to Arizona and talked the park ranger into letting us stage the show. To make it hard on whatever crowds might want to show up, the ranger restricted the concert to the West Rim, which is off limits to the general public. Nonetheless, about a thousand people hiked overland and got to the site to watch us film the sun coming up over the East Rim, an event almost never seen by anyone other than an American Indian. We shot through the day, catching the full sweep of the sun to the West. Songs were sung at different hours as the sun produced different moods. And as the sun was setting, we taped two lovers standing atop a mega wall of amplifiers against a purple haze.

The band sang: "*Champion, Where Are You?*"

After the concert we drove back to New York with *Satan*, who taught *Kiss* how to eat fire.

For awhile we lived in a radio-TV commune on 14th Street and Second Avenue in a building called The U.S. Senate. The commune owned the old Second Avenue Yiddish Theater, then called The Phoenix, where Ann Corio held court while doing "*This Was Burlesque.*" When she left, the theatre folded until two off-Broadway actors bought it. They fed and housed us in the U.S. Senate, while two blocks down on 12th street they were remodeling the theater.

Because most of the people working on remodeling were performing artists and not real tradesmen, at least not the kind who should be reupholstering 499 seats, someone gave the order to unscrew every seat in the house and stack them up in the foyer.

Then they had us rip all the staples out of all the seats, take off all the Naugahyde, and pull out all the stuffing.

It was our job, that is, us and Satan, to put those seats back together, restuff them, recover them with Naugahyde, and use that plier device to stretch and restaple. The color was orange. The job tooks weeks, eight hours a day.

Then the time came to put the seats back.

We started with the first row, but none of the seats fit. Nobody had bothered to mark the seats as to where their original places were. Thus we had 499 seats and not the foggiest idea where to put them.

As we sat around with the rest of the crew, understanding what purgatory was, Satan, who had a rock band on Bourbon Street in the Sixties, started picking up the seats, studying them, and separating them into size piles. Some of the seats were minutely bigger than others. After the sorting he took the largest seat off the first pile and walked around looking for the largest empty hole. It took him four days, but he put every single seat back in its exact spot. We know that because when we got down on the floor we had to turn thousands of screws into thousands of holes. They all fit.

The new theater with the bright orange seats opened with "*The Best Little Whorehouse in Texas*" in its off-Broadway debut.

On June 23, 1978, Jim's 39th birthday, we raised the money to produce a live rock concert, called "*Rock Wars*," on the highest man-made stage in the world: the helicopter pad atop the South Tower of the World Trade Center in Manhattan.

Every rock star who had nothing better to do that night was at the party. The Y*ear One Band* and *For Shakes Sake* from Brooklyn played from dusk until midnight. People brought their own everything, and down on the107th floor the Trade Center opened a sumptuous bar and smorgasbord. It was an incredible, perfectly clear night with a full moon and a grand piano.

People called the radio station that was broadcasting the live performance and said, "We can hear it over here in Staten Island," and somebody else said they could hear it all the way into New Jersey.

The next day the New York *Daily News* said: "The World Trade Center was made for three things: *The Wiz, King Kong*, and the *Rock Wars* party held last night."

Ken met an artist at the 14th Street commune who called herself Shakti. She was a medical doctor from Australia who was tall, blonde and beautiful. She had painted murals on the walls of the theater we worked in, so Ken asked her to illustrate the story we had written about rock and roll, where the Children-at-Arms come from the Center of the Galaxy to reunite the Beatles. For the next fourteen months we, including Satan, lived and worked together on the *Rock Wars* storyboard. It eventually turned into a 96-page, full-color Doubleday Dell trade paperback that sold 42,000 copies before John Lennon was shot and killed at The Dakota.

Rock Wars died with the most intelligent man in rock.

Ken wrote an epitaph for Lennon and it was reprinted in *Billboard* Magazine and in The Washington *Post* (see it in the back of this book). Yoko Ono wrote Ken a letter telling him that she had hung a copy on her wall.

7

THE PETERSEN MEMO

*"Though a good deal is too strange to
be believed, nothing is too strange to
have happened."*

—Hardy

In the spring of 1979, Jim filed a Freedom of
Information Act request for anything under his
name at any government agency. A few months
later, a file three inches thick came in the mail
that included everything we had given to the
FBI. There were also FBI memos about the
stacks of evidence we had sent in.

There was a notation in the folder that 37 pages
of the file were sequestered "in another agency."
We called an agent at the Miami field office of the
FBI and asked: "What does that mean?"

"The CIA," he said.

We wondered why. What does the CIA have to

do with vote rigging? What has this to do with
national security? And what the hell is on those
37 pages?

We also found among the papers a memo of
instructions from Henry E. Petersen, assistant
U.S. Attorney General of the Criminal Division of
the Justice Department.

UNITED STATES GOVERNMENT DEPARTMENT
OF JUSTICE

MEMORANDUM

TO: Acting Director, DATE:: 5/16/72
        Federal Bureau of Investigation
FROM: Henry E. Petersen
        Assistant Attorney General
        Criminal Division

SUBJECT: UNKNOWN SUBJECTS:
KENNETH COLLIER - VICTIM
ELECTION LAWS

This is to recommend that the Crime Records
Division advise U.S. Representative Claude
Pepper (Democrat-Florida) of institution of this

investigation at the request of the Criminal Division Department, regarding a possible Election Laws violation. Investigation at this time is being limited to interviews of: (*The names were blacked out.*)

<u>Background:</u> James Collier and his brother Kenneth have furnished several statements concerning what they believe to be a violation of the Election Laws Statute. The violation allegedly occurred during the September1970 Florida primary elections when Kenneth Collier was a candidate for U.S. Congressman running against the incumbent Claude Pepper on the Democratic ticket. The Colliers contend the elections were "rigged" because immediately after the polls closed, Miami television stations predicted the final vote percentages of each candidate and the projected vote totals. The television stations' predictions were allegedly 100% accurate. Professor Ross Beiler of the University of Miami and Mr. Elton Davis of the Cavanaugh Computer Corporation apparently programmed the computers for the Miami television stations which predicted the election outcome. The Colliers allege Beiler and Davis participated in a scheme to rig the above mentioned primary. Statements obtained from the Colliers regarding their allegations have been forwarded to the Criminal Division which has requested Beiler and Davis to be interviewed to ascertain their possible involvement in alleged scheme to rig this election. If either Professor

Beiler or Mr. Davis acknowledges that he did particpate in rigging this election, the Bureau should attempt to ascertain the manner in which this rigging was effected, for what purpose it was effected, and who directed that the election be rigged.

ACTION: Departmental Attorney Craig C. Donsanto was contacted and advised as a matter of courtesy. *It is recommended the Crime Records Division advise Congressman Pepper that at the specific request of Assistant Attorney General Henry E. Petersen, Criminal Division of the Department of Justice an investigation has been instituted.* (End of memo)

Henry Petersen was to become semi famous later on as the federal investigator in the case against the Watergate burglars. *This was the first indication that Petersen was fully involved in the vote fraud investigation prior to his Watergate assignment.*

8

VIDEO VIGILANTES

*"Some circumstantial evidence is very
strong, as when you find a trout in
the milk."*

—Thoreau

A new decade, the 1980s, found us living up
at a yoga ranch near South Fallsburg, New
York, in the Catskill Mountains, studying
karate, yoga and meditating. Shakti, whose real
name was Elizabeth, was with Ken and they
were married at the ranch by Swami Vishnu.
Their daughter, Unity, was born there in
November of 1980.

One of the students at the ranch owned a
bean sprout business which he wanted to sell.
He taught us how to grow sprouts in bathtubs
in dark rooms, harvest them, bag them and sell
them by the pound.

Sprouts brought in so much revenue that we

decided to leave the ranch and start our own route in Manhattan, Queens and Brooklyn. We made money instantly. Our "*Heartland Sprouts*" became the best-selling alfalfa and mung bean sprouts in the city. Winter came and Jim decided to go back to the warmth of Miami and leave the business to Ken and Shakti. He lived in the black belt quarters of Larry Pizzi's Shori Goju dojo, near the Lincoln Road Mall, and managed the karate school.

In the summer of 1982, a revival was planned for the California rock group, *Mamas and the Papas*, with Spanky of Spanky and Our Gang playing the dead Mama Cass and McKenzie Phillips, the daughter of John and Michelle Phillips, playing her mother's part.

Ken read about it in *Billboard Magazine* and invited John Phillips to do a show on top of the World Trade Center. They met on the helicopter pad on top of the Trade Center one cold day in February. An icy wind off New York harbor whipped around the two of them. John said no to the venue. A nice warm concert in Florida seemed a whole lot better to him.

Ken called Jim: "John will play Florida if you can raise the money."

"Hell, I don't have a penny."

"That never stopped you before."

So Jim raised twenty thousand dollars, found the auditorium, bought rock radio advertising, and had the tickets printed and distributed.

Ken sold the sprout business to an organic

food dealer in Queens and came down in time for the concert.

The new *Mamas and Papas* did all the sentimental old hits, like *California Dreamin*, and *Monday, Monday*. They made the audience glow with nostalgia. The press loved them. But that same night a rock group called The *B-52s* opened at *Pirates World* about 20 miles away, and almost everybody who didn't remember the Sixties, which was everybody under 25 years old, went to listen to The *B-52s*. We had an artistic success and a financial flop.

In 1982 we got back into the newspaper business. We had seen posters all over town with the banner, "*The Fighting MacKenzies*." The poster pictured a young, pretty blonde woman flanked by two men. It looked like an advertisement for a singing group out of the Forties. The poster said that Christina MacKenzie was running for a seat on the Metro Dade County Commission, and that her father Donald and his brother Douglas were running her campaign.

After reading their literature, Jim figured her to be honest but naive. He saw "*The Fighting MacKenzies*" as either a crock or as a possibility to recruit professed fighters into the frey. He telephoned Christina to warn her about vote fraud in Dade County and to hear her reaction.

Don MacKenzie got on the line.

"Who are you?" he asked.

Jim explained vote fraud in Dade County.
Then Ken took the phone and got deeper into
the discussion. After a while Ken's voice raised
in tone as he got short of temper. It was the
sound of two hardheads bashing. From the start
MacKenzie made it clear that he wanted to take
control of any future negotiations between us.
But Ken couldn't possibly let someone he
thought was an amateur, who didn't have a clue
as to what was really happening, start dictating.
It degenerated into a screaming match and we
hadn't even met the guy.

Suddenly, MacKenzie shifted gears. "Meet me
in my office at the Hialeah *Home News* and we'll
talk about it," he said calmly.

"What do you do at the *Home News*?" Ken
asked.

"I'm the managing editor."

That afternoon we met MacKenzie. He was a
Scotsman built like an Isuzu. He had a barrel
chest on a frame that stood about five feet seven
inches tall. His red hair was combed into a flat-
top pompadore and it was never messed up in
public. He habitually wore a black suit, black
vest, white shirt and dark necktie, even in the
summertime. On less formal occasions he wore
his Marine Corps major's camouflage jacket.

MacKenzie was born in Detroit and he spoke
in the unaccented way that Detroiters (who
make good radio announcers) speak. He had
been a legislative aide to Michigan Congressman
Guy Vander-Jaght before abandoning politics to

bring his family to Florida in the early Seventies. There were hundreds of "war stories" about MacKenzie as an FBI and CIA operative, but most of them shouldn't yet be told in print.

Within a few weeks we were members of the Hialeah *Home News* staff, along with Bill Tucker, a rewrite man who was so fast and stylish that his talent was legendary in the Deep South. He looked like a wrinkled Chinese fighting dog with a fat black cigar sticking out of his grumpy jaws.

The Hialeah *Home News* was a 40-year-old suburban newspaper that once served the community news to the crackers and horse people near the Miami Airport and the Hialeah Race Course. Now it was owned by an ex-FBI agent who had installed his buddy, MacKenzie, as managing editor

The paper had a tradition of looking into stories other county papers wouldn't investigate. It was the last bunker of independent journalism in Dade County.

We now had a forum for the first time since we lost our Dell book contract and the *Planet* folded. And we had an editor who was on our side.

"Are you one-story guys?" MacKenzie asked.

"No, we'll do other stuff," Jim assured him, already feeling at home in the glass-walled city room. "We had a paper called The *Daily Planet* in the Seventies. What have you got in mind?"

"They got a moratorium on building down on South Beach. Nobody's allowed to improve their property under penalty of arrest. You want to look into it?"

We agreed as long as we could also crank up *Votescam* stories. The next day we found ourselves knee-deep in Miami Beach politics.

It was October.

For the "South Beach" section of Miami Beach, which is south of 16th Street and all the way down to Government Cut where the big boats and cruise ships come into Biscayne Bay, there was a moratorium, declared by the Miami Beach City Council, on any kind of home improvement or building. The property values of the old Art Deco hotels and apartment houses plunged. If you couldn't fix them up, you had to rent them to the most indigent of the Cuban exiles (the ones nobody else wanted). They trashed the buildings and rents hit bottom. Property owners lost their nest eggs. We wrote that this local depression was a vicious plot by the creators of the Dade County "master plan" to choke out the old owners and then buy up the land and the buildings for a fraction of their real value.

It would take several years of crusading against this injustice before Miami Beach Mayor, Norman Ciment, ended the moratorium. The damage had already been lethal.

One day in late October the *Home News* editor-in-chief, Elmer Rounds, a six foot plus,

250 pound Southerner with a droll sense of humor, handed us a press release from the Republican National Committee. The first word we saw was **REWARD** and the number $5,000.

"What can you do with this?"

We read the release signed by RNC chairman, Richard Richards:

"It has saddened us to learn that vote fraud still exists in certain areas of this country," Richards said in a letter to fifty Secretaries of State.

"Since the right to vote is the keystone of all other rights we cherish as Americans, any dilutions of the vote by fraud or error must be stopped."

The RNC reward offer said that any citizen who gave information leading to the arrest and conviction of any official who violates state or federal laws against vote fraud would receive $5,000. It went on to say:

"We have established telephone numbers that will be manned by attorneys who will assist in putting them in touch with the proper state and federal officials who will proceed with such complaint."

"I can't believe it," Ken said. "Do you think someone in Washington has finally gotten off their ass?"

"MacKenzie brought you guys in to deal with that story, so look into it," Rounds said.

We hadn't gotten a major break in the *Votescam* story for eight years, but a day before the 1982 primary we received a pamphlet in the mail entitled *Don't Get Punched Out*, written by Robert Corcoran, a radio newsman from the West Coast. The point of it was that the card-counting computer is a "black box" operation that had been used to rig elections in California and other states. He warned that a very dangerous situation was developing in America. The vote, he warned, was being stolen in counties from Maine to California.

He said that anyone using a punch card to vote with had no idea what was going to happen to their card after they punched it. There were no safeguards. In the California races Corcoran had studied, there was no way to verify a vote because fraud was so easy to perpetrate and so hard to detect.

In Dade County we had also heard from "concerned citizens" who came to us after witnessing the new-fangled computer vote being counted. They told us that members of The League of Women Voters, a private political club, were sitting up there in the Data Processing Center on Galloway Road, punching holes in the vote cards. It was exactly that kind of fraud that *Don't Get Punched Out* warned about.

It seems these "volunteers," were actually worth $15 an hour per head to the League's treasury. Their salaries were paid by the Dade elections division from taxpayer money directly to the League.

We knew that if such an activity were taking place, it was expressly forbidden by state and federal law, which prohibits any *"handling or piercing of the public's ballots by anyone except the voter."*

One of our early informants was an older woman who entered the Data Center after getting her name pre-approved by the election supervisor. Without a security check, she said, she couldn't have gotten in.

"You mean in order to see the vote counted the board of elections has to pass on you first?" Ken asked. "That's unconstitutional."

"That's what they told me," she said.

She reported seeing members of the League using little black pencils issued by the election division to punch out new holes in the vote cards. She explained that new holes could either become a new or different vote, or invalidate an existing vote by punching out both sides.

"Are you sure?"

"I saw it with my own eyes," she said.

"Five thousand dollars per person arrested and convicted," Jim salivated. "How do we get it?"

"Well, it seems to me that we need to get proof that they're punching holes in the ballot cards and bring it to the RNC."

"How are we going to get in the building, it's a bunker. And even if we got in, how do we prove it?"

"Videotape." Ken suggested.

"Great idea. But first let's call the elections supervisor and see what he has to say about the League punching holes."

The new supervisor was David Leahy, a man in his thirties, with dark blonde hair done in a close bouffant.

"We'd like to videotape the proceedings at the Data Processing Center," Jim said.

"You haven't been issued credentials, Mr. Collier," he replied patronizingly.

"What kind of credentials?"

"Only candidates, and those with credentials, are allowed to be up there. And no cameras or video equipment is allowed."

"That's patently unconstitutional, and illegal on top of it. People have a right to see their vote counted, David." Jim tried to level Leahy's attitude by using his first name. "You can have a secret ballot but you can't have a secret count. We're coming over to videotape."

"If you try to come into the building you will be arrested by the guards at the gate." Leahy hung up.

Jim turned to Ken: "We need a plan. We can't get in that building past the guards, past the video cameras, without getting busted.

"We're going to need some kind of credentials."

"We could say that we're *Herald* reporters."

"But we need credentials."

"No," Ken figured, "all we need is a *Herald* reporter covering us...in other words, we've got to get the *Herald* to take Leahy's arrest threat seriously and assign a reporter to cover it."

"That's right. If we get in with a *Herald* reporter they can't stop us."

We went to see Jim Savage, the editor in charge of investigative reporting for the Miami *Herald*. His office was a cubicle in the *Herald* city room overlooking Biscayne Bay. Savage was a testy guy in his fifties and he listened as we laid out the three different votescams we had investigated: *The Blank-Backed Canvass Sheets*; *The Forgeries and The Printomatic*. We put it all up on a blackboard. A reporter named Bob Lowe, a Hawaiian who had won two Pulitzers and wasn't yet thirty, took notes. Savage assigned Lowe to go up to the Center and wait until we showed up with our video camera. The assumption was that he'd do the story about it if we got in, and maybe even if we got turned away.

MacKenzie rented a color, sound, hand-held video camera.

On election day, November 2, at about 6 p.m., we drove to a precinct in a schoolhouse on Miami Beach and walked in with the video camera. MacKenzie, wearing his FBI-style dark suit, drove up behind us in his brown Buick Regal. We didn't take any pictures inside because it was too early. The polls didn't close until 7 p.m. But we told the precinct captain that we were going to videotape his precinct after 7 p.m..

Jim said: "We'll follow your precinct's cards from the time that they open the ballot box shortly after the polls close, until the votes are finally reported at the Data Processing Center. We just want to follow its route."

"You can't stay in here after seven," the captain said. "We lock the doors."

"You mean you lock the public out?" Ken asked.

"Yes, so that nobody interferes with the counting process."

"That is illegal, my friend." It was MacKenzie's voice and it was firm. "Go call Leahy and tell him we're going to stay here because it's illegal to lock the doors against the public after seven."

The captain's face was serious and red. He went into his office, we hoped, to call Leahy.

As soon as he left, we disappeared down the road. We drove to a different precinct a mile away and at 7 p.m. we entered with the video camera and said that we were from the *Herald*. Nobody stopped us.

Ken taped the precinct captain opening the voting box full of punchcard ballots that were stuffed inside their security envelopes. Several of these ballots fell to the floor and Ken shot the image of ballots under precinct workers' feet. They were busily taking the rectangular computer ballots out of their security envelopes, then stacking them in piles of 100 with the beveled edge to the upper left.

"Madame, in the green pants," Ken said. "There is a ballot under your foot."

She reached down and picked it up.

MacKenzie noticed another ballot on the floor a few women down. He whispered to Ken.

"Lady in the red pants, there's a ballot under your foot," Ken said.

She apologized and picked it up.

"Zoom in on the pencil in that lady's hand," Jim told Ken.

There were ten workers in the schoolroom and each had been issued a black pencil by the precinct captain.

Ken taped eight of the workers as they put the pencils in their pockets and two who held them like a cigarette between their fingers.

MacKenzie whispered to Jim:

"Those pencils…don't say anything, but if we weren't here filming, they'd be having a hole-punching party right now. Those instruments are not supposed to be in their hands."

The pencils were the first illegality caught on tape.The camera had recorded some pretty rough handling of the cards, but not a single piece of "chad" – those little pieces of paper that get punched out of the holes – was anywhere on the table. Yet, according to our informant, members of the League were in the Data Processing Center at that very moment for the expressed purpose of cleaning "tons of chad" off the backs of vote cards.

The piles of cards were then placed in metal "security" boxes which were locked with a numbered plastic and wire seal, like the ones on an electric meter. At that point, the security boxes were thrown in the back seat of the precinct captain's car and driven, with MacKenzie and ourselves following, to the central collection point at Miami Beach High School.

We all arrived at the high school at 7:35 p.m. and MacKenzie asked for a time check on camera.

We followed the box and its attendants into the gymnasium, as about twenty other precinct captains were coming in with their boxes.

The camera recorded a heavyweight guy with giant gold rings on his fingers put a white bag under the table between his legs. It was a Burger King hamburger sack. After a few minutes he took a handful of something out of the bag. The camera zoomed in as he placed it on the table. The something turned out to be about 20 red plastic numbered seals like the ones on the metal security boxes.

A woman in her sixties examined a security box brought in by a precinct captain.

"Your seal is broken," she said.

"Yes, I know," the precinct captain replied.

Ken focused on the male clerk who had brought the seals in the paper sack.

"What are the extra seals for?" Ken asked.

"These?"

"Yes. Those."

"Oh, they're just in case any come in broken or something." He shuffled them lightly about with his fingers.

Ken panned to the woman.

"May I ask how that seal could possibly have become broken on the short ride to the high school?"

A long pause for thought.

"Well, it's possible," she answered.

"Can you tell us what purpose that seal serves if it can come in from the precinct broken?"

She stopped, looked quizzically at the camera, and said:

"Well, if it happens, we just put another one on."

"And then you record the new seal number as if it never happened?"

"That's right."

There was the *second* crime caught on tape.

With the registration procedure completed, two uniformed Metro cops put the boxes in the back seat of their squad car. They took off like a bat out of hell, ran lights, and we couldn't follow.

"If we hadn't been there," MacKenzie said,

gunning the engine of his Buick, "she would have put new seals on those security boxes that came in broken. But she couldn't commit a third-degree felony in front of the camera, so she let the box slide through with a broken seal."

We drove up to the front of the Data Processing Center at about 8:45 p.m. The police cars were unloading the security boxes full of ballots onto four-wheeled dollies.

We got out of the car and MacKenzie went to park. Ken turned the videocam on the police.

"Who you with?" one of the cops asked.

"The boss sent me," Ken said casually.

We followed one of the four-wheeled dollies behind the workers who were pushing them into the front door. There was a security desk and video camera located in the lobby between us and the elevators. A woman behind the desk was issuing I.D. badges, while a uniformed guard stood next to a sign that read: "You must have I.D. to enter this building."

"A New England town meeting, it isn't," Jim remarked.

"Where are you guys from?" the guard asked.

"The *Herald*," Ken deadpanned with his finger still on the video button.

"Yeah, we're going up to see Bob Lowe," Jim added, seeing Lowe's name on the security list.

The woman asked our names and we told her.

Then the guard leaned over to a security helper and said out of the side of his mouth: "Call Leahy."

The helper started to dial.

Jim turned around and saw a blue suit, vest and dark sunglasses coming through the door. He turned to the woman with the badges and said, "He's from the FBI."

She immediately issued the three of us building passes reserved for the *Herald*. We attached ourselves to another dolly full of boxes and headed for the elevators.

The videocam caught the sound of a telephone ringing behind us, and a loudspeaker boomed:

"Security chief to the lobby! Security chief to the lobby!"

But the elevator doors closed and we were in.

We got off on the third floor and followed the dolly into a well lighted room about the size of three tennis courts. A lot of people were working at tables.

Young guys in T-shirts lifted the security boxes off the dollies and placed them on tables in front of women who would break the seals by twisting them or cutting them with heavy shears. They would then open the boxes and take out the stacks of ballots and place them in cardboard trays without tops.

Ken asked of one of the women:

"Where is the League of Women Voters?"

"Through there," she pointed.

8:50 p.m..

We entered a big, carpeted room. There were reels of computer tape in racks on our left. On

our right were about twenty men and women
dressed for business. They were recognizable as
the county bigwigs: judges, members of the
election division, the Mayor of Miami and others.
In front of us was a row of seven machines
about three and one-half feet high.

These were called BMXs, or ballot
multiplexers.

The camera saw six empty machines. They
were unlighted and appeared turned off. At the
seventh machine was a heavyset young guy in a
white shirt. His machine made a clacking noise.

As we approached him, the camera recorded
about 500 punchcards stacked in a hopper on
the right top of the machine. A thick, black
Magic Marker line was drawn across the top
edges of the white cards. We were later to learn
that only *already counted* punchcards were
marked with a black line.

We watched as the cards were sucked from
that hopper past a photoelectric cell that shined
a light through the punched-out holes and
recorded the position of the holes on a tape.

The camera rolled as the man took a card
from the already counted side on the left and, in
a sweeping arc, transferred it back to the
uncounted side on the right. The machine was
still clacking away.

Then he looked up and saw the camera.

Ken asked: "What are you doing?"

He didn't answer. Instead he glanced over his
shoulder with a "Do I Tell Them Anything?" look

on his face. Ken swung the camera around and focused on a man with a goatee and eyeglasses.

"Who are you?" he asked, like the Caterpillar asked Alice.

"It's not important who we are. Who are you?"

Jim looked at his badge. "He's Joe Malone."

"You're Joe Malone the computer chief who programmed this election?" Ken asked.

"No, I'm not."

"You mean you're denying who you are?"

We knew Joe Malone from our research but had never met him.

The *Herald* called Joe Malone the "*God of Elections*" because without him an election could not be programmed for counting.

"You'll have to leave the room immediately; you're not allowed to be in here." Malone said.

Another voice piped up: "You've got to get out of here."

Ken turned the camera right into the face of David Leahy.

With that, a burly, blond Metro police office grabbed Ken's arm. Ken whipped the camera around, got a picture of the policeman's head, badge and uniform, and asked:

"Are we under arrest?"

"Not if you leave peaceably right now."

The policeman escorted us into a large room adjacent to the counting room. As we walked through the door, the first person we saw was Bob Lowe, with pen and paper in hand, grinning.

"Oh, there's Bob Lowe." Ken tried to provoke a reaction. "Bob, did you get into the secret basement where they take the reel of tape to have it counted?"

Lowe didn't bite but kept grinning.

The policeman pointed to a glass window in the wall.

"You can look in through this window here."

The BMX room from which we had just been evicted could be seen in total through the window, but everything going on was much too far away and the view was blocked by people. That window was as close as the public was permitted to the counting process.

Ken took a quick shot through the window.

"Nah," he said, "this is no good."

And he walked back to the door.

Three uniformed policeman were blocking the doorway.

At this point Ken got even more provocative as he kept shooting.

"What have we got? Malaria? If the police apparatus can be in there, why can't we? Have you been ordered by your bosses to keep us out? Do you take orders from them?"

"Yeah, and I give orders, too," drawled one of the cops.

"What happens if I try to come back in?"

"You'll be arrested for trespass after warning. Read the statute and the process."

Ken turned and panned the room. There was a purple velvet rope which kept the public from the rest of the room. And on the other side of the rope was a large area we hadn't even noticed. In it were about 70 men and women, casually dressed, seated at long tables.

The camera focused on a woman with a box of ballots in front of her.

"Are you from the League of Women Voters?"

"Yes."

We saw people riffling through stacks of *beige* vote cards. These were not the same as the *white* cards we had just witnessed being run through the BMX machine.

Jim's attention was drawn to a woman sitting directly in front of him. She had a black pencil in her right hand and was busy poking a new hole in a card. Then she reached around the back side of the card and pulled away the piece of "chad" that dangled by a thread.

Ken asked: "Why are you poking a hole in that card?"

"Because it didn't go all the way through."

Jim, acting as Ken's peripheral vision, told him to pan the room.

"Get the chad all over the tables and on people's clothes."

Ken began to videotape people holding the punchcard ballots up to the light and, using those black pencils, punching holes in them."

"*Get 'em outta here!!*" The security guard, who had been too late to catch us in the lobby, stuck his hand in front of the camera.

Ken said: "Hey, pal, get your hand off my lens."

With that, four cops grabbed us, two on each, and force-walked us out the door and back to the elevator.

"I'm not under arrest, am I?" Ken still had the camera rolling.

Instead of the elevator, the police marched us down three flights of steps, and all the way back to Galloway Road into the dark night.

"If you come back," one of them said, "you'll be arrested."

As the cops walked away, Bob Lowe stuck his head into the frame. He had followed the action out to the street.

"You've got to get into the basement to see what happens to the tape after it comes out of the BMX machines. We didn't get that far. Will you do it?" Ken asked.

"Yes," Lowe promised.

That night back at the *Herald*, Lowe wrote that there was "a blizzard of chad on the floor beneath the feet of the volunteers," indicating the massive extent of hole punching after we left. Lowe claimed that he named the League of Women Voters as the volunteers and that he wrote about us being dragged out. But the city desk, on Jim Savage's order, stopped it.

MacKenzie's brown Buick loomed out of the darkness. We jumped in. We had gotten proof of election rigging on tape. We crowed.

9

SHOTS IN THE DARK

"There's nothing like a good plan that comes together."

—The A-Team

Within two weeks we were back on the road to Washington. We had an appointment at the offices of the Republican National Committee and its legal counsel, Mark Braden.

The RNC offices were not far from The Library of Congress on Capitol Hill. Braden turned out to be a short man in a small office. We were seated on a low couch across from his desk that forced us to look up at him.

"We shot a videotape of members of the League of Women Voters who were punching holes in computer-counted ballots," Jim opened. "We'd like to show it to you."

"The League is above reproach," Braden said,

sitting up straight. "They do a great job for America."

He told us he once worked as the chief elections official for the State of Ohio, and he maintained regular communications with the League through its national president, Dorothy Ridings. He had worked with her on several occasions, including the presidential debates.

Ken asked:

"Are you aware that the League spent years of time and effort and money to lobby the punchcard system through the legislature of nearly every state?"

"I don't see anything wrong with that."

"Not even if the payoff and *quid pro quo* for their efforts was a nationwide sweetheart contract in all the major election venues hiring the League to pierce the public's ballots on election night?"

He was silent. Then he mulled something over and said:

"You know, the RNC hasn't any particular clout with anybody in the government. We have to keep our nose out of governmental operations. If we even attempted to get involved in the job the Justice Department is doing we'd be in hot water."

"Will you look at the tape?" Jim asked.

"No. It's not up to me."

"But the reward offer says that you have attorneys that you'll put us in touch with. Who are they?" Jim asked.

"That would be up to Frank Fahrenkopf, the President of the RNC".

"How do we get to see him?"

Braden was looking at his watch. Finally, "Look, why don't you contact the Justice Department on your own initiative and ask for Craig Dansantis, or something like that. I believe he's the chief vote fraud prosecutor attached to the Public Integrity Section."

He mispronounced Donsanto's name, as if he didn't know the man.

We had met and briefed Donsanto in March 1972. He refused to act then. Now Braden was sending us back to the man whose job, it appeared to us, was to keep the stopper in the bottle of vote fraud.

Braden clearly had no intention of helping. For us, it was ridiculous to see someone in his position, with the power to telephone the U. S. Attorney General or the President, trying to sell us the idea that he couldn't spur any government action.

The first words of the reward offer, written by former RNC Chairman Richard Richards, stated: "*It has saddened us to learn that vote fraud still exists in many parts of this country.*"

Well, Braden was the one the RNC directed us to, but he was *not* saddened by vote fraud. His sympathies were clearly in league with the League.

We sat in stunned silence, trying to figure out how we could salvage anything from this trip.

Jim assessed Braden's obtuseness and realized that there would be no record of the meeting, except for the sign-in log in the lobby. And if there was no proof, it would be easy for them to say, "Hey, they never came to see us ."

So Jim said:

"Why don't you call Donsantis and tell him to see us?"

"I've got no clout with Justice," Braden said in a whiney voice. "What do you want me to do, call the President, too?"

"Yes," Jim said, "or at least the Attorney General."

"If I do that, the RNC will be in hot water."

"That's a crock," Ken said.

We looked at each other in exasperation.

"I've got nowhere to go," Jim leaned back on the couch, stretching out his legs, "so I'll just sit right here to get this appointment on the record."

"I'll call the security guard."

"Go ahead."

Braden rang for security. The look on his face was angry and hurt. Very few people who are given the runaround in Washington refuse to walk away meekly. Politicians and bureaucrats count on that "responsible" behaviour, and to encounter confrontation on the part of the public makes them doubt their own potency.

Braden sat and fumed until the guard came. The guard took our names and we asked him to put our "sit-in" on the building's log book, the time and whom we saw.

"It's already on the log book when you sign in," he said.

"Remember that we were here in Braden's office," Jim said, getting up from the couch, "because you may be subpoenaed."

"I'll remember," he assured us. "Now please leave or I'll have to call the police, and they'll remember, too."

We laughed. Then Jim walked back to the couch and sat down.

"Go ahead."

Ken sat on the arm of the couch and watched the expressions on everybody's face, then he said:

"If we turn this into a police matter, which I think is probably a very good idea, we could get it in the papers, maybe on television…"

"I don't think the Washington *Post* goes in for Sixties politics anymore," Braden said, feet on desk, hands folded behind his head.

Jim turned to the guard.

"See, a police record will guarantee that we attempted to get Braden to see us, because we suspect that he's going to deny it."

Ken closed the debate: "Why don't you just write a report and give us a copy, so that we don't have to say that you guys somehow colluded to wipe out this meeting?"

Braden decided we weren't bluffing. He told the guard to write a report stating that we were trespassing in his office, and that he had to call the cops. That was Braden's pound of flesh, but we left with a copy of the report.

On the way home in the Maverick, we talked about what a sorry fucking state the country was in when a citizen has evidence of vote fraud and nobody will do anything about it.

We knew that Donsanto wouldn't do a damn thing. And we didn't tell Braden that we knew Donsanto. We figured: why give him more ammunition to use against us in any future claims? You can bet that if we went to the Justice Department on our own, the RNC would later claim that we weren't entitled to their reward offer because we didn't use their attorneys…the ones they promised would put us in touch with the proper authorities *who will proceed.*

In the Fifties there was a movie titled *Brotherhood of The Bell* that starred Glenn Ford. It was about members of a fraternity in California who belonged to *The Bell*, which was an evil good old boys' network. Only members of that fraternity could become powerful judges or politicians in California. Glenn Ford discovers its existence, but it's his word against theirs, and the most powerful and prominent people in the state are all in cahoots.

"It's the fucking *Brotherhood of The Bell,*" Jim said. "Everybody's in it and nobody can talk."

"Yeah," Ken agreed, "but Glenn Ford finally gets somebody to break."

"But only after his family leaves him and he's a broken man."

We weren't happy, and in a way, we also felt dirty, like we had uncovered terrible shit and had gotten it on us.

Ellis Rubin and Janet Reno were unfinished business. Reno, in the intervening years, had been elevated to Dade's State Attorney. We wanted to find out what had driven Rubin out of Reno's office eight years before.

A newspaper crusade has a way of quickening the blood in veteran newspapermen, and big Elmer Rounds turned out to be spoiling for a fight.

When we told him what happened in Braden's office, Rounds wasted no time in dedicating the resources of the *Home News* to combat.

For nine straight weeks we hammered Janet Reno with an onslaught of articles. We charged her with cover-up. Every story challenged her to answer questions about her conduct with Rubin in 1974, when she told him *"the statute of limitations has run out on the vote rigging crimes."*

Research proved that Rubin had presented her with the evidence of vote rigging 48 hours short of two years. So the *statute of limitations had not run out.*

Finally, after nine weeks, Reno was forced to

issue a statement. She called upon Governor Bob Graham (Katharine Graham's brother-in-law) to appoint a special prosecutor to "look into the charges" that she was consistently protecting vote-rigging friends. She said her own landslide victories in two consecutive elections held four years apart, "disqualifies me as an objective person to judge the merits of the Collier/Rubin charges. And since I am being accused each week in a community newspaper of being engaged in obstruction of justice for not choosing to prosecute, I am requesting this special prosecutor to investigate my role in this, since I cannot be expected to investigate my own activities."

We saw this as a smart ploy by Reno to wash her hands of the entire matter. If she should ever be asked to discuss the issue, she could squelch the subject by claiming: "A special prosecutor is looking into it."

And that was that.

We called Don MacKenzie "the Leprachaun" because if you took your eyes off him for a second he was gone.

MacKenzie loved to play politics, but he didn't fit in with any political crowd. The downtown Metro cronies bored him, and they couldn't be sure what his agenda was. He could be a friend and confidant to the most saintly and the most currupt, without necessarily tipping off one side to what the other was up to. His unique ability to pal around with all castes in the Miami heirarchy – from the high rollers he took out on his yacht, to low lifers hustling for dollars – made him a friend to all. Indeed, friendship was MacKenzie's stock in trade.

Elmer Rounds often found MacKenzie sitting outside his office plotting how to get rid of him.

It started when Rounds printed one of those CIA war stories about MacKenzie, essentially blowing Don's cover. Then, when Rounds wrote an editorial favoring a politician that MacKenzie didn't like, MacKenzie snuck in at night and pulled the offending paragraphs from the story and replaced them with an ad.

The Leprachaun had struck.

When Rounds saw the paper the next day, he was livid. MacKenzie, who came up to Rounds' chest, was equally pissed. He looked up at the 6'3", 200-plus pounds of Rounds and said:

"I'll kick your ass down those stairs if you ever get in my way again."

Within days MacKenzie announced that he had bought the paper and that Elmer had gone upstate to run a printing plant.

MacKenzie moved into Rounds' office.

During the nine-week Reno attack, we also renewed our relationship with Ellis Rubin. He never did tell us what happened in Reno's office that day in '74. He simply said: "I asked her to do her duty and I left." He wouldn't go beyond that statement.

He once told us a story about being a young naval officer who wanted to join the CIA. He went through all the formalities, but because he had stuttered as a kid, the CIA was worried that under some incredible pressure, he might revert to form and find himself stammering at the wrong time. According to Rubin, he was therefore rejected by the CIA.

But MacKenzie told us stories about Rubin's position as CIA bureau chief in the Caribbean basin. He also told us about his own exploits as pilot and expedition leader to several Caribbean countries. Having just met MacKenzie, we weren't sure if he was bullshitting, but one day, Jim got ahold of MacKenzie's "little black book" and found the home phone numbers of top agents.

If MacKenzie was right, and Rubin's stuttering story was simply created to deflect serious inquiry into his background – then Ellis Rubin is, by now, a Thirty-Year Man in the Company.

What Rubin never told us was that his call to Robert Rust in 1972 got us the appointment with Donsanto. He also never mentioned that he was a personal advisor to Richard Nixon, and that he could easily put through a phone call to either the White House or Key Biscayne. We found out these facts years later in conversations with him.

When you consider that Rubin filed a federal lawsuit on behalf of Cuban prisoners held for ransom in Cuba after the JFK/CIA Bay of Pigs invasion failed – and that he was the lawyer for the Watergate burglars, except Gordon Liddy —

it makes a good case that both MacKenzie and Rubin were well connected, to say the least.

Rubin viewed the *Votescam* tape and within days issued the following itemized report:

OMBUDSMAN'S REPORT
By: Ellis S. Rubin, Esq.

1. CONCLUSION: Computerized voting by punchcard thwarts the will of the people. A cancer is growing on our most precious franchise. It must be eradicated.

2. FACT: In 1972, Circuit Court Judge Henry Balaban appointed me to the post of Dade County Ombudsman to investigate and report on any alleged irregularities in the Dade County voting system.

3. HISTORY: In 1974 I submitted physical evidence and a report to the Dade County State Attorney's office. I recommended prosecution of those public officials connected with three specific methods of vote fraud which I demonstrated both to the press and to Assistant State Attorney Janet Reno. No official action resulted.

4. CURRENT: On this past election day, November 2, 1982, some

disturbing events surrounding the general election were videotaped. You will be shocked and sickened to see seventy workers from the League of Women Voters sitting at long tables at the Dade County tabulation center using pencils to punch holes in thousands of paper punchcard computer ballots prior to their being counted. These women do not take oaths to perform this task, are not elected, and in fact, are not authorized by state law to be there at all.

The report went on to itemize the several State and Federal laws that Rubin found to be violated on the tape, including the contraband-seal incident; the BMX card-reader operator covertly rerunning a blank deck through the counting mechanism; the League poking and scraping at the ballots, and the forced removal of two reporters from the premises.

Taken all together, Rubin's findings might normally have been expected to tickle the antennae of prosecutors at the State Attorney's office. Or at the very least they would have been the catalyst for a Grand Jury investigation. But, as the Seminoles we went to elementary school with used to say: Dade County politics is "tough as a snapping turtle and lower than turtle shit."

By January of 1983, the *Home News* had lost most of its advertisers. The all out attack on Reno and the Dade County elections department had caused overt pressure to be put on local merchants, and they didn't want to fight City Hall.

At that point the paper was taken back by its former owner. In less than three months his wife turned it into a pious religious publication.

Early one morning, Jim and MacKenzie cruised out to the Gulfstream in MacKenzie's fifty-foot yacht. They trolled for shark. They talked about what it would take to introduce a new paper to Dade County.

They decided to start the Miami *Herald-Tribune* out of MacKenzie's pocket. He found partners who owned all the paraphanalia needed to start a small tabloid.

"If the FBI would be interested in a story, that's the story I want to pursue," MacKenzie ordered.

But it was just four issues later that our thinking clashed with the partners. So we went to Miami Beach and left the mainland to MacKenzie.

We started our own newspaper called the Miami Beach *Herald Examiner* with offices in the karate school. MacKenzie subsidized our first issue and we sold ads after that to keep it going. The *Examiner* was fearless in naming names and exposing crooked politicians, developers, the power structure, the news media. It only attacked people big enough to attack back.

The *Votescam* story was always on the front page.

Shakti, who we now called Liz, drew ads for local merchants. They were so good that we sold every one of them. Within one week the paper was in the black. We gave MacKenzie the *Votescam* stories to use in the *Herald-Tribune*. Between us we covered Dade County.

The paper was given away free, and the political awareness was feverish. The elderly transplanted easterners on Miami Beach followed gossip among the local players like soap opera addicts. The paper grew from eight pages at the outset to a steady 16 pages, paid for completely by advertisers.

Soon the pressure against our crusading started to hurt. At first it was subtle, such as the loss of tire pressure in our vans on delivery day. Sometimes it was overt, such as having our newspapers stolen from drop points and trashed. Or having our advertisers telephoned by someone claiming to represent the State Attorney's office and *suggesting* that if they continued placing their ads they were in danger of being indicted. The word *indicted* scared away some of our customers, but many were survivors of Nazi intimidation and they didn't threaten easily.

Then one day we got a tip: the politicians on the Miami Beach City Council were meeting in secret with the City's power brokers two days before their actual city council meeting.

Our informant attended these secret meetings, he said, but he didn't approve of what was going on.

He told us the meetings were held in the plush board room of the Senior Corporation, a land development firm with offices in the Flagship Bank Building on the Lincoln Road mall.

"The council members," he said, "are violating the Florida Sunshine Law." The law states that *no elected official may meet privately with any other elected official on the same council to discuss how they would vote at the next meeting.*

"They're getting together in private on Monday night before the Wednesday public meeting. So Wednesday's meeting is fixed in advance. And that pisses me off real good," our informant told us.

On the following Monday night we were in Ken's van in the parking lot of the bank. We waited for the Miami Beach City Council members to appear.

Within the 30 minutes from 7 to 7:30 p.m. we photographed five of the seven council members entering the building. The mayor didn't show up. The *Herald Examiner* in its next edition ran a story about the secret confab in direct violation of the Sunshine Law and promised the photographs would appear in the next issue.

The story described how members of the Miami Beach Council met with powerbrokers like Dan Paul, the lawyer for the *Herald*, the ex-police chief of Miami Beach who was now a private lobbyist, the heads of both the Miami and Miami Beach Chambers of Commerce, and several lawyers and speculators with property interests on the Beach. Also in attendence were the owners of the local television stations. The public was not invited and the press bigwigs who were in the *sub rosa* session did not report it in their media. This entirely private affair was illegal, and if prosecuted could pose the threat of a jail term for everybody involved.

Photos of those attending a secret meeting – even though published in a 5,000 circulation weekly – seriously troubled almost everybody in that room.

In our off-hours from writing and delivering the paper, we unwound by shooting pool in the Bingo Bar on Miami Beach. Whole nights could pass trying to hold the table against Big Red, or some lucky tourist with a hot eightball instinct.

One night a guy we knew walked into the Bingo. He put his quarters on the pool table, sat down on a stool at the back of the room, and quietly waited his turn to play.

The green-shaded light over the pool table left the edges of the room in darkness. We were standing in those shadows when he got up and ambled over. He pleasantly informed us not to run the pictures taken outside the bank building. If we did, he promised an abrupt and permanent ending to our careers. We had no trouble believing him.

(Back in the Sixties Art Kunkin, publisher of the L.A. *Free Press*, printed the names of all the narcs in Los Angeles. So Jerry Powers got the names of all the Miami narcs from an insider in the State Attorney's office and threatened to print them in our next issue of The *Planet*. He was told that if he did, he would end up floating in Biscayne Bay. He chose the side of discretion, not valor.)

We left for Washington the next day.

One week later MacKenzie, who had printed all our *Votescam* stories in the *Herald Tribune*, was driving home after dark. He pulled into his driveway. Just as he opened the door and stepped out, he heard a bullet punch the old Buick.

He dropped to the ground to use the door as a shield.

Three more bullets tore into the car. The last bullet cut through the metal of the door and, crumpled and spinning, hit MacKenzie in the kidney area. He was badly bruised inside and out, but miraculously, the bullet only penetrated an inch.

The Leprachaun had escaped again.

The next day the *Miami Herald* refused to report on it. The *Herald Tribune* and the *Herald Examiner* never published again.

10

WATERGATETOWN
1984-1988

*"Anybody who isn't paranoid in
Washington must be crazy."*

—Henry Kissinger

It was a May afternoon in Washington. We parked our disreputable pair of 1968 VW vans at the corner of Constitution Avenue and 14th Street, N.W., near the Washington Monument.

The thermometer read 95 degrees in the shade and it was humid. You could smell the sweet decadent perfume of the magnolia trees with their huge white flowers. Ronald Reagan was President and the booty-shakers were in charge of the nation. It was a city where your power status was measured by the car you drove, and we drove vans that hadn't been washed or painted since Woodstock.

When our vans were parked together in the

shadow of the Monument, they looked like a commercial for a beer company that says, "IT NEVER GOT BETTER THAN THIS."

Jim said: "It's going to be a long winter if we don't have a plan and if we don't get any breaks."

Ken missed Liz and Unity. After hearing about the guy in the Bingo Bar, Liz decided it was time to take Unity away from the madness. Ken was in a constant black mood, and it was Jim's lot to keep him focused on both *Votescam* and personal survival.

We had "exhausted all local remedies" when our newspapers were put out of business in Miami, so the only move left was finally to call the Justice Department's Public Integrity Section and ask for Craig Donsanto. If he actually got on the line, there was an outside chance that we could get an appointment with him. And if we found ourselves in his office, there was a chance we could pull the thread on the reward offer.

The *Votescam* video now seemed crucial to our future. Dispossessed from our former lives on such short notice, we swore that we would survive in the Capitol by grit and wits. We could normally have counted on MacKenzie to help keep us afloat, but his bruised kidneys put our friend in the hospital "incognito" for several weeks.

Ken called the Justice Department.

"Craig Donsanto, please. Mr. Collier calling at the instruction of Mark Braden, chief counsel of the Republican National Committee."

"Donsanto, here."

"Is this the Craig Donsanto we know and love?"

"I presume this is one of the Collier brothers from Miami. How are you? What brings you to Washington this time?"

"Of all things, a reward offer put out by the Republicans for admissible evidence of vote fraud. We've got the evidence. We need you to confirm that it's admissible."

"What kind of evidence is it?"

"Videotape. It's really some fascinating stuff."

"Do you want to drop it off?"

"No, we want to be there when you view it. We've missed you all these years. We can talk about old times. We'd like to get your comment on a couple of memos Henry Petersen wrote, using your name, just before Watergate. You remember Watergate?"

"N-o-o-o-o comment," he said coyly.

The mention of Henry Petersen and curiosity to find out what the prosecutor of the Watergate burglars had to say about him, lured Donsanto to invite us over.

"All right, why don't you bring it by tomorrow afternoon and I'll take a look."

As we drove around Capitol Hill looking for a place to park the vans for the night, we wondered about Donsanto's "no comment" in reference to Watergate. We knew the connection Petersen had with both *Votescam* and Watergate, as the FOIA file showed he was the chief investigator in both cases.

We had only a day to plan. We went over to the Washington *Times,* the town's only rival to the Washington *Post,* and met with managing editor Woody West, who had invited us to show *Votescam* material if we ever came to town. West assigned a reporter to our story.

An hour later we were scoffing club sandwiches and iced tea in the dining room with reporter Gene Goltz, a two-time Pulitzer Prize winner who told us he was amazed that we could obtain instant access to a Justice Department official.

"What have you got on Donsanto, or what does he *think* you've got on him?" Goltz asked.

"Something about Watergate, Gene, but it's a long story."

We asked Goltz to go with us to see Donsanto as a professional witness. Goltz was game.

The building guard alerted Donsanto to our arrival, and as the elevator doors opened he was there to greet the three of us. He was still melon-headed. He ushered us into a nearby library conference room where there were more introductions. Donsanto had invited two witnesses of his own – Patricia Prilliman, an FBI agent from the local office, and Nancy Stewart, an assistant prosecutor in the Justice Department. The six of us took seats at the conference table. Prilliman, Stewart and Goltz were poised to take notes.

Donsanto had spent the previous twelve years consistently declining to prosecute any but the most amateur vote fraud. The only exception to this was convictions in Cook County, Illinois, against some officials who knowingly voted "dead people."

"How long is your tape?" Donsanto asked.

"It's about 45 minutes. It's totally convincing," Jim said.

"If it's so convincing, why haven't you taken it to '60 Minutes'?" That wooden grin again. "Seriously, you know that my door has always been open to you."

Coming from Donsanto, that comment was as sincere as a Mafia kiss. Ken, who was nursing broken dreams and a bad temper, decided to take the offensive.

"Your door may have been open," he said, "but according to FBI files, you've made it your business to *close* all cases. The tape is another one of our efforts to find out why. We've come to the conclusion that wherever the computer is, the American voting system is shot through with corruption." Donsanto's cheery face flickered darkly. Had he allowed himself to be set up in front of witnesses? Worse yet, were the Colliers acting in behalf of some government investigative arm, trying to pin a case of obstruction of justice on him?

We handed him a sampler of the vote fraud evidence gathered over the past decade: a Blank-Backed Canvass Sheet, a forged Canvass Sheet, a Printomatic Return Sheet and a TV computer read-out used by Channe1 7 in the original *Votescam* of September 8, 1970.

"We're asking you," Jim said, "why you haven't done anything about all this?."

Donsanto felt the heat.

"Why are 37 pages of the Justice Department file on the Miami vote frauds deleted from the FBI files we got from Freedom of Information?" Ken asked. "And why are they censored by *'another government agency'*? Are we talking about an agency that can't be named because it's the CIA?"

Donsanto checked notations from his file.

"Yes," he said. "The coding here indicates that the material is under national security."

It was the first time a Justice Department official admitted that vote fraud investigations had a national security lid. Why?

Ken pressed harder.

"Are we talking about a domestic vote fraud probe ordered by Henry E. Petersen into the culpability of three Miami TV stations—one of them owned by Katharine Graham—being of vital interest to the CIA? We think so, because only the CIA would hide its involvement in domestic affairs."

Donsanto stammered. "It's a matter of national security, a call I never made."

His eyes narrowed. He peered over at Goltz.

"Who did you say you represented?"

"The Washington *Times*," Goltz said. "I showed you my press card when we got off the elevator. If you don't want me here for some reason, I'm willing to leave."

Donsanto slammed his notebook and rose to his feet.

"That's it! I didn't realize you were a *reporter.* This meeting is over. And don't bother calling me for any further meetings, you won't be put through."

"But what about the t-a-a-a-a-pe…?"

Before the question was completed, Donsanto was out the door.

Prilliman and Stewart just stared at each other.

Just then Donsanto popped his head inside the doorway.

"If you have any further questions direct them to Mark Shaheen in the Public Relations office on the 10th floor," he said.

We drove back to the *Times* in Goltz's battered old Chevy.

"Is this a story, Gene?" Jim asked.

"I think it is. But it's going to be up to Arnaud de Borchgrave." He was referring to the spy-editor of the Washington *Times*. "It's his agenda and he's CIA. Chances are good they'll never print it."

We stopped at a Holiday Inn on New York Avenue where *Times* reporters liked to drink and play liar's poker.

"You guys should get your video on television. Go to the networks."

Goltz promised to write a story on the meeting with Donsanto. If he ever did, it never ran.

That night we found an acceptable, unobtrusive place to park our vans. The Union Station was undergoing renovation and the ellipse out front was available. Like small elephants in tandem we pulled the bulbous VW's into two adjacent spaces and settled in after a lengthy rehash.

At 10 a.m. the next day we put a call through to the news desk at ABC Television. It turned out better than we could have hoped. ABC's supreme court correspondent Tim O'Brien took the call. We explained the reward offer, and the runaround we had gotten from both the RNC lawyer and the Justice Department.

"You've got my curiosity piqued," O'Brien said. "Why don't you bring the tape over?"

"We understand you're an attorney, Tim?"

"That's correct."

"Wonderful. We'll be right over."

O'Brien let us know up front that he couldn't guarantee ABC would do the story. He explained that would be a decision made by others.

However, if we had what we claimed, he thought it would be a story of explosive national significance.

"I put in a request for a screening room and engineer," O'Brien said. "While we're waiting, I'd like to take a look at exactly how they worded the Reward Offer."

We gave him a copy, plus other materials including the final issue of the *Home News* featuring more than a hundred still photos of the *Votescam* video. He read them with intense concentration.

A buzzer sounded.

We trailed O'Brien through several corridors. As we entered the screening room, he was reading a copy of Rubin's report.

"We've got slow motion, stop motion and picture enhancement here," the engineer said.

As we got to the part where the stocky guy at the BMX machine lifted the white card from the *already counted side* and stuck it back to be counted a second time, we asked the engineer to stop the action.

"An FBI agent in Miami showed us this," Jim said, "look at this…" he pointed to the screen, "the hole in that phoney white card is running vertical. Later, when we get to the League punching out holes in real cards, you'll see the ballots are beige, not white, and *those* holes are running *horizontal*."

O'Brien was impressed. As we left the screening room, he said: "I can't deny that you delivered on that tape. The only question is what do we do next, and that's a decision I'm in no position to make."

"That's what bothers us," Jim said. "You're an attorney with the legal expertise to know felonies when you see them – backed up by Rubin's Ombudsman's Report – still the decision to go with the story isn't yours to make?"

"Welcome to network news, gentlemen," O'Brien said.

He asked us to stay for lunch on the company credit card after he made a few calls. It wasn't long before he came back with word on the fate of our story. He had phoned Braden and assured him that in his opinion as newsman and lawyer, our videotape had everything the RNC was looking for in the Reward Offer.

Braden gave him the "Catch-22" excuse. There would be no way the RNC would ever consider paying out reward money unless there was prosecution and conviction. And as far as he knew, there were no prosecutions planned either by the Justice Department or local authorities. His main concern, according to O'Brien, was whether or not ABC was going to broadcast the story.

O'Brien's call to Donsanto perplexed him.

"I've known Donsanto for years, and this was the first time I've heard him resort to 'no comment.' Usually he's quite gregarious."

"Do you think ABC would ever run the story?" Ken asked.

"Frankly, I have serious doubts," he answered. "The reason for their reluctance has more to do with loyalty to the League than the news value of your story. Understand that ABC subsidizes the League and hires their membership *en masse* on election night. It's not surprising they'd want to protect its reputation."

After lunch we said we'd call for the results of his efforts with the top ABC brass.

"This stuff is really great," O'Brien said, "and I admire you guys for getting it. But you've got to remember something."

"What?"

"When you're dealing with the networks, you're dealing with a shadow government."

We crossed the gilded expanse of carpet in the Mayflower lobby, heading from the world of expense accounts into the uncertainty of the afternoon. What next? The power lunch was over. It was drizzling. Miami was a painful memory. The battery in Jim's van was dead. Time was leaden, unforgiving.

It was obvious what had to be done. We had to obtain a base of operation, housing, a phone, respectability, credibility, and income.

The first thing we needed was a shower. One place we figured might have "complimentary showers" was the Shakespeare Theater on Capitol Hill. Ken, who was born on Shakespeare's birthday and could quote vast passages of The Bard, pretended to be a Shakespearean actor. He eloquently talked his way backstage where he found what he was looking for, fully equipped dressing rooms. After that, we would take turns keeping guards occupied while one of us would sneak backstage for a shower.

The fifth floor reading room of the Library of Congress annex on Third Street was an air-conditioned oasis, filled with the entire collected wisdom of the ages until 6 p.m. We were able to accomplish invaluable research, between naps of the head-on-arms variety, generously overlooked by the library staff. It was a place suspended in time.

Each small increment of routine we established boosted our morale. Driving us was the conviction that the evidence we had so painstakingly gathered on election fraud since 1970 must not be allowed to dissipate and be forgotten.

The answer to our financial dilemma appeared in the Library of Congress reading room for current periodicals. We came upon a copy of the *Spotlight*, a weekly political tabloid distributed nationwide. Although our research showed its editorial policy was strictly right wing, it had a million readers weekly, and, surprisingly, on staff were such liberals as lawyer Mark Lane, writer Andrew St. George and ex-CIA spook Victor Marchetti (who was exposing CIA abuses). Best of all, its office was located directly across the street from our temporary headquarters in the Library.

There were certain phone booths in the

Library building which were lucky and others definitely to be avoided. Ken telephoned the *Spotlight's* senior editor, taking care to use the lucky booth. Editor Vincent Ryan immediately invited us over.

We proposed a year's worth of *Votescam* stories, one each week.

Ryan's enthusiasm was tempered by space considerations, and the requirement that *Spotlight* lawyers (including Mark Lane), go over every inch of our material. Once we jumped those hurdles, the articles could start running, and only then would we be paid.

"How long?"

"Maybe six weeks."

Now we had articles to write and the possibility of money coming in before winter. However, just as quickly as the cool atmosphere of Ryan's office faded from our skin, replaced by Washington's sticky humidity, we realized that the most lofty enterprise depends, in the last analysis, on the bottom line.

The street people we met during the next six weeks in Lafayette Park, across from the White House, inspired us to hold out against gainful, steady employment until The *Spotlight* gave us a room and typewriter. Lafayette Park used to be the front lawn of the White House until Pennsylvania Avenue cut through it from east to west. The park runs two blocks along Pennsylvania Avenue and is one block wide from north to south. It's surrounded by the Court of Appeals, a yellow stucco church, and a row of old townhouses. There are several fountains, chess tables, curving walkways, benches, old trees, and a big statue of General Lafayette who helped America win the Revolutionary War.

From all over the country, for every imaginable reason, rooted in idealism or frustration, protestors appeared with their signs and banners in the park. They felt they had grievances that only the President could redress — if only he would gaze out his front window and give a shit. There were giant plywood signs on which were written the words that defined somebody's cause. When some really serious issues of life and death, war and peace, arose in the news, the Buddhists in saffron robes would come to the park with their skin drums and produce a steady, relentless, incessent *"Boooooom, booooom, booooom, booooom, booooom, booooom."* It drove the President nuts.

"Can't you stop those drums?" Reagan was quoted asking.

"No," the Interior Department police replied, "not constitutionally."

In the evening, the MacKenna's Wagon dispensed free sandwiches and Kool-Aid to these individualists, anarchists and assorted true believers of every stripe. At night, after we departed in our vans to Capitol Hill, the denizens of Lafayette Park faced arrest and imprisonment if a park ranger caught them so much as napping. No camping or sleeping was allowed. The authorities acted under orders from the White House to keep the riff-raff moving.

The unofficial Mayor of Lafayette Park was William Thomas, a stone sculptor and jeweler from Albuquerque, New Mexico, who wore long dark hair and a beard. Thomas could peddle a bicycle around a corner no-handed, while eating soup with a spoon from a cup. He was a man of infinite balance. His wife, Ellen Thomas, had once worked for the National Wildlife Federation as an executive secretary who could type 125 words per minute. She was intelligent and gutsy.

Thomas took great pride in the ethic of fighting back, no matter the odds, no matter the resources of his adversary. His own personal cause was against nuclear weapons, but he championed anyone who wanted to use the park to stage a protest, 24 hours a day.

Reagan's Secretary of the Interior, James Watt, issued a regulation removing the overt act of sleeping from protection of the First Amendment. Thomas doggedly pursued legal actions against officials responsible for arrests – from suing Watt himself down to the arresting officers.

Thomas, whose real name was William Thomas Hellanback, learned his legal basics in Washington's best public law libraries. He would pore over books to develop a defense against being thrown out of the park. They had already uprooted him from his niche in front of the White House gates on the other side of the avenue. One day, while he was still on the White House side, his ten-foot tall wooden sign caught fire. Perhaps it was arson. The conflagration so riled up the Secret Service and the Park Police that a regulation was promulgated to keep all protesters on the other side of the street. And thus a place where people had been camping with protest signs since the War of 1812 was ruled off limits.

That eviction, however, launched Thomas into his role as street lawyer. He began to explore the necessities of *pro se* law. That's when no lawyer will take your case and you can't afford one anyway so you do it yourself.

Thomas claimed he was sitting "vigil" in the park, and would stay there until there were no more nuclear weapons – years, decades, if necessary. The Park Service said: "No, you can't." Protest people like Thomas were an eyesore. Yuppies who came to the park to eat lunch were offended visually. The bureaucracy was offended because life wasn't orderly. The President and his wife across the street were offended by it all.

Thomas is one of the most famous and most photographed Americans. People from every state and around the world, including foreign press, constantly check to see if our country's only continuous anti nuclear protesters are still at their post. Tour buses schedule stops so that visitors can talk to Thomas and ask questions.

"When they go," said a Norwegian newspaper, "so will democracy."

The Park Police arrested Thomas and Ellen about every four months for falling asleep on vigil. Most of the time Thomas got out of jail immediately, and then he would go right back on the sidewalk. Eventually, he detected the telltale pattern of a conspiracy to take away his First Amendment rights of free speech and assembly, so he filed a federal conspiracy case. Ellen corrected and typed his legal briefs.

Ellen met Thomas in 1984 while on her way to cocktails at the Washington Hotel. A protest sign in the park caught her eye and she stopped. One of the street people told her about a philosopher who lived in the park, and since she was researching a play about a street philosopher, she was immediately intrigued.

Within three weeks, Ellen had left her job, her buttoned-down life, and was living with Thomas in Lafayette Park. They were married in a Quaker ceremony.

Ellen had a wild, angry streak, but she also had a whimsical side, which she let loose on memorable occasions. The story of Casimer Urban, Jr. is a case in point.

In the summer of 1984, Casimer Urban, Jr., was arrested for protesting the Supreme Court decision on the Lafayette Park "camping" regulation. The High Court confirmed that homeless people couldn't sleep in their tents. So for five days Casimer Urban, Jr. pretended to sleep in front of a sign that read:

WELCOME TO REAGANVILLE, 1984 WHERE SLEEP IS CONSIDERED A CRIME.

Once arrested, Casimer told the magistrate that he wanted to represent himself. Instead, the magistrate appointed a public attorney who immediately suggested that Cas be put into St. Elizabeth's Hospital for 30 days psychiatric observation.

Exiled to the St. E's cuckoo's nest, Cas imitated Jack Nicholson. He was disrespectful, wise-assed, honest and funny. The psychiatrists decided he was a paranoid schizophrenic and injected him with Prolixin, which can cause the side-effect of catatonia. Cas was in danger of being kept in the cuckoo's nest for good without ever standing trial.

Ellen was scared for him. And angry. She decided that anger was fruitless in trying to get Cas out, so she would use theatrics instead.

In October, she decided to climb a tall sycamore tree. Sometimes she perched way up high, sometimes on a lower branch. Then someone gave her a hammock and she slung it from limb to limb. She kept just out of reach of the park police. Ellen lived in a ski suit and took care of personal business in a cup. After a week, the park police and a D.C. SWAT team arrived at

4 a.m. and plucked her out of the sycamore with a cherry picker. She was taken to jail, charged with *general injury to a tree*, which she denied, *attachment to a tree*, which she admitted, and *camping*, which she denied.

However, a law student who had passed under the sycamore and talked to Ellen, took the story to a professor at a local law school. The professor took Cas' case and got him out.

That night there was a wild party that must have kept Reagan up 'til dawn. *Boooom, Boooom, Booooom, Booooom, Booooom!*

Between us and William Thomas, a street law firm was forged: Collier, Collier & Thomas. We were our only clients. But some of the biggest shooters in America, who collectively represented billions of dollars in assets, were destined to become defendants.

11

POWER CORRUPTS

*"May you have a lawsuit in which you
know you are in the right."*

—Gypsy curse

Our office in Lafayette Park was a lean-to on
the sidewalk; our desk a packing crate and our
typewriter a Royal, circa 1929, well-oiled and in
splendid working condition.

Ellen got us the typewriter from Mitch Snyder.
He was Washington's homeless advocate who
fasted in the park to within an inch of death
when the government refused to give him five
million dollars to renovate a building for the
homeless. Dick Gregory was his fasting coach,
and just before Snyder was to suck his last breath,
and just before the election Reagan gave in.

Snyder would serve hundreds of dinners to
the homeless in the park Thanksgiving and
Christmas that year. We stood in a cold, dripping

rain, waiting for stuffing and cranberry sauce, Jim told Snyder: "It's taken me a lot of years to work my way down from the top." We had gone broke going for broke.

All through that summer in the park we prepared a series of lawsuits. They were filed against defendants whose actions to suppress the *Votescam* video coincided with one another.

By fall, the *Spotlight* had run five of our Miami stories on vote fraud. They included an investigation of Computer Election Services (CES), the San Francisco firm which controlled most of the vote-counting apparatus in 1984.

Our first lawsuit was against the RNC. As we saw it, the reward offer was a binding contract. We wanted our day in court to show the video to a jury. Let them judge who was acting in good faith to expose vote fraud and who was trying to cover it up.

The lawsuit against the RNC also gave us breaking stories every week. Our stories were filled with excerpts from sworn depositions of prominent functionaries and politicians. There was also the chance we could use the law's discovery process to reveal further leads into the heart of vote fraud. We promised *Spotlight* editors that at least three more lawsuits would be filed in early 1985.

We submitted the following complaint to the court:

PLAINTIFFS: (Collier)

V.   **CC CA10395-81**

DEFENDANTS: Repub. Nat. Comm. et al Civil Action No.___

1. JURISDICTION OF THIS COURT IS FOUNDED ON D.C. Code Annotated,1973 edition. Sec,.11-921

COME NOW THE PLAINTIFFS and say:

1. **THAT** Plaintiffs are residents of the District of Columbia, appearing in pro se.

2. **THAT** Defendant is an unincorporated association with its principal offices located in the District of Columbia along with its Chairman and its principal legal office.

3. **THAT** Defendant caused to be published a nationally circulated press release in October,1982 to the effect that a "Reward Program" was being offered to "individuals who give information" related to violations of certain State and Federal laws against "vote fraud." (Please see EXHIBIT "**A**" which is attached hereto and made a part hereof.)

4. **THAT** Defendant wrongfully and negligently contracted with Plaintiffs via the generally circulated press release referred to in Paragraph 3, guaranteeing to "...put them in touch with the proper State and Federal officials who <u>will proceed</u> with such complaint," when, in fact, Defendant had no authority to make such a promise, thereby luring Plaintiffs efforts through misrepresentation.

5. **THAT** Plaintiffs acting solely on the guarantee that their efforts would receive the official action as cited in Paragraph 4 herein, embarked on a mission to infiltrate and videotape the activities of a vote-racketeering ring operating with apparent impunity within the United States,

doing so at the risk of our lives and at the peril of
our families. Our efforts produced vital
information.

6. <u>THAT</u> Defendant, by and through its chief counsel
and agent, Mark Braden, acknowledges in writing
(May 30, 1984) its knowledge of Plaintiff's
substantial compliance with the "Reward
Program," absent an arrest in the case, admitting
Plaintiffs had "obtained information." (Please see
EXHIBITS, attached hereto and made a part
hereof). Defendant BRADEN and Defendant
FAHRENKOPF co-authored the memo's content.

7. <u>THAT</u> defendant failed to make any effort to get
State or Federal proceedings started.

8. <u>THAT</u> as a result of the foregoing
misrepresentation Defendants have caused
Plaintiff to suffer impoverishment, mental
anguish, anxiety and permanent threats to their
lives. Wherefore, Plaintiff demands judgment
against Defendant in the sum of $<u>20,000,000</u>
(TWENTY MILLION DOLLARS) with interests and
costs.

_____

_____

                                      Plaintiffs

_____

It didn't take long for the complaint to reach the
most important figures in the Republican
braintrust. We know this because a White House
log was released less than a year later which
chronicled the activities of President Reagan's

national security advisor, Admiral John Poindexter.

The log revealed that less than 48 hours after the complaint was filed, alleging the existence of an organized "vote-racketeering ring" operating within the United States, RNC chairman, Frank Fahrenkopf, sent a memo to Poindexter discussing the implications of such a charge.

Poindexter, in turn, consulted with William Casey, Director of the CIA, and together they drafted a "*National Security Directive Decision*" (NSDD 245) for immediate approval of the President. The thrust of the Directive was to involve the Reagan administration in the question of whether the computerized portion of the U.S. voting system was secure, or whether it was open to manipulation and fraud.

When the Directive was signed by Reagan, it was classified "Top Secret." A year later, The New York *Times* discreetly published a minor story revealing that the administration was aware of the dangers of computerized voting. The *Times,* however, did not assign a follow-up on the story.

David Burnham, the reporter who discovered the Poindexter logbook and managed to get the following into the paper September 9, 1985, left the *Times* shortly thereafter.

U.S. PROBES ELECTION COMPUTER MAKEUP

N.Y. Times News Service

WASHINGTON - A branch of the National Security Agency is investigating whether a computer program that counted more than one-third of all the votes cast in the United States in 1984 is vulnerable to fraudulent manipulation.

The National Security Agency is the nation's largest and most secretive intelligence agency.Its principal job is to collect intelligence by eavesdropping on the electronic communications of the world and to protect the sensitive communications of the United States.

Mike Levin, a public information official for the agency's National Computer Security Center, said the investigation was initiated under the authority of a recent presidential directive ordering the center to improve the security of major computer systems used by the nonmilitary agencies such as the Federal Reserve Board and the Federal Aviation Administration and for such private purposes as banking.

The target of the Computer Security Center's investigation is the vote-counting program of Computer Election System of Berkeley, Calif.,the dominant company in the manufacture and sale of computer voting apparatus. In 1984,the company's program and related equipment was used in more than 1,000 county and local jurisdictions to collect and count 34.4 million of the 93.7 million votes cast in the United States.

"We have no interest in any particular election." Levin said. "We are only interested in the possible misuse of computers to compile election results."

Frank Fahrenkopf, the newly-named chairman of the RNC, resented being named as a defendant in what he considered a nuisance suit. The $20 million in damages we sought as relief could conceivably affect Fahrenkopf's personal holdings if misrepresentation was found to be implicit in the terms of the reward offer. For while Fahrenkopf was not the signatory on the reward offer we saw in 1982, nonetheless he found himself obliged to put his signature to an identical document promulgating another offer in 1984.

Thus, with his house and car literally on the line, Fahrenkopf found himself less able to avoid taking a personal interest in the progress of the Collier suit.

As events in court piled up, Fahrenkopf took an increased role in stage-managing the RNC effort to get our tar–baby suit off their backs. At first he relied on a junior attorney in his office, Michael Hess, to file a simple Motion to Dismiss. He expected some judge at the Superior Court of the District of Columbia to glance at the pleadings and, with a snort of disapproval, throw the case out.

When that didn't happen, he called Hess into his office for further consultation. Their only alternative was to file for a summary judgment, a legal maneuver which, if successful, would have the same effect as a motion to dismiss. The only drawback, from Fahrenkopf's point of view, was that months would pass before a ruling, enabling the Colliers to strengthen their cause with support drummed up by their newspaper stories.

What at first had presented itself as a pimple of a case, had become a full-time boil. Meanwhile, Fahrenkopf called a meeting of the intelligence community's public adjunct, the Center for Strategic and International Studies, (CSIS), of Georgetown University.

The mission of the CSIS is to provide the world media with certified experts to comment on developments in international relations. In providing this "service" to the networks and newspapers-of-record, CSIS imparts whatever "spin" to the analysis might satisfy CIA requirements.

Accordingly, a domestic mission of the CSIS in 1985 was to marshall its brainpower to help Fahrenkopf with ways and means to better manage the major media. Powerful personalities in news and politics would weigh in with advice, and their perceived expertise would form the basis of an *ad hoc* election commission.

Fahrenkopf met with CSIS executive director Robert Hunter to discuss details of a proposed series of conferences among select CSIS luminaries and special invitees. The working title of the 1985 project was: "<u>The National Commission on Elections</u>." Its mission was Fahrenkopf's goal: ***"Developing ways and means to overhaul the U.S. voting system to better conform with the realities of a mass-media environment."***

To better explain what Fahrenkopf really meant by *"the realities of mass-media environment"* we have to give a little history. We have to go back to that day in Dallas when John F. Kennedy was gunned down.

The Establishment line that a *"lone gunman"* was responsible for the murder was being attacked by various newspapers around the country. The CIA could not tolerate any dissension from the official government edict.

Therefore, in the immediate years following the November 22, 1963 assassination, a lid was slammed on all investigative reporting about the case. In fact, the relationship between the one time vibrant *adversary press* and the U.S. government was ominously frozen following the fatal gunblasts.

So notorious was the plot against JFK, and so prominent were the figures who had a hand in executing it – and later covering it up – that today, 30 years later, coercive and rigid conformity still chills the Establishment press from labeling the Warren Report a time-worn joke.

As history shows, immense collegial pressure was exerted upon TV and press managers in the wake of the assassination to ignore, suppress and discredit critics of the Warren Report. During that period not one word of dissent from the Warren Commission's conclusions was permitted on a single network television program in the United States.

In 1966, *The Associated Press* devoted the longest article it had ever originated to an intelligence-inspired attack upon several prominent critics of the government-approved version of JFK's death. After *Rush To Judgment* (in 1966) by author/Warren critic Mark Lane was published, the CIA adopted a program to destroy it.

CIA document No. 1035-960 read as follows:

"We do not recommend that discussion of the assassination question be initiated where it is already not taking place. Where discussion is active, however, addressees are requested:

To discuss the publicity problem with liaison and friendly elite contacts (especially politicians and editors), pointing out that the Warren Commission made as thorough an investigation as humanly possible, that the charges of the critics are without serious foundation, and that further speculative discussion only plays into the hands of the opposition. Point out also that parts of the conspiracy talk appear to be deliberately generated by Communist propagandists. Urge them to use their influence to discourage unfounded and irresponsible speculation.

To employ propaganda assets to answer and refute the attacks of the critics. Book reviews and feature articles are particularly appropriate for this purpose. The unclassified attachments to this guidance should provide useful background material for passage for assets. Our plan should point out, as applicable, that the critics are 1) wedded to the theories adopted before the evidence was in; ll) politically interested; lll) financially interested.

Mark Lane later wrote: *"Coinciding with the CIA offensive to cover up its involvement in JFK's death was an urgent speech by ex-CIA director Allen Dulles to Chief Justice Earl Warren. The CIA, having executed the President who was about to dismember that agency and withdraw all U.S. advisors — as they were then called — from Vietnam, approached Earl Warren carefully and with premeditation.*

"On January 12, 1964, just as the Commission began its work, the CIA advised Warren that it was certain that Oswald had acted alone but that complicating factors, if publicly revealed, might very well threaten the peace of the world. The CIA confided to Warren that Oswald had been meeting in Mexico City with the Soviet

KGB officer in charge of assassination in the United States. The spectre was raised to a credulous Warren that World War III might result if an enraged American public was informed of the single "Communist Plot" against its beloved fallen President — that some kind of violent retaliation would be politically inescapable.

"Warren, confronted with that scenario agreed to hide the evidence 'for at least 75 years,' take all testimony in closed sessions, designate the transcript 'top secret' and issue a false report. That was all done in the interest of national tranquility and international peace. The motives may have been defensible, but the 'facts' upon which Warren's briefings were based were CIA inventions. Warren sacrificed both his reputation and the truth as the result of an elaborate CIA disinformation effort."

In other words, the major media in this country has been co-opted by the CIA. It was that covert CIA action that Farhenkopf was referring to when he said the U.S. vote-counting system had to conform with the realities of the media.

There was a strict protocol with respect to the order in which Fahrenkopf contacted the invitees to the CSIS National Commission on Elections. First, he was careful to secure the commitment of those he considered superstars in the political firmament. Then he used such commitments to persuade those on the "B" list to come aboard.

This meant getting semi-official input from his party's titular leader, Richard M. Nixon. Nixon's interest in politics had only increased over the years, and his influence related to the conduct of elections had become bigger since he resigned from office.

Protocol requires that a former President rates deference one notch higher than a future President.

Fahrenkopf reached the former President at Nixon's home in Saddle River, New Jersey, and received approval of the Election Commission concept. Nixon requested that he be represented at the proceedings by his reliable friend Melvin Laird, his Vietnam-era Secretary of Defense. Fahrenkopf was only too pleased to comply, as Laird's cabinet-level ranking set a high tone.

Fahrenkopf's next approach was to George Bush, Vice President and heir-apparent. Virtually all the Republicans participating in the Election Commission activity took it for granted that when they were dealing with Bush, they were dealing with the next President. Thus, with Bush's acceptance of the plan to overhaul the U.S. electoral system, a message was effectively delivered: Bush stood ready to manipulate the levers of power from without and within to achieve his place in history.

The secret CSIS-sponsored hearings were scheduled to take place in privately rented hotel ballrooms in Washington throughout the rest of 1985. Bush requested that he be represented by his own man – the most knowledgeable computer wiz in or out of government – John Sununu, Governor of New Hampshire. Sununu would act as working chairman and occupy a position at the center of the dais.

While the Republican chairman created a roster of media moguls, former politicians, attorneys and consultants, we were exercising our prerogatives to subpoena witnesses and conduct "discovery" sessions.

The first person we served with papers was Richard Richards, the RNC chairman prior to Fahrenkopf. It was his signature on the reward offer of 1982 that made it binding upon that committee. The following questions were put to Richards in the office of his lawyer in Washington, to which he was obligated to answer under oath:

Q. *When you permitted the reward offer to be disseminated over your name and signature, is it true that you were attempting to further the interests of the Republican Party for whatever benefit it might yield?*

A. Yes, the promulgation of the letter was designed to do just that — to further the benefit of the party and of the Republican National Committee.

Q. *You were acting within the scope of your authority when you issued the reward offer?*

A. That is correct. I had the authority to do that.

Q. *Did you hold yourself as an authority or expert on vote fraud?*

A. We hired experts to develop the language in the letter. As Chairman of the party with authority to make decisions on behalf of the Republican National Committee, I endorsed their findings and signed the letter.

Q. *Did you assume that the RNC had taken on a fiduciary duty to any potential claimants that may respond to the reward offer?*

A. I think that's a fair statement, yes. I assumed that we had a duty to be fair and honest and straightforward to a claimant.

The questioning went on to probe Richards interpretation of *"will proceed"* as stated in the offer. He said there should have been a better word, since the RNC had absolutely no authority to make that promise. When asked if there was a difference between the two phrases, "may pay us" and "will pay us," he conceded that the word "may" gives discretion to act, while the word "will" is mandatory. As to whether it was fair that a claimant without a legal degree, relying upon the exact words "will proceed with such complaint" would draw a 180-degree difference in inference if the RNC used the words "may proceed," Richard responded, "The word "will" probably overstates the case in this letter because a better word would have been "may" or "could" or "can."

We asked our final question.

Q. *Would it have been reasonable, in your opinion, for someone reading the text of the reward offer, to have been induced to take action under the exact wording as it appears, relying on the credibility of the Republican National Committee to back it up?*

A. I do not know. We intended to honor it if someone met the requirements. What they may have thought about when they read it and how much credibility they gave to the RNC, is wholly within their knowledge. I do know that you gentlemen have so far failed to obtain any arrests or convictions. There is no doubt in my mind that therein lies the reason why you have not achieved elegibility to qualify for the reward.

Richards' final comment represented the heart of the RNC case. Their defense was based on the proposition that because there were no arrests and convictions, we hadn't fulfilled the requirements spelled out in the reward offer.

Our position was clear-cut. We had been wrongly induced to take action by the false guarantee which Richards admitted to in his deposition. Furthermore, it was blatant misrepresentation to promise prospective claimants that authorities "will proceed." They lured participation under false pretenses.

We argued that when we produced the videotape the evidence was so convincing that convictions would have been likely. However, for reasons explained in the three other lawsuits we filed in 1985, Craig C. Donsanto prevented such prosecutions and thereby blocked our chance to qualify.

The second lawsuit we filed was against Donsanto himself, with the U.S. Attorney General (William French Smith) included as a party defendant. The likelihood of our winning the suit, which stemmed from Donsanto's refusal to view the *Votescam* video, was problematical. Nonetheless, we hoped to demonstrate that the Justice Department's chief vote fraud prosecutor *purposely* stood in our way.

Of the four lawsuits we filed, the Donsanto case was the only one to claim jurisdiction of the federal court. This meant that federal government attorneys would be required to defend, and that the ultimate decision would be rendered by the U.S. Court of Appeals. On that bench was a key judge with direct links to Donsanto dating back to the Watergate era — *soon-to-be Supreme Court Justice Antonin Scalia.*

The third lawsuit in our barrage was headlined on the *Home News Wire*:

VOTESCAM WRITERS SUE ABC
By Kenneth and James Collier

WASHINGTON - The *Votescam* affair continues as the latest in a series of damage suits filed in the Washington D.C. Superior Court by these reporters. This time the defendant is ABC, charged with interfering with a reward offer by the Republican National Committee. The RNC had been seeking citizens' information on vote fraud.

Central to the $250 million case (Ed. This figure represented a dollar a citizen) is the charge that ABC persuaded the RNC to breach the terms of the reward offer as it applied to these reporters'submission of evidence. We had provided the RNC with a videotape showing the League of Women Voters tampering with ballots in a federal election.

According to the complaint, Tim O'Brien, ABC's Supreme Court correspondent, alerted superiors to the Colliers' *Votescam* Video after viewing it. He received permission to telephone Mark Braden, the RNC chief counsel, and learned that the RNC had no intention of making any moves to assist these reporters in persuading the Justice Department to initiate prosecutions.

The complaint alleges that the phone call imparted a two-way message between the political committee and the TV network. Since the RNC disavows any responsibility for performing under the terms of the Reward Offer, ABC won't have to do a TV piece embarrassing the League of Women Voters, which is in ABC's employ.

Thus, the "understanding" reached in the O'Brien-Braden phone call amounted to ABC's self-serving "interference with the contract offer."

During the course of 1984, we repeatedly contacted O'Brien about the lack of interest ABC News was exhibiting. On the surface he seemed to honestly sympathize. He assured us that if we succeeded in suing the League of Women Voters, ABC would be forced to put the story on national television.

Then, in mid-1985, in an historic decision by ABC, they sold the entire network to the New Jersey-based Capital Cities Communications (CCC), a company much smaller than ABC, in a so-called "friendly takeover."

"If the sale goes through," Ken reasoned, "they could find some way to get out of the lawsuit."

"You mean they could say that Capital Cities didn't know anything about what ABC used to do?"

"Yeah, it's a case of 'We're sorry, but we weren't around then.'"

We decided to exercise the only option we had: stop the sale until our lawsuit could be decided by the courts.

We filed a "petition to deny sale" with the Federal Communication Commission. We charged ABC with attempting to evade responsibility for its part in keeping the *Votescam* video from the public, thereby engaging in a coverup of vote fraud. The ABC-CCC sale price involved some $4 billion – and the principal financier behind the deal was Warren Buffet – a board member and mega-investor in Katherine Graham's Washington *Post* Company.

We also decided to depose Tim O'Brien and put his views about our evidence on the record. The transcript of his sworn statement is distilled, and begins with a question Jim asked O'Brien in the office of ABC's attorneys, Bergson, Borkland, Margolis and Adler.

Q. *May we have your comments on the Votescam Videotape?*

A. I felt that was your best stuff. What I liked for its news value was where you captured the moment and picked up one of the League of Women Voters poking the ballot. I mean, you like to think that no one is going to touch your ballot after you cast it. I still have reservations as whether that is a proper practice. It struck me as something that is possibly improper. For all I know she was doing exactly what she said she was doing, yet I didn't find that quite right. Why should she have been there? Your videotape troubles me.

Q. *Did you take any action after viewing the tape?*

A. I took a number of actions. I encouraged you to keep me posted on what was happening because it seemed to me there was a possibility this could develop into a story. I discussed your evidence with some of my colleagues. It's certainly not that no one was interested; they were.

Q. *Exactly who did you discuss it with?*

A. I talked to some of my colleagues and our bureau chief. To Ed Fouhy, who was our producer, yes, and to Victor Newfelt, a senior producer and our Washington senior producer, John Arrowsmith. Also spoke to a producer in New York, Charlie Stewart, who specializes in doing stories for future use. My discussion with Fouhy lasted about five minutes. I offered to show him the videotape, but he expressed concern about using tape shot by freelancers. He suggested that I stay close to the story and see if there was something we could do on our own. Charlie Stewart returned my call and his question was: "Well, what about these guys? What about their story?" And I told him, quote, "What I'm telling you now is that they have something."

Q. *Did you make any further contacts after viewing the tape?*

A. I called Mark Braden, chief counsel over at

RNC, to find out exactly what their position was on the reward offer. His first response was that he thought you had done some good work. In fact, I felt in my brief conversation with Braden that he wanted to help you along; that he wasn't fighting it. I can recall now, in fact, that he said he would like to see you get the reward. I called Donsanto at the Justice Department, but he refused to comment. So if you are asking me if I just totally disregarded everything and dismissed you guys as a couple of lunatics, the answer is "no." I thought your videotape was airworthy and I was intrigued by Donsanto's silence.

Q. *Has anything happened to dispel your feeling "disturbed" over the contents of the videotape?*

A. No. If anything, the feeling has deepened. I think our election system is the cornerstone of our democracy. I think if we had evidence that ballots were being handled in such a fashion as these appear to be handled, nationwide, that would be a story. I would stipulate to that. I suspect that there may even be a producer here or there who might be waiting for me to say, "Let's go with this." And I would also concede it is possible that there is a Justice Department cover up as long as Donsanto refuses to be interviewed. It is possible that everything you are saying about Donsanto's Watergate past is correct.

The fourth lawsuit was filed against the League of Women Voters. The suit asked for $150 million in damages. This compensation was for the League attempting to cover up its illegal practices by actively lobbying in Washington to discredit our journalistic credibility.

As an exhibit in the suit, we introduced a page from the federal election statutes applying to the prohibition of outsiders in the official vote-tallying process.

"The proceedings at the central counting location shall be under the direction of the county canvassing board, and shall be open to the public, but no person except those employed and authorized for the purpose shall touch any ballot or ballot container, any item of automatic tabulating equipment, or any return prior to its release."

The *Votescam* videotape was offered as proof that the law was broken by the LWV and by those who paid them to handle the ballots.

The suit contended that the LWV is secretly ushered into the inner sanctums of the U.S. voting process on national election nights in thousands of jurisdictions across the county. They are told that handling computer card ballots (and, yes, even punching holes in them) is perfectly permissible.

This "ballot-cleaning" privilege enables the LWV to command an illegal insider's position in the U.S. vote process, which is exploited by the League in its drive for increased membership. The suit explains the "sweetheart" deal the LWV nets for its coffers.

By mid-1985, it had become the goal of the federal government and three law firms in Washington to get our lawsuits dismissed.

But in June, Superior Court Judge Colleen Kolar-Kotelley ruled against RNC arguments and refused to dismiss the case. She stated in her one-line opinion that there were "*issues between the parties that can only be resolved by holding a trial.*"

Unless something intervened to delay it, a trial was due within 180 days.

The RNC had lost its first round and removed their lawyer, Hess, from the case. It immediately hired an outside law firm, Carr, Goodson & Lee, to seek a continuance while it "familiarized itself with the case."

As soon as we received notice of the RNC's decision to change legal counsel, we contacted their new lawyer, Lawrence Carr. We wanted a meeting to check out the adversary.

Carr had no objection to being called "Colonel," his highest military rank. He was jovial, white-haired and confident, maintaining an erect military bearing even at rest.

By contrast, we were somewhat less than

kempt, blue-jeaned, T-shirted and fifteen minutes late for our first meeting.

"Sorry, Colonel, it's the heat of the summer," Jim explained. "It's especially brutal in the park, our home, office and headquarters."

"Well," mused Carr, "I can see you've been laboring under adverse conditions. If I didn't have the obligations I've got I'd happily be out in the field with you."

Ken measured him.

"No doubt you're being well paid for taking on this case, Colonel. May we presume to ask what kind of retainer it takes to put you on the side of the angels?"

Carr was unflappable.

"Now, it kind of depends on which side that is, gentlemen. Don't forget, I'm a hired advocate who takes on either side of an issue, depending on who's footing the bill."

"But in this case, Colonel," Ken pushed, "doesn't it go against your grain to have served your country so faithfully in the Marine Corps — yet now you're being paid to cover up evidence of vote fraud?"

Jim leaned in. "Colonel, vote fraud is undermining your country's most sacred franchise. How can you live with yourself?"

Carr ran a hand through his shock of white hair and smiled.

"Without conceding any portion of your premise, the short reply is the tried and proven, 'It's an ugly job, but somebody's got to do it.'"

This calculated joshing went on for about five minutes. Then the meeting ended. The symbolic battle lines were drawn.

Throughout 1985, while the four lawsuits were moving like molasses through the courts, our readership responded to the *Votescam* series with tips and encouragement.

We received a letter from a man named Robert Plimpton, a millionaire who lived in Palm Beach, Florida. Plimpton was affiliated with a civic group who found themselves locked out of mainstream political influence in the county. They had long suspected that part of their problem stemmed from rigged elections.

He suggested we get in touch with Pat Robertson's 700 Club, and offer them the use of the *Votescam* video. He thought Robertson's Christian Broadcasting Network might want to show its 23 million viewers "the true state of the U.S. voting system."

When we met with CBN's Washington-based bureau chief, John Black, he took the time to view the entire 45-minute presentation. Then he candidly discussed what could happen if the issue of vote fraud ever really surfaced in America, if it were broached by Pat Robertson.

Robertson's plans to seek the Republican nomination for President in 1988 would certainly be affected. In fact, Black felt that if the *Votescam* video was released prematurely by the "700 Club" it could backfire. The result would be a "sour grapes" syndrome attached to Robertson years in advance of the election.

Black wanted CBN to air whatever portion of the tape it chose, whenever it chose. That way, Pat Robertson could never be accused by his detractors of covering up its existence. Within a few days we had a check for $2,500.

Robertson opted to keep the tape under wraps for more than a year. There was never a mention that CBN was in possession of evidence impugning the honesty of the U.S. voting system.

Then, on November 3, 1986, the eve of the off-year general election, Robertson invited the former New York *Times* reporter David Burnham on the "700 Club" television show for a discussion of vote fraud in America. Burnham authored the *Times* article that revealed the top secret White House investigation of computer voting nationwide. A three minute portion of the *Votescam* video was played on the air, showing highlights.

Apparently, however, Robertson was using the tape to fire a mere warning shot across the bow of the Establishment in preparation for his own bid for the Presidency in 1988. Nothing more was heard of the vote fraud issue from that day on.

And that was that.

We appeared often on radio shows from

Miami to San Francisco. Our subject, "How The American Vote Is Rigged," almost always provoked great listener response. People felt that we might be hired guns that travel, so they invited us into their towns as "vote vigilantes" to help them find evidence of vote rigging. They wanted ideas about how to uncover the fraud they felt sure was lurking in the electoral system.

The second most frequently asked question we encountered from radio and television listeners (after *"Aren't you guys afraid of getting killed?"*), was:

"Why don't you go to '60 Minutes' with your evidence?"

In fact, as you remember, we did make an approach to "60 Minutes" anchorman Mike Wallace. It's fair to say that his opinion of the story's value was overwhelmingly favorable, but for reasons only he can explain, he was never able to air it.

Eleven years after we met him in Alan Becker's office in Miami, the following article appeared in The *Spotlight* in September, 1985, attempting to tweak the journalistic conscience of Mike Wallace.

AN OPEN LETTER TO MIKE WALLACE

Dear Mike Wallace:

We are taking this extraordinary measure of addressing an open letter to you because the *Votescam* affair has gotten to the point where newsmen of your caliber and prestige must eventually go on record as either opposing the ominous presence of vote fraud in America, or continue to condone it by covering it up.

In fact, this story comes as no surprise to you. Members of your advisory production staff have previously provided you with a complete report on the earliest roots of the *Votescam* case. In 1974, you met with Florida State legislator Alan Becker and you said in the presence of several freelance newsmen that this "may be the biggest vote fraud scandal ever to rock the nation." Writer Gaeton Fonzi quoted you to that effect in *Miami Magazine,* July 1974.

However, since that article appeared, leading off with your quote, you have been strangely silent. Over the ensuing years we have consistently offered your producers and investigators solid prima facie evidence, including the *Votescam* video. It clearly shows a series of indisputable felonies being committed by trusted election officials during the vote-counting process in a federal election.

These reporters were under the impression, as are so many trusting Americans, that you are always open to exposing the corruption of public officials as long as you have the cold, hard evidence.

We are left to publicly speculate why you have

allowed this trust in your watchdog role to be grossly undermined by your subordinates (possibly your superiors?) to the point where this open letter has become necessary, aimed at embarrassing *"60 Minutes"* into doing the *Votescam* story.

As you know, the League of Women Voters is shown on the tape caught in the act of unauthorizedly and illegally altering ballots. This widely unreported election night activity, if committed by any other special interest group, would be a cause for prosecution and perfect subject matter for a nationally renowned TV "magazine" such as *"60 Minutes."*

Unfortunately, that is not the case here, as your own employer (CBS) apparently seeks to protect the LWV from scrutiny, due to the business relationship CBS has long maintained with the League's specially privileged election night vote-reporting services.

In fact, on election night, your network virtually depends on the League's input to the News Election Service (NES) of New York, a joint venture among the networks, for all broadcastable vote totals as reported directly to the CBS computer from a centralized source owned by CBS, ABC, NBC, AP and UPI.

Unfortunately, you may not be able to touch this *Votescam* story. CBS attorneys may have confirmed to you that all three major networks are so dependent on the League for election night totals that an unmasking of their criminal behavior would end the networks' convenient relationship. In turn, it would result in the networks having to rely on official sources for their election night reporting.

Moreover, such an unmasking of the secret election-night activities of the League would concurrently lead to the exposure of the Big Three networks as actually abetting the perpetration of a massive, centralized "preprogrammed" vote fraud on the American people.

We both signed it.

And that was that.

12

STRANGE BEDFELLOWS

> *"Democracy substitutes election by the incompetent many for appointment by the corrupt few."*
>
> —Shaw

One day in the spring of 1985, we received a message from Don MacKenzie. The return number was the *Home News*. During the brief interval before MacKenzie came on the line we were puzzled. Had his wounding slowed him down to the extent that he had to take a job?

It had been about a year since the ambush in his driveway sent him into hiding. He had done a good job keeping out of sight, since all our best efforts hadn't been successful in finding him.

He told us that while convalescing, he had done some thinking.

"...and I came up with the conclusion that the most important story in America today is germinating. It may take five more years, but it's guaranteed to explode. One of these days, in a way that none of us can predict, there's going to be a vote fraud scandal in this country..."

He had been talking about *Votescam* articles he'd seen in the year since his shooting, and credited our "Open Letter to Mike Wallace" with propelling him to use his insurance money to buy back into the game.

"...so I bought the *Home News*."

MacKenzie had also managed to make a deal with a Dade County distributor to expand geographic coverage of the paper.

"What we'll do is start using Washington datelines. But all the material has got to be credited to the *Home News Wire*, with at least one major story on the progress of your lawsuits every week."

"What kind of Washington distribution can we get?"

"I'll ship you 2,000 papers and you can establish a route through Congress, the White House press room, the National Press Club, etc. Anywhere they'll be seen regularly by opinion makers and their staffs."

"What's the story with advertising? Are you going to be able to subsidize it if you run into resistance?" Ken asked.

"From what I can tell, you have lawsuits underway worth a few hundred million. They have a way of getting settled out of court. Then you can reimburse me."

"Don, what if the cases get dismissed?" Jim asked.

"In the end they'll try to steal it from you. I'm willing to gamble."

On that note we said goodbye, but not before MacKenzie added:

"Take some advice. Tie all your defendants into a conspiracy and you can triple the damages under the RICO Act."

Within one week we were busy delivering the *Home News*, with the story of our lawsuit in it, to every major office in Washington. It took five hours to walk the halls of the House and Senate office buildings, distributing the papers to a hundred senators, four hundred-plus Congressmen. And then we tackled the twelve floors of the National Press Building.

The journalists who worked there represented their hometown newspapers. They might be from Tokyo or Moscow or Cape Town or San Francisco, and they ranged from young to old walruses.

Most of them sat around clipping the New York *Times* and the Washington *Post* in order to rewrite certain stories with their own bylines. When we showed up, it afforded some of these poseurs a schoolyard laugh to think a newspaper not sanctioned by the Establishment press had anything worth telling them. One woman journalist put her hand to her throat and pretended to gag when we walked in. The nastiest were the Denver *Post* and the Boston *Globe.* They locked their doors to keep the *Home News* out.

Happily, there were those less self-righteous who saw the merits of our investigation and avidly read each week's paper.

One of the most difficult places to leave the paper was the City Room of the Washington *Post.* It wasn't often that we managed to penetrate the security of their lobby-level guard post. However, once in a while, a distracted security man would assume that somebody with a stack of papers was a messenger on official business. One particular issue was headlined: "BOB WOODWARD'S SECRET." *

Our mission was to place a copy on Woodward's desk and on the desk of Ben Bradlee, the managing editor and Woodward's

---

*It suggested the famed reporter was harboring a secret about the Watergate Affair. The story connected Assistant Attorney General Henry Petersen, head of the criminal division, with all the participants in several conspiracies. Petersen was a registered Democrat working in a Republican Justice Department. He was referred to as "The Mole." It was Petersen who had his finger on the button in both the Watergate and *Votescam* investigations. He was also a personal friend of Katharine Graham. Petersen told Mrs. Graham that Richard Nixon had proof that her television station in Miami had been involved in election rigging and that Nixon was pushing to have her FCC license revoked. Our report continued that Mrs. Graham needed to stop the President before he stopped her. Mrs. Graham's problem was that the Watergate break-in was just a third-rate burglary. The charge had to be elevated to a federal offense in order to destroy Nixon. The answer to her dilemma came with the subsequent bugging of Watergate.

Watergate editor. We cradled the papers in such a way that the headline showed, then confided to the guard: "The brass upstairs are waiting for their copy of this."

He glanced at the papers. "Nobody told me anything"

"Nobody told you they're waiting?" We kept moving.

"The only way you can get 'em up there is to put them in the mail room," he called after us.

After that, the 100 executive cubbyholes in the *Post* mail room became destinations for the *Home News*.

We started getting requests for lectures and personal appearances.

Letters came into the *Spotlight* from all over the country telling similar stories – the *Votescam* series had awakened their interest in

---

According to FBI files given to us by Ellis Rubin, the Watergate was never bugged. Rubin filed a federal suit on behalf of Frank Sturgis, one of the burglars,in an attempt to clear Sturgis' name so that Sturgis could get his gun permit back. Rubin's suit was based on FBI documents stating there had been six sweeps of the DNC Headquarters in the Watergate, three by the FBI and three by the telephone company. Neither located a bug on any phone.
Mrs. Graham, our report contended, knew from FBI reports as of July 5th that there was no bug on Watergate phones, and if she knew, then so did her two reporters, Woodward and Bernstein.
Thus, during the three-month period between the June 17th capture of the Miami crew and the September 12th convening of the Grand Jury, when newspaper coverage of the burglary was virtually nil, Mrs. Graham directed her forces to maintain the "bugging story" despite its outright fiction. Just three days before the Grand Jury was scheduled to convene, R. Spencer Oliver experienced an overwhelming urge to dismantle his telephone in the DNC. It took only a second or two to loosen the circular mouthpiece and — presto —there was a phone-bugging

safeguarding the votes in their hometown, but
no cooperation came from election officials or
local media.

They asked: "What options are available?"

We became authorities on fighting entrenched
local officials who had ceded their authority to
outside election consultancy firms.

A group from Titusville, Florida (on the
billion-dollar Space Coast), called Jim
complaining that their election supervisor,
Shirley Baccus, lived in a $750,000 house on a
$66,000 a year salary. The implication was that
she couldn't possibly afford that lifestyle on what
the county was paying her, and that perhaps she
was getting money from some outside source.
They asked Jim to investigate.

Titusville, located between the Intercoastal
Waterway and the ocean, is the bedroom

---

apparatus in plain view. According to Oliver, he was shocked
beyond telling, and he immediately called his secretary to verify
his finding. Then he had a staff photographer record it, including
in the photograph a newspaper headline of the day to prove that
the find took place on September 12, 1972.

Federal Judge Joyce Hens Green, in ruling on Sturgis' appeal,
found that everything Rubin had contended was true. But the
Judge wrote that "it was too late to ask for relief" and she
dismissed the appeal. Jim arranged a Rubin press conference in
Washington for the Press Corps.

The 13th floor lounge at the National Press Building was packed.
Rubin showed the FBI documents, explained the suit and
presented Sturgis for questioning. Not a single word was ever
written in any paper.

Our report ended with an interview with Oliver. He claimed he
was unaware of the existence of the FBI documents. After we
informed him that the bug he reported on his phone was
conclusively determined by the FBI to have been an obsolete "toy"
— devoid of the power to transmit any messages beyond the walls

community for the federal space workers at Cape Canaveral. Most of them are on government salary.

"If the government rigged elections," Jim was told at a meeting his first night in town, "it's all right with most of them, as long as their federal paychecks keep coming."

What Jim found while rummaging through public records was an invoice from a Moline, Illinois, outfit named Fidlar and Chambers. It seems that although Bevard County had a $20 million mainframe computer to count votes, it still hired an outside consultant at $100,000 plus, per election, to come in and operate the same kind of punch card system seen on our video tape. *This was all done without public knowledge or public bid. Fidlar and Chambers' activities were, in every sense, illegal.*

Jim discovered that Fidlar and Chambers similarly serviced hundreds of other venues

---

of the room — we asked him:

"Can you explain how Alfred Baldwin in the Howard Johnson motel across the street received 200 detailed communications from this device, when the FBI said it had no capacity to transmit?" He had no answer. We followed up by asking:

"What was the fate of the 200 separate communications Baldwin was supposed to have intercepted from the bug on your phone?" He answered, "To my understanding, nobody has ever heard them because they got burned up by somebody."

"If the bug you found in September was legitimate, why was it never introduced as evidence at the trial?"

"That was a decision made by Henry Petersen."

When we asked Bob Woodward to comment on the story, he said: "Don't start a war with me on this."

throughout the Southeast and Midwest on election night.

They brought in their own computers and computer modems, which meant they could get telephone access to the Bevard mainframe computer from a motel room. They also brought in the software that instructed the computer how to count the votes.

Few chief election officials in the U.S. are technically qualified to understand computer language. They and the public are totally dependant on the integrity of these outside firms.

This was the first time we discovered the use of private companies to count votes in state and federal elections. In the ensuing years we would find that DFM in Irvine, California, counted the vote for most of that state.

According to Ralph Anderson, president of Fidlar and Chambers, he has about a dozen other competitors.

Is it, we asked ourselves, an implausible scenario to imagine a candidate with a treasure chest approaching these shadowy organizations to buy his way into office?

With the information Jim gave them, the group went to the local newspaper but was informed that no investigation was warranted.

"Can you prove they're rigging elections?" the editor asked.

"No," he was told, "but the public should know that this is all going on behind closed doors."

The editor wouldn't budge.
And that was that.

In the autumn of 1985 we were paid expenses to travel to Cincinnati by a group named the Cincinnatus Party. Concerned citizens, represented by lawyer James Condit, Sr. wanted us to videotape and evaluate the Hamilton County, Ohio, election system. It was another punchcard operation and they suspected corruption identical to what we had uncovered in Miami.

Condit had obtained a court order from Common Pleas Court Judge Richard Niehaus. It was issued as part of "discovery" in a suit Condit had filed seeking to ban voting by computer in favor of returning to old- fashioned paper ballots. The court order okayed observers, but did not mention the use of videotape. However, it specified we could monitor "*all phases of the election including testing and counting.*"

We drove from Washington to Cincinnati in an old clunker borrowed from a friend. You could see the road through the rust holes in the floor, but it got us there.

Cincinnati is a city on the Ohio River that is probably most famous nowadays for being the home of a fictional radio station, WKRP. We found a motel and could hardly wait for Election Day to dawn.

We discovered that the county also had a $20 million election system, that apparently required 40 League of Women Voters volunteers to make it work. Jim Condit Jr. was the leader of the Cincinnatus Party, which was conservative and outside the mainstream. He wanted videotape on whatever abnormalities or felonies we could find.

Just as we did in Miami, we started out at a precinct and followed a vote card to its counting house.

When we got to the central location where the precincts sent their ballots to be consolidated before they were brought downtown to be counted, we were locked out.

"You can't bring a video camera in here," an official said.

We then drove to the courthouse where the ballots were to be counted. There we were told by Judge Neihaus that we could observe, but not with a camera. We argued in vain. The judge stood firm. He threatened to have us arrested if we turned on the camera, which was fitted with a very bright, white light.

Ken simply disconnected the light. Since any observer would think the camera wasn't working, Ken was able to shoot videotape pretty much as he pleased.

The videotape revealed a battery of League of Women Voters volunteers using 98-cent tweezers to pluck out tiny tabs of chad from punchcard ballots. It seems the League provided a veritable "road show" – performing this dubious function wherever called upon.

The women pointed out that the vote card was blistered on the back.

Ken focused the unlit camera on a card which showed about seven little "pocks" on the back. They were in the exact same spot on every card. The women were tweezing these pocks off each card because the blister prevented the card from passing through the counting machine.

It appeared that that the Port-o-punch* had been used to quickly punch a slate of seven candidates. Since the cards were stacked, the pieces of chad could not fall freely, so League women were hired to remove them. Later that night, on Channel 9, our videotape of the tweezing was shown. The following morning a story appeared about our taping activities in the mainline Cincinnati newspaper.

PARTY CLASH AT BOARD OF ELECTIONS

BY HOWARD WILKINSON
The Cincinnati Enquirer

"The Cincinnatus Party's monitoring of

---

*Back in Miami, we had reported on "hole-punching parties" using the IBM Port-o-punch, a device that could punch identical holes in a pad of 50 cards. Although there was not a statute labeling it a crime, the Miami election supervisor gave the ballots to precinct captains to take home as much as a week in advance of any election. We were told that a good time was had at parties where people would punch out a slate of candidates, thus necessitating the need for The League to clean up the vote card. Both of these latter acts are crimes.

Hamilton County vote counting produced a confrontation at a Clifton polling place and a verbal battle at the board of elections Tuesday night.

Hamilton County Common Pleas Judge Richard Niehaus called the four board of elections members and Cincinnatus attorney James J. Condit, Sr. into the back rooms of the board offices just as the polls were closing Tuesday night. He took the action after precinct workers at the Clifton firehouse-precinct 15-D-complained that computer experts hired by Cincinnatus Party supporters were disrupting their work.

"There was nothing in my court order that said they could participate in any way in the voting process," said an angry Niehaus while waiting for Condit to arrive at board offices.

In August, Niehaus had ruled in a four-year-old civil suit that the Cincinnatus Party and its representatives could observe Tuesday's vote-counting process. A lawsuit by former Cincinnatus city council candidate, Jerry Schutzman, claimed that because no board employees were on hand at the Regional Computer Center while votes were being counted there was a potential for fraud.

About 7 p.m., Ken and Jim Collier, two computer experts from Washington, D.C., hired by Cincinnatus to monitor the election, walked into the Clifton polling place with a videotape camera.

When the polls closed, precinct judges complained to the board of elections that the Colliers had insisted that the ballots at that precinct be hand-counted. James Condit, Jr., this year's Cincinnatus candidate, said: "That is absolutely not true. They did not ask for a handcount. The judge's order said we could observe all phases of the ballot-counting process and that is what we are doing."

THE COLLIERS showed up at 7:30 p.m. at the office of elections director Elvera Radford, where Niehaus was waiting to talk with the board members.

Niehaus ordered the Colliers not to use their videotaping equipment and a brief shouting match ensued.

After consulting with the Cincinnatus attorney, Niehaus said his court order limited Condit and the Colliers to observation only.

"If they want to do anything else, they have to file a motion in court, and videotaping is not covered by my order," Niehaus said.

BOARD MEMBERS were angered by the confrontation at the Clifton firehouse and at the board office Tuesday night.

"They've got to stay within the judge's order," said Democratic chairman and election board member John "Socko" Wiethe. "I expected there would be problems with this."

Condit and Schutzman did not claim in the suit that the results of previous elections had been tampered with, but they argued that because Regional Computer Center employees were employed by incumbent Cincinnati City Council members, there was potential for abuse.

Elements of the story did not jibe with our interpretation of events; still, it was an acknowledgement that controversy was engulfing the Cincinnati-area election officials. And for the same reason it had become a noted cause in Miami: the League was being inserted into the public vote-counting process, and this violation went unreported by the local press.

The story served us nicely. We sent a copy to Tim O'Brien at ABC News, along with a copy of an audio tape of a radio show we appeared on the day after the election. The show's host, Jan Mickelson, issued a challenge to anyone associated with the League to phone in and justify how a private political club rated a special insider's position in the voting system. He also invited the Hamilton County State's Attorney to appear and "show cause" why the LWV shouldn't be prosecuted for ballot tampering.

The response from the public kept the lines lit up for hours. They unanimously expressed their outrage, with the net effect that within 24 hours, Elvera Radford, the local elections officer, resigned the post she had held for more than a decade. No other action ensued.

And that was that.

13

FULL CIRCLE

> *"Whenever a man has cast an eye on office, a rottenness begins in his character."*
>
> —Thomas Jefferson

When we opted to sue four prominent defendants, we had no illusion that we would prevail in court. The suits were more a symbol than a worrisome threat to the TV networks, the League, the Justice Department and the Republican National Committee.

Initially, each of the defendants sent the paperwork to their legal departments for routine disposal by seeking a summary dismissal. They told the court that a great waste of time would be incurred if the case proceeded, since there was *"no likelihood that the Plaintiffs can prevail on the merits."*

When their attempts at dumping the litigation

via simple paperwork failed, they were forced to consider a chilling prospect – seeing the cases through to a jury trial. Due to the court's denial of their dismissal motion, our opponents were forced to yield important figures for our questioning under oath. If the cases later came to trial, these people would find their words being used to sway a jury on the merits of our case, not theirs.

We felt that some mechanism would have to be uncovered whereby all corporate players named in our charges were discovered to be meeting on a regular basis. Their agenda would be how to coordinate and crush all the Collier suits, and how to best strengthen their grip on the U.S. electoral process. In other words, we wanted to put all the conspirators in one room, the same as we did in Miami Beach at the Senior Corporation Board Meeting.

All of which brings us full circle, back to the moment when Frank Fahrenkopf was advised by George Bush to involve New Hampshire Governor John Sununu in putting together a Commission on National Elections.

The only reason we found out that secret meetings were indeed being held, who participated and what was said, is because a source close to the official stenographer's records at CSIS sympathized with our efforts to police the U.S voting system.

To us, obtaining the following transcript and

printing parts of it verbatim on the *Home News Wire*, was a journalistic coup. Especially rewarding because the transcript we received quoted CSIS' most prominent figures, candidly debating the necessity for removing the League of Women Voters from future sponsorship of the Presidential Debates.

No major publication in the country ever reported on the following story which appeared on the *Home News Wire*.

LEAGUE OF WOMEN VOTERS DROPPED

By James M. Collier
and Kenneth F. Collier

WASHINGTON D.C. - These reporters have obtained a transcript of a secret meeting held in Washington wherein certain top media executives and highly placed government officials of current and past administrations, came to the decision to remove the League of Women Voters (LWV) from its traditional role as sponsor of the Presidential Debates.

The decision to drop the LWV from its long-held (since 1960) insider's position in the presidential selection process was made on November 26,1985, after a series of candid discussions among members of the Georgetown University affiliated Commission on National Elections (CNE). The commission was formed by the Center for Strategic and

International Studies (CSIS) an Establishment think tank.

Curiously, the decision to deprive the LWV of its role in presidential debates was barely publicized in the press or on TV, despite the fact that it required an historic joint communique from the two national party chairmen to make the outster official.

It appears the lack of publicity surrounding both the CSIS meetings and the decision to remove the League from the debates was an accomodation to the LWV, whose then president, Dorothy Ridings, was a member of the panel and a lone dissenter to its findings.

In fact, at one point in the proceedings, just prior to the time when the subject of the LWV outster was addressed, Commission co-chairman Robert Strauss (former chairman of the Democratic National Committee) reminded the group of assembled notables that confidentiality was the order of the day. He put it this way:

"Let me say that there's no press in here today. There will be none today. So we can speak with some considerable candor."

This statement was made by Strauss despite the fact that several of the most powerful owners and operators of the U.S. press and TV network news were sitting at the table with him. In effect, what Strauss was saying in his supposedly never-to-be quoted remark is that the high profile media moguls who were present for the secret meeting should not consider themselves as representing the "press."

The list of media barons who cheerfully went along with Strauss's proposal for "candor" in the absence of the working press reads like a Who's Who of American journalism.

KATHARINE GRAHAM, chairwoman of the Board of the Washington Post Co., which publishes the Washington Post and Newsweek.

LAWRENCE K. GROSSMAN, president of NBC News since 1974, past president of the Public Broadcasting Service.

ROONE ARLEDGE, recently named group president for ABC News; producer of "World News Tonight," "20/2O," "Nightline" and "Viewpoint."

ROBERT PRESTON TISCH, president of Loews Corp. since 1960. He recently acquired a controlling interest in the Columbia Broadcasting System, CBS.

WILLIAM LEONARD, chief consultant to CBS News, vice president for government relations, former head of the CBS News Election Unit and former producer of "CBS Reports."

HAMILTON JORDAN, currently political commentator for Cable News Network; former chief of staff to President Jimmy Carter.

Also present at the meeting and active in the decision taken by the group to quietly distance itself from the LWV by means of deliberately keeping the working press from publicizing the commission's near unanimous verdict to do away with the League were:

LANE KIRKLAND, president of the AFL-CIO since 1979.

FRANK FAHRENKOPF, JR., chairman of the Republican National Committee since 1983.

PAUL G. KIRK, JR., chairman of the Democratic National Committee since 1985.

TONY COELHO, four-term Democratic representative for California's 15th congressional district.

WENDELL H. FORD, two-term Democratic senator from Kentucky.

CHARLES S. ROBB, former Democratic governor from Virginia.

JOHN H. SUNUNU, two-term Republican governor of New Hampshire.

A discussion by the Commission took place at the Madison Hotel's Arlington Room on October 15, 1985. Nearing the conclusion of the proceedings, Mrs. Graham turned to Laird and openly criticized the way presidential debates had been run in the past:

Mrs. GRAHAM: I would just like to ask one question. I think the formulation of who is asking the questions has gutted the debate so totally that by the time they have gotten through getting rid of everybody they dislike for the panel, everybody who can ask a question is gone and it's terrible. I think it's a scandal.

LAIRD: That's what we're trying to solve.

FAHRENKOPF: We are not sure…whether we ought to go to a traditional debate format.

JORDAN: Kate (Graham) makes the point I'm

trying to make. The more of these things left in the air three years out present opportunities for candidates to wriggle out of debating.

STRAUSS: It's the hope of the parties working on this that they'll come to an agreement on that, which will substantially improve the debate process itself, including the selection of examiners and the format it will take.

LAIRD: Well, I would think that a candidate who feels committed to a particular course such as agreeing in advance to debate, many years ahead of time, has lost some control of their campaign. I agree with you, too, (Presidential) debates are not the greatest thing in the world. Everybody seems to think that we think that debates are the most wonderful things that ever existed, that they are the only (meaningful) part of the campaign. We have tried to downplay that as much as possible.

STRAUSS: Let me make another point, too. I'll guarantee you that the two party chairmen could handle that better with some third (political) party than the League of Women Voters (could). During the Carter campaign we (at the DNC) couldn't cope with it all. We had nothing to get our hands on. I almost drove the League crazy and they me.

Mrs. RIDINGS: What you're telling me is that Frank (Fahrenkopf) and Paul (Kirk) are going to deal with sponsoring the debates?

That's the most ridiculous thing I ever heard. How ever could they deal with a credible third (political) party?

JORDAN: Dorothy, we were presented the reality in 1980 that the John Anderson campaign was viable. That the incumbent president of the United States had to debate a man if he had over 10 percent in the polls. That was a very arbitrary decision that the League made that we had to live with and wrestle with. I really believe that the way to credibly and effectively administer the debates is to do it through an agreement between the (two major) parties.

LAIRD: Then there's fairly general agreement that we can do it better through the (two major) political parties?

Mrs. RIDINGS: Mel, I disagree with part of it. I think it's an absolute mistake to say that the chairmen of the two (major) political parties are going to get together two years ahead of time and decide how the ultimate candidates of those parties...

LAIRD: They may not get together. But if they do get together I think their recommendations can be a very important part of this report.

Mrs. RIDINGS: You are trying to make rules way ahead of the game.

STRAUSS: That's exactly what they hope to do. Once you do it that way then you don't have to make decisions in the context of what's good or bad for anybody They are made with blinders on.

Mrs. RIDINGS: You're asking my opinion? I

think it would be foolish for any candidate to agree ahead of time to do that.

KIRKLAND: The object is to have a debate. I think the possibilities are considerably enhanced if the networks are involved in the negotiations. Even if a candidate might consider overriding a decision made by his party chairman, I think one would be a little more concerned about overriding a decision in which the networks are involved. *That's my view of the relative focus of power in this country.*

STRAUSS: I think, and I think you would agree with me, Dorothy (Ridings), that this discussion should stay within this room. *If we could keep it out of the press it would be important and significant that it not be (in the press) - (that) we not read about it in the next few days' press.*

Mrs. GRAHAM: I just wish to point out that things leak. They don't necessarily leak from those of us who are here at this table.

STRAUSS: You don't need to tell me.

Mrs. GRAHAM: I'm not taking responsibility for it.

STRAUSS: But if we could keep it in this room - it has been kept in this room for a month already, so there is no reason why it can't be for another month. Yes? In other words, if the (two major) parties work out an agreement to take over sponsorship of the debates, rather than have it mailed out, I'd want it to stay in this room and not read in the papers or see it on TV until we (the commission) agree to it.

After the session was over and the CSIS think-tank had unceremoniously disposed of the League, Frank Fahrenkopf buttonholed Nixon's ex-defense chief, Melvin Laird, in the cloakroom. Fahrenkopf was worried. The U.S. Court of Appeals in Washington had recently (September, 1985) handed the Colliers a cause to celebrate. It ruled unanimously to remand the case against Donsanto to the District Court "for further proceedings."

This meant that unless something intervened, Donsanto and Attorney General William French Smith (also named as defendant) would have to appear in court. It would create the publicity bonanza which they rightly assumed we needed in order to expose the story. It was a doomsday decision that would have to be neutralized.

Fahrenkopf had done a lot of thinking since he had personally taken on the developments in our cases. We believe that he conferred with Carr and together they devised a way to poison the waters of the Donsanto/Smith suit.

It was to be a "killer memo" inserted into the court file, authored by a highly rumored imminent nominee to the Supreme Court. This "killer memo" was to be written and filed by Federal Appeals Judge Antonin Scalia,*

---

* It was a young Antonin Scalia who was in charge of the Office of Telecommunications in the White House in 1971 when the exonerating Craig Donsanto from any charges of wrongdoing in the Collier case, thus signaling all judges dealing with our case in the courts below, that the "Great Persuader" (as Scalia is known), wanted a dismissal to result before the case came up for hearing in Federal District Court.

When we first filed the lawsuit against Donsanto and Smith it was dismissed. Then a two-judge appeals court panel, made up of Judge Skelly Wright and Judge Ruth Bader Ginsberg, remanded our case to Federal District Court. It was supposed to be heard by whichever judge received the case in routine rotation.

Therefore, Scalia knew that his input was not required or requested. Only if two judges split their decision is a third opinion called for. Scalia's two cents would be gratuitous.

Now Scalia had to be persuaded that the risk incurred by stepping in and unilaterally acting to influence the lower court, for two Justice Department friends, was worth the payoff.

Carr and Fahrenkopf knew that any overt move by Scalia, such as issuing a memo in behalf of former colleagues to get them off the hook, was dangerous. It could someday result in conflict-of-interest charges against Scalia. But if

---

Collier telegram was sent to Richard Nixon. As the President's chief counsellor in these matters, Scalia's job was to put the telegram through the proper channels, which included both Nixon at the White House and Donsanto at the Justice Department.

the prize was big enough to warrant the gamble, they figured Scalia would likely go along.

That left the question for Carr and Fahrenkopf as to precisely the nature and timing of the payoff.

We believe there was no less than a guarantee from the Republican hierarchy that Scalia would be next in line for the nomination to the Supreme Court in 1986, instead of his mentor and former law professor, Robert Bork.

On a sheet of paper was the proposed "killer memo," a one paragraph statement by Scalia which read:

I concur only because I believe that summary affirmance should not be by less than unanimous vote. In my view, it is plain from the face of the pleading that the law pertinent to prosecutorial discretion fully supports the district court's dismissal of the action.

SCALIA, Circuit Judge

As any lawyer can see, Scalia used a subterfuge here: first, he said that *"summary affirmance should not be by less than unanimous vote."* That means he was agreeing with Wright and Ginsberg. Thus, he had no reason to write anything else but "I concur."

Then, he put in the "killer line" – that Donsanto had full discretion not to see our evidence and that our case should be dismissed. *(When in fact Donsanto was mandated to see*

*our evidence and then decide if he should act
upon it).*

Without question, in the absence of the
memo, Donsanto and the Attorney General
would have been ordered to appear at a hearing
— yielding us a dramatic forum in which to air
the government's hands-off attitude toward
prosecuting vote fraud.

An unprecedented 60 days after the two-
judge panel's original order, Scalia surreptitiously
entered the memo into our file. It was
undocketed on unbonded, unwatermarked
paper, with no time stamp, with Xerox doodles
on the back. All it lacked were tomato stains.

Shortly thereafter, Scalia was nominated for
Justice of the Supreme Court.

We didn't let it go without a fight. We sued
Scalia, challenging his integrity and the cronyism
that led to the tampering of records. Scalia's
corporate counsel, Edith Marshall, argued that
Scalia, in fact, did what we claimed he did, but
because he was a judge he had a perfect right to
do exactly as he pleased. We countered that
Scalia was not acting as a judge when he snuck
the memo into the file 60 days after the fact.

Ken testified against Scalia at his confirmation
hearing. We needed approval by the Committee
Chairman, Senator Strom Thurmond, in order to
be a witness against the judge. If the Judiciary
Committee found no merit in our charges, we
would not have been permitted to testify.

Listening to the indictment against Scalia, Senator Thurmond, in an unsolicited move, asked: "Do you want two more minutes?

Ken replied: "Yes, Sir. I am an investigative reporter, here to find out if this nominee is going to be challenged this afternoon, as we were, in order to come to these hearings.

"We asked the attorney defending Judge Scalia against our lawsuit: 'Will our charges be denied?' Six weeks have passed since the filing. It's had a chance to mature, Senator, but it has resulted in not a denial on the merits of the suit, which attacked the integrity of Judge Scalia, and put him as a co-defendant with the RNC.

"His attorney then assured us that Judge Scalia has immunity to do whatever he pleases, whether on the bench or off, and if he didn't legally file the memo, it was the only concurrence (memo) that was never filed in the history of Appeals Court."

Thurmond thanked Ken and, predictably, our case was later dismissed.

Today, Scalia sits on the Supreme Court of the United States. A man who cheated his way there on a deal with the Republican National Committee, and cheated his old professor, Robert Bork.

This is the man who makes decisions over the lives of 250 million Americans.

And that was that.

Throughout 1985, as public interest levels were

being raised on the topic of vote fraud and a dialogue opened in the courts and in print, the time was nearing for a hearing in early December before Superior Court Judge Nicholas S. Nunzio.

The hearing would determine if our arguments were strong enough to warrant "punitive damages" from the RNC, or whether (from the RNC point of view), the case should be dismissed in a summary judgment. It would be the first open-court test of the charges.

There were about 100 people in the courtroom when the hearing opened. Carr went first and recounted our case to Judge Nunzio. In fact, Carr sold our case better than we could have. He detailed every nuance to the Judge. He was eloquent.

His strategy appeared to be a recitation of just how strong our case actually was against his client, the RNC, hoping that Judge Nunzio would get the point and dismiss the litigation before too much damage was done.

For example, after recounting how many agencies had studiously ignored the evidence, he said:

"Your Honor, that hasn't stopped the brothers in their quest for prosecutorial proceedings. They have continued to write about this. Every detail of what happened in that tape has been in many, many publications.

"Not only do we have these official

organizations seeing the tape, but the Colliers have made every detail clear in a set of published photographs. Still nothing to this date has occurred."

Carr was living up to his reputation. He had no notes. It was just an extemporaneous display of style. He submitted an outright falsehood in saying that any agency had ever seen the *Votescam* video, and it was so smooth that he was totally believable. We were as fascinated as the audience.

"Once again, addressing the language of the reward offer. One of their claims has been that they were induced to make the videotape, and they relied upon the offer's wording. They say because of this inducement, they actually undertook life-threatening action when they operated their video camera. In fact, they show later there was a shooting of the publisher of the Hialeah *Home News*, which was crusading in behalf of their cause.

"But the credibility of their notion of danger becomes less when you realize that in the last three to four months, they've risked exactly the same thing in the State of Iowa. They went to Iowa with their video equipment and again took footage they claim shows vote fraud. They've also recently gone to the State of Ohio, where they've videotaped the League of Women Voters doing exactly the same thing as they discovered in Dade County.

"I honestly believe that the Colliers are

dedicated to fighting vote fraud as they see it, as it exists. However, your Honor, I also suggest that it's not completely nonselfish, because for one reason, they're making their own news.

"What happens here today without question will appear in some newspaper within a week. They've used the tactic of asking for punitive damages against my clients because they feel that if they're ever allowed to really get into the financial records of the Republican National Committee, there will be tremendous material there for yet other articles."

This was a correct conclusion, but also an attempt to get Judge Nunzio to dismiss the case. Not because it lacked merit, but because the Colliers could make money selling a story they had pursued for over a decade. It was a step away from Ayn Rand's indictment of society, foreseeing the man who invented fire being burned at the stake, and the man who invented the wheel being turned at the rack.

Carr sat down and Ken fired our first question to the court in rebuttal.

"Counsel this morning has stated that we should have known better than to think that the RNC could follow through or deliver on its promises. Why did the RNC promise what it could not deliver?"

We told Judge Nunzio that we had researched the law of estoppel. It held that if a promise is made without the intention of fulfilling it, or where the party making the promise is in a position to know about its inability to deliver, the other party may sue for punitive damages.

That statement brought Carr's hand to his temple. He started giving Roman hand signals to the Judge, because where we may not have been able to prove actual damages (money out of pocket), if Judge Nunzio granted punitive damages, the cost to the RNC could be enormous.

The Judge said to us:

"You say it is a contract. Mr Carr's argument is that it was an offer of a reward; that it was not a contract *per se*."

We then read from the deposition of Richard Richards, former RNC chairman. It was evident from his statements that every element of a contractual relationship between us and the RNC had been admitted under oath.

At this point Judge Nunzio caught Carr's hand signals. He rose half-way out of his chair, hefted our case file off his desk and became very agitated.

"First of all, if I had this file downstairs, it was reviewed by somebody else. I would never have entertained oral arguments – but somebody else reviewed this."

(*In other words, the Judge would have never allowed this dialogue in open court, but he was trapped with a hundred spectators listening.*)

"But somebody else reviewed this; I happened by chance to be the motions judge and they were reviewing it and somebody set it for hearing; I did not. I think that I could have adequately ruled on this on the pleadings and therefore… "

(We could hear the death knoll coming in Nunzio's halting cop-out about not reading the file. Indeed, the Judge had not come prepared.

What he was telling Carr was that he was caught off guard, and that he would have preferred to dismiss the case before it ever got to court. We made a last frantic attempt to be heard.)

"May we *voir dire* the judge about your previous experience as a Justice Department prosecutor…?"

Nunzio slammed in with: "Mr. Collier, please take your seat."

Jim desperately jumped in. "If the Court please, may I have one statement?"

"All right, what is it?"

"I just want it on the record for this Court, that the videotape evidence referred to as the *Votescam* video – which the Court may be on the verge of concluding without viewing – is such compelling evidence that the Christian Broadcasting Network recently purchased air rights. And the tape we put together in Cincinnati was conclusive of vote fraud. The fact that those women were using tweezers…"

"I'm not concerned with that."

"…to pluck tabs out of the ballots, creating illegal votes…it got on local television and caused the Elections Supervisor, Elvera Radford, to quit her post and resign the very next day."

"You must understand, both of you, that I'm not trying your case. I'm listening to arguments and nothing more."

"I would like to proffer further argument to help buttress the good work we have done," Ken said

Judge Nunzio sat back and smiled. "You know you act like a man who feels as though he has lost."

Carr jumped up, not sure as to what Nunzio's motives were, or what Nunzio was about to do. Carr's slickness had disappeared.

"Very briefly your honor, it's quite possible there's voter fraud on this tape. I don't know, I'm not prepared to judge it. It's been presented to officials all the way from Florida to Washington. They haven't acted on it. I didn't know they sold it, not just to that organization, to many other organizations. Nobody's acted on it. We rest on that."

Judge Nunzio then handed down his ruling.

"This is the way I see it. The Colliers may well have a point with respect to Donsanto. If he did not do his job, then in effect, it is material that he chose to block their contract. But I do not see a case of punitive damages here.

"I'll grant the RNC partial summary judgement because the plaintiffs have failed to demonstrate any wanton, malicious, reckless or outrageous acts."

He looked at us. "Your case is alive, Messers Collier, only with respect to those material issues concerning Mr. Donsanto and whether there was a contract there. Thank you very much."

We had cleared the last hurdle before the final scheduling of a jury trial. As we left the courtroom, we assisted Carr with the big double doors leading out, careful to gauge his attitude in the face of defeat at the hands of amateurs. He was not happy.

Suddenly sprouting an aggravated half- smile, he reached for the most portentous comment yet:

"Don't count your money."

We had watched him squirm as Judge Nunzio handed down his decision. His hand signals were expended to no avail. Now the full-blown trial which Carr had been hired to avoid loomed imminent.

14

STAR CHAMBER SESSION

"When I use a word," Humpty Dumpty said, "it means just what I choose it to mean— nothing more nor less."

—Lewis Carroll

The next step on the way to trial was a pretrial conference scheduled for three weeks hence on January 6, 1986. The purpose was to formally clear the decks of any unresolved questions by defining the specific points of law to be decided at trial.

The only way Carr could derail our progress would be to "reach" the pretrial judge and attempt to have the case dismissed. When the judge turned out to be an unapproachable journeyman pretrial specialist, known to be "unreachable," Carr had to bypass him.

He had his assistant, Kyle Kane, research the biographies of every judge on the Superior

Court. It wasn't long before a standout candidate emerged, one whose integrity might be sublimated long enough to rationalize "doing a favor for a friend."

It was Judge Henry F. Greene, a 1981 Reagan-appointee to the Bench, whose employment at the Justice Department spanned thirteen years and brought him regularly into the orbit of Craig C. Donsanto.

On January 6th, at 11 a.m., the day of the pretrial, we were standing in the court clerk's office with Carr and his assistant Kane, when the phone rang. Until this time the case had been assigned to the official pretrial Judge William Thompson. The clerk who took the call advised us our case had been reassigned to Judge Henry F. Greene. We had no idea at that time why we were re-routed to a "special pretrial judge," but we had no choice but to go along and play out developments.

Warning lights started flashing when we were told that the pretrial conference would be conducted in a little used annex-portion of the court-house located several blocks away. All of the other people standing nearby, who had been reporting for pretrials every half-hour, were sent to Judge Thompson in the main courthouse.

"Why are we being treated differently?" Jim asked.

"Judge Greene's orders are being followed," the clerk replied.

Carr and Kane, who had been hovering just behind us at the counter, registered no surprise at the last minute event.

"Follow me," Carr said "I know where he's sending us. It's over in Building A".

We trooped out of the main courthouse in Carr's wake and silently followed his footsteps imprinted in the ankle-deep snow. When we arrived at the appropriate building, Carr mumbled something to the guard at the side door and he waved us through, rather than requiring us to enter by the front door where metal detectors and video cameras were installed to record who went in and out.

Carr guided us to a self-service elevator. When we arrived at a private door with no markings, we noted that it was just behind a courtroom which was undergoing renovation. Later we learned that the "Moot Court" exercises of several local university law schools were conducted in it – but no official Superior Court hearings had been held there in nearly two decades.

Carr knocked and opened the door without waiting for a response. There, was Judge Henry F. Greene and his secretary waiting for us. Oddly, however, the seats they were sitting in seemed to be awkward, as if this were an entirely alien situation they founds themselves in. The secretary was seated in the Judge's chair behind a massive desk, while Judge Greene sat in an informal wooden armchair. He had arranged two other armchairs in a semi-circle a few feet from his own.

He beckoned Carr and Kane to take the seats closest to him, while we were relegated to sit on a bench across the room, against the wall. Judge Greene spoke first.

"Look at the size of this file. I had some spare time to fit in a pretrial conference, but I thought that the clerk would just send me a 'slip-and-fall.' Instead, what do we have here? A matter involving the Republican National Committee!"

"Sir, could someone tell us why we're here and not in Judge Thompson's office?" Jim questioned.

"Do you have a tape recorder on you?" Judge Greene asked.

"No, we do not."

"Then sit down and shut up."

We attempted to challenge this star chamber session.

For those who may not be familiar with the term, the dictionary defines *star chamber* as *"formerly an English court which met in secret session without a jury, and handed down arbitrary rulings that were extremely severe. Abolished in 1641. Therefore, any investigative body that is similarly unjust."*

"Do you happen to be represented by counsel?" he asked us.

"We are representing ourselves, your Honor."

"Then my advice is you'd better get a lawyer if you don't like the way things are going in here."

   With that, we were ordered to return 72 hours later for a *de novo* hearing – that means all the evidence presented to Judge Nunzio would have to be represented to Judge Greene in 72 hours – even though court rules required one week's written notice to both sides. It was ground already settled and these guys were illegally forcing us to go over it again.

   We left the dark and dank old courthouse and walked around in the afternoon snow. We had been dragooned and keelhauled in that room. Now we felt sick and furious. There seemed to be two choices: first, we could file a motion challenging the 72 hours.

   "But if they buy another judge and we don't show up for their bullshit *de novo* hearing, we could find ourselves back in Lafayette Park with no case," Jim said.

   "Or," Ken suggested, "the other choice is to show up and get the transcript and use it to impeach Carr and Greene."

   "I'd like to get Carr disbarred."

   We opted to show up.

W hat follows are excerpts from those sequestered and illegal proceedings.In his opening statement, Judge Greene fully admits that he was not the assigned pretrial judge.

COURT: This matter first came to my attention on the first day I was assigned to my new civil assignment on Monday of this week, January 6, 1986, when it was certified to me about midday for a pretrial hearing...

(In fact, this case had never been certified to Judge Greene.)

...when it came to me, about six inches of file walked into my office. Unless I was going to keep counsel and the parties waiting for two or three hours, it made sense for me to at least get some initial impression from both sides as to where this matter stood. Then I would recess to take a more informed look at the file...

(Translation: "I just got this and I didn't know what I was dealing with.")

...both parties are seeking a portion of Judge Nunzio's ruling to be overturned. The Colliers sought punitive damages against the RNC, and Mr. Carr filed a parallel motion seeking full dismissal.

(Judge Greene knew that we were not seeking any portion of Judge Nunzio's ruling to be overturned. We simply wanted a pretrial conference. It was Carr who was seeking to have Nunzio overturned.)

KEN: Your honor, if we were to win our motion for punitive damages, no harm would be done to Mr. Carr's position. But if the Court reconsiders the issue of overall liability once again by conducting a new hearing from "square one," as Mr. Carr is seeking, we will be the only party in jeopardy of dismissal. It is a patently unfair situation we find ourselves in, with little to gain and everything to lose. Mr. Carr has everything to gain and nothing to lose.

COURT: So, you were not satisfied that there was an adequate hearing before Judge Nunzio?

KEN: It was satisfactory on the issue of liability only. If we had been given sufficient time to argue our point for punitive damages, we would have simply listed the egregious willful, wanton, reckless and malicious nature of the tactics used by the Republican National Committee to avoid honoring their reward offer.

We then went on to give the shopping list of all our grievances that should have led to punishment of the RNC. We told Judge Greene that Carr had viewed our evidence and never once had suggested that it didn't meet the highest standards of admissibility required in a criminal trial. Then we turned to Carr:

KEN: Mr. Carr, we challenge you to do so now.

COURT: Let's try to keep our eye on the ball. The ball in our view is the reward offer. That's where this litigation starts, and may well be where it should end.

Judge Greene read the reward offer in its entirety, then added: "the reward offer further indicates, *"We have established phone numbers which will be manned by attorneys, who will assist in putting (claimants) in touch with the proper State and Federal officials who will proceed with such complaint."*

KEN: Yes, we did use the phone number to call Mr. Braden at the RNC in November 1982.

COURT: Are you contending that Mr. Braden did not put you in touch with the proper official?

KEN: Yes. Mr. Braden did utter the name of Donsanto, but not in the context of putting us in touch with him. The utterance of a surname of someone in the Justice Department is a far cry from putting a reward claimant in touch with him.

COURT: You're contending now that Mr. Donsanto was not a proper official to have been sent to, even though he is a vote fraud prosecutor?

KEN: Yes. It turned out that he wasn't.

COURT: It turned out that he wasn't? Are you contending they knew he was not a proper official to be sent to with your evidence?

KEN: Your Honor, once we were rebuffed and told not to return, Donsanto became inappropriate – the wrong official.

COURT: You seem to insist on making Mr. Donsanto a party to this litigation. He's not. He has not been interpleaded, he has not been made a third-party defendant. And while there may be a pending investigation of him by the Justice Department, or the FBI, or the KGB — I don't know who's investigating him...

(Let's not forget this is an illegal hearing and there was no need to interplead Donsanto. Donsanto was being sued in the Justice Department case.)

KEN: The OPR – Office of Professional Responsibility, sir.

COURT: I don't discern its relevence to this litigation. Now, let's finally assume for purposes of argument that the last of the words "will" that appears in this reward offer means exactly what you contend it means.

That is, that it amounts to a guarantee that the RNC would make sure that federal officials would proceed with your complaint.

KEN: The RNC's intentions were clearly set out in the plain language of the offer. Only now, in this litigation, do we find out that they did not intend it to mean exactly what it says on its face.

COURT: I don't mean to be facetious, but you seem to think that the relationship between the RNC and the government, if there happens to be a Republican President, is about the same as between the Communist Party and the Politburo in the Soviet Union. In other words, whatever the party in power says, goes. Is that your position?

KEN: Your Honor, while we appreciate the Court's colorful analogy, we respectfully submit that in modern day Washington, to deny the existence of "clout" would be the height of naivete. Let's not forget that the opening phrase of the reward offer states: " *We, the Republican National Committee, are saddened to learn that vote fraud exists in many areas of the country"*. But when it comes to two citizens, in this case my brother and myself, actually going out into the field and risking all to prove that vote fraud does exist – the RNC wants to forget about it. If your Honor would just agree to see the videotape, it would be clear as to why we pursued this case. Here you have the League...

COURT: Okay, Mr. Carr, let me ask you why the language in the reward offer means what the Plaintiffs contend it means? Why isn't that sufficiently outrageous or malicious conduct to qualify for...why isn't that kind of intentional misleading of the Plaintiffs sufficient to make this a punitive damages case?

(With the above remark, Judge Greene articulated our side of the case for the first time, but before permitting Carr to respond, added the following hint that "down the line a little bit" he would provide his own rebuttal.)

...I think there is a substantial issue here, which we'll discuss on down the line a little bit as to whether any reasonable individual could so interpret the language. Mr. Carr, would you concede that if it means what they say it means, punitive damages should have remained in this case?

CARR: I would not concede that the punitive damages element would remain in the case. I don't think it goes to the level of maliciousness and fraud that are required.

COURT: In other words, are you saying that if the RNC meant it to appear to the reader to be a guarantee, and knew that it wasn't, and knew they couldn't make a guarantee, that's still not enough to get them over the hump to make a punitive damages claim?

CARR: I don't think, under the case law here, that it rises to that level in the contract field, your Honor.

(That colloquy was merely "code" for the record. Judge Greene was telling Carr that he understood the seriousness of our case. Between them a charade was being conducted. The Judge knew very well that he was about to overturn Judge Nunzio's original ruling that we were entitled to a jury trial on the merits of the case.)

COURT: Thank you. I'm almost certain that I can recall a punitive damage case, in which the Court of Appeals vacated an award, holding that even in a fraud case, punitive damages are not necessarily appropriate. I've heard all I want to hear now. I have some strong inclinations as to how I'm going to rule, but I want to wait until I find this case, because I think it exists…

(Translation: "After lunch I will give you a piece of dictum that's going to dismiss your case."

After the recess, Judge Greene wasted no more time in giving us any benefit of the doubt.)

COURT: Now get this. It is my view, as a matter of law, that no reasonable person could interpret the language "Who will proceed with such complaint," as anything other than predictive. That no reasonable person could construe that language as a guarantee by the RNC as to what federal officials would do. I guess that is really the crux of the matter.

KEN: Your Honor, may I say something?

COURT: Mr. Collier, if you interrupt me again, I'm going to get a marshal over here and hold you in contempt of court. Now I have just so much time to deal with this matter. I've heard far longer from you than I've heard from Mr. Carr. You're on notice.

(What came next was akin to finding ourselves in a hall of mirrors. Judge Greene proceeded to manipulate and distort the meaning and content of the English language.)

COURT: It seems to me that the word "will" when used as a verb has several connotations. There is a Supreme Court definition which just recently came out about the word "will"...

(Judge Greene was trying to say that the Supreme Court had recently ruled that the bedrock of contract law, the word "will", was no longer to be trusted.)

...In preparation for this, I was looking in a dictionary of English usage last night, and the word "will," has several connotations. Sometimes it does have connotations that amount to a guarantee, but in another context, has only a predictive connotation. That is, "it will rain today." If I tell you, "it will rain tonight" or "will snow tonight," the word "will" is being used in a predictive connotation, because there's no way I can guarantee that it will rain or it will snow tonight. It seems to me likewise, the word "will" as used the last time in the reward offer, clearly has a predictive connotation. I find this as a matter of law.

(Judge Greene just shattered centuries of common law.)

KEN: There is nothing predictive in the word "will" according to Black's; it's promissory, and there's nothing in Black's Dictionary about anything predictive.

(We then read to Judge Greene the statement of former RNC president Richard Richards when he said that by signing the reward offer, he intended the provisions of that document to be binding upon the RNC.)

COURT: Well, I've already concluded…you know, I may be wrong. The court of appeals will tell me if I'm wrong, but I've already concluded that the word "will" is not a word signifying a guarantee. It is a word, in my view, that can only be reasonably interpreted by any reasonable person as signifying a prediction as to what will happen.

(Finally, Judge Greene fired off the following.)

COURT: Any allegations of improper activities

by Mr. Donsanto at the Department of Justice are irrelevant to this Court's decision. The only question concerning Mr. Donsanto is not what he did with any information he received, but whether he was, in fact, a proper public official, and that is conceded by the Plaintiffs in this case.

The Plaintiffs have repeatedly asked the Court to review and examine the videotape and I have declined to do so, because whatever is on that tape is irrelevant to the Defendant's motion for summary judgment. I must assume that there is evidence on that tape of voting irregularities and voting fraud. I want to make it perfectly clear on the record that I am not reaching that conclusion as a factual matter, but that I have to assume it for purposes of this argument and I have done so, consequently, it is not necessary for me to examine that tape.

(We waited until the very last moment before using the same futile attempt we used on Nunzio – to "make a record" of the fact that Judge Greene was connected to Justice Department cronyism.)

KEN: Your Honor stated in chambers the other day, relating to your former experience in the Justice Department as an official or something of that nature, which we did not understand. I want to know if you could clarify that for the record, because we do fear summary judgement, and we fear that it might come here and now.

COURT: Your request is denied, Mr. Collier.

KEN: Have you ever worked for the Justice Department, Sir?

COURT: I worked for the Justice Department up until 1981, and I will not respond to any further inquiry.

And so, Judge Greene ruled there was no contract. No contract, no law-suits, no scandal. Carr's goal had been accomplished. Donsanto had been successfully protected, and all the suits we had filed to illuminate the dimensions of vote fraud in this country were eventually eliminated.

We sued Judge Greene and asked the Chief Judge of the Court to hold a full investigation into Greene's and Carr's activities in that backroom court.

We filed ethics charges. We filed charges with the bar association. All court investigators agreed that we were correct in the Star Chamber assessment. With no surprise, they all refused to take action.

We appealed to the Supreme Court. (See Writ in appendix).

We had been a flea in their side. Virulent but not deadly. As we walked out into the bitter cold Washington winter, it was the ending of an era.

For us it was also the end of any possibility of letting the People know why the American dream was failing and the infrastructure of our country was being destroyed.

Americans witnessed crack-cocaine being sold in the streets, crime, unemployment, family breakdowns, and they had no idea that this lack of leadership was due to a calculated computer chip.

On that dismal afternoon, we could not have foreseen a light at the end of the tunnel. It would shine with the advent of the Nineties.

Book Two

The Unified Field Theory
1990-1992

"*A theory is good if it satisfies two requirements: it must accurately describe a large class of observations on the basis of a model that contains only a few arbitrary elements, and it must make definite predictions about the results of future observations.*"

—Stephen W. Hawking

15

PIECE OF THE PUZZLE

> *"Exit polls ... I'd make them criminal offenses."*
>
> —Ross Perot

Throughout the Eighties we had been searching for more clues to that elusive piece of the puzzle; the one piece that would complete the picture and prove to be the smoking gun.

Now in the Nineties, we believe that piece is the Exit Polls.

In 1970, when we were first introduced to the so-called "magic machine" used to predict perfect vote totals in Dade County, we didn't realize that a slightly altered version of that trickery was already being conducted by the television networks in exit polling.

It seems that Louis Harris, the father of exit polling in America, was hired by CBS in 1964, shortly after the JFK assassination, to create the first exit polls. He told us that Huntley & Brinkley on NBC had dominated the election coverage for years, relegating Walter Cronkite to secondbest.

Harris was instructed to conduct exit polls for the Rockefeller/ Goldwater presidential race, and it was expected that Cronkite would beat Huntley & Brinkley to the election-night punch.

In a telephone interview, Harris recalled that back in 1964 he devised an effective method of conducting exit polls. He simply had voters put beans in jars labelled with each candidate's name. He used seventy-two sample precincts and at 7:01 on election night, Cronkite was the first to accurately tell the public who won the presidential race and by what percentage.

From that point on, Cronkite on CBS remained the dominant election-night personality, all based on beans in a jar.

Harris also told us that afterwards he was treated like a pariah by the other networks because he was the creator of exit polling. It was a concept that would ultimately force ABC and NBC to find a way to compete.

In 1982, when we investigated the television networks' abilities to call election results at 7:01 p.m., based on "exit polls," we were told that we could not be given any information because it was proprietary; that meant the networks were competing with each other and they didn't want to give their secret sample precincts away; nor were they about to reveal any information to renegade reporters not officially sanctioned to investigate.

Over the years, we were repeatedly asked the same question by news department personnel at all three networks: "Who told you to call?"

Only Warren Mitofsky, the chief of the exit polling division at CBS, who replaced Lou Harris in 1966, repeated the company line:

"This is not a proper area of inquiry."

He would repeat the litany over and over throughout the years as we continued to push for answers.

Because all three networks projected the same numbers within minutes of each other, the question grew: *did they all use the same sample precincts?*

As far as we could determine from our phone conversations with their news departments, only CBS actually did exit polling of some kind. ABC and NBC personnel indicated that they didn't have sufficient staff to handle it. But Warren Mitofsky was always the man very much in charge at CBS.

It came as no suprise when, in 1989, the networks finally admitted that a consortium was formed in which ABC, NBC, CBS and CNN would pool their "resources" to conduct exit polls. That network pool was named *Voter Research and Surveys (VRS)* and it was headed by Warren Mitofsky. In fact, VRS and NES (News

Election Service) both filter their numbers through the same mainframe computer located on 34th Street.

Between NES and VRS, the networks have total control of the vote -counting process in this country.

Where Harris used beans in a jar, Mitofsky uses Chilton Research of Radnor, Pa. For years we tried to be hired as exit pollsters for the networks, but we were told that Chilton employs other subpolling organizations in various states to do the actual hiring of field personnel. In spite of our consistent efforts, the answers to the following still remain a mystery:

Who are those subgroups who subsequently hire exit pollsters? Just how many exit pollsters are actually hired? What are the names of the field organizations who hire them? Where are the precincts they work in? How are those sample precincts chosen?

Mitofsky (VRS) and Chilton refuse to explain how they operate by claiming they are private groups *and don't have to tell the American people a damn thing.*

In the New Hampshire 1992 primary this spring, VRS claimed to poll 3,800 voters using 38 precincts. That averages 100 people surveyed per precinct, or approximately 100 responses to about 30 questions. The New York *Times* ran a blurb reporting the survey was conducted from noon until early evening (say, 6 p.m.). That averages about 18 people per hour, per precinct, filling out questionnaires in the cold of New Hampshire. A VRS spokesperson assured me that "our pollsters don't fill out the forms, we make the voters do it."

According to VRS, voters are more than willing to answer long questionnaires after they leave the polling booths. They are happy to divulge their income, religious and sexual preferences, and a host of other personal information, including the names of the candidates for whom they just voted. So much for the secret ballot.

When we called election supervisors in New Hampshire and other states around the country during the 1992 primary season, we were told that they never saw anyone they could actually identify as an exit pollster; furthermore: "nobody lines up in the cold in New Hampshire or South Dakota, in winter winds, to answer a long list of questions."

One of the questions on the form was: "What is your income?" In New Hampshire, the VRS survey listed 80 people in the over $75,000 per year category. One election supervisor assured us: "there probably aren't that many people left in the state with that kind of income, and most wouldn't answer questions for some stranger in a parking lot.

"Most people hurry to vote before work," the Manchester supervisor said. "Some vote in the early morning before work, others at coffee breaks and lunch hours. The rest vote in the cold dark after work and then rush home for dinner."

So who are these thousands of people with the time, patience and inclination to stand around answering questions for VRS?

VRS claims they only use about 30 to 40 sample precincts per state, and they interview as many as 3 to 4,000 people per state.

Again, simple math shows that people would have to be consistently lined up virtually every hour to be interviewed in order for thousands to become statistics.

On Super Tuesday in the 1992 primaries, some time after 6 p.m. the exit pollsters would have had to total up about 100 questionnaires apiece (assuming everything was balanced) that is, take the 75 responses times 100 sheets of paper and get a total. That's 7,500 numbers per person to total. If all precincts were not balanced (with 100 questionnaires apiece) then some precincts would have, say, 150 forms, while others would have only 50. The pollster with 150 forms would have to total more than 11,000 numbers.

Pollsters were instructed to call polling results back to a Radnor 800 number. The telephone company verified that only 67 telephones rotated off that 800 number. At about 6 p.m., the pollsters would have to go to a phone, call

Chilton, and repeat that long list of numbers back to one of those 67 operators.

Since VRS claims that thousands of people were polled in seven states, our math indicates that it was *impossible* to garner and call that much information back to Chilton operators and have the results on the air at 7:01 p.m.

Lee C. Shapiro at VRS (Lee C. is what they call her around the office) is Mitofsky's top aide and we've shadowboxed several times over the past decade. She always responds with the company motto: *"this is not a proper area of inquiry."*

But the last time Jim called, he got some unexpected information. "We use clipboards for the people who fill out questionnaires," Lee C. said. "They answer the questions and drop the paper in a box."

"Does Chilton issue official clipboards and pencils?"

"No, not clipboards, exactly," she backed off.

"Well, do the people fill them out on their laps, on other people's backs, on the hoods of cars?"

"You'd be surprised how many people can't wait to fill out our forms."

"But Lee C.," Jim prodded, "how is it that every precinct totals exactly the right percentages? And even more interesting is that all the people who fill out your forms fit the same percentage mold. Why don't all Jerry Brown's people fill out forms in some precincts, while the Clinton people refuse? Even if the precinct is representative of the national norm, who says the voters filling out questionnaires have to be a perfect mixture of that balance?"

"Because we create a statistical analysis that picks those precincts."

"But you don't pick the people who leave the polls on a cold winter day who answer your questions," Jim said. "What's more, when all the networks were supposedly competing, before they admitted to a network pool, they all still came up with the exact same numbers at 7:01 p.m. And those numbers always agreed perfectly with the actual vote totals that NES tabulated after the polls closed. Did everybody use the same precincts?"

"Sometimes they used the same precincts."

"Okay, then give me two precincts in Pennsylvania that I can go to in the next primary and see for myself how it's done. That can't possibly spoil some great cosmic plan."

At that point Lee C. Shapiro simply disconnected. It was obviously not a proper area of inquiry.

According to Walter Goodman in the New York *Times,* (November 11, 1989) "It is easy to understand voters...asked to tell somebody with a clipboard how they voted, might have replied with less than courtesy."

The article comments on people not telling the truth as to whether they voted for black or white candidates. Especially if a black person is being asked the question by a white person with a clipboard, or vice versa. That also goes for voters stating their religious and sexual preferences.

"A professor of political science at the University of Richmond called it 'the fibbing factor' "

Besides voters protecting their privacy, Goodman speculated:

"Might it be that some television viewers were being mischievous? Disgruntled at being deprived of an evening's excitement, might some have figured out that the way to restore a bit of zest to election night would be to mislead the polltakers? Here was an opportunity for people exasperated at being told what they were thinking, night after night, on all channels, to do the telling...what a kick to kick the experts. Let all polltakers beware."

For the last few years, we have attempted to enlist the aid of top reporters from major newspapers around the country to help us penetrate the secret world of VRS. Among those contacted were: *Hunter S. Thompson, San Francisco Chronicle; David Rosenzweig, L.A. Times; Lionel Barber, Financial Times of London; Harold Meyerson, The Los Angeles Weekly; Martin Gottleib, The New York Times, Joan Konner, Dean of the School of Journalism, Columbia University.*

Although no help was forthcoming from any of these people, Rosenzweig sent us an excellent compendium of stories the L.A. *Times* had researched on computer vote fraud in July of 1989. Why the L.A. *Times* did not crusade on the subject, since they had this comprehensive material, is a question that begs to be answered.

16

THE THIRTEENTH FLOOR

> *"When you have eliminated the*
> *impossible, whatever remains,*
> *however improbable, must be the*
> *truth."*
>
> —Conan Doyle

When we settled back to watch the 1992 New York primary election returns, we were at the end of a 22-year mission, and we really had no intention of getting further embroiled in investigating vote fraud. Besides, New York State uses lever machines, and those old dinosaurs are very hard to rig.

But as we watched ABC in New York tell the public that eight percent of the vote was already counted by 9:15 p.m., just 15 minutes after the polls closed, we couldn't resist a telephone call to ABC.

"How'd you do that?" Jim asked the man in charge.

"I use Associated Press figures," he said.

Jim called AP only to find out:

"We use News Election Service's figures and the *police feed*."

With that, the investigation was back on and we were once more drawn into the fray.

How did NES report eight percent of the vote in just 15 minutes? Jim figured that it would require either computer terminals in the 13,391 state precincts that could instantly send vote totals back to NES in New York. (Eight percent of the precincts would be almost 1,100 precincts.)

"Or," Jim added, "a phone bank at NES headquarters that could receive telephone calls from correspondents in those same precincts."

The only problem with the computer theory was there were no computer links in school houses or fire stations where most people vote.

That left phone banks.

We decided to call NES executive headquarters and ask how they arrived at that eight percent figure so early.

We didn't harbor much hope of getting a straightforward answer from NES. When Ken told Robert Flaherty back in the Eighties that we were writing a book on vote fraud, he promised:

"No one will publish that book."

This time Jim called NES executive headquarters and asked for Dennis Zire, the computer operator. He asked for the location of the phone bank that received raw vote totals from the precincts in New York State.

"Who wants to know?"

"I'm with the Jerry Brown campaign," Jim improvised.

"It's none of his business," came the reply.

Ms. Susan Bucksbaum at Voter Research and Survey (VRS) said the League of Women Voters supply the personnel who phone in raw precinct totals to a phone bank at NES, but she claims not to know where the phone bank is located. Only after some coaxing did she volunteer that it "might be at One World Trade Center."

Not surprising, she wasn't sure if the League was reporting vote totals to NES directly from the 13,391 state precincts or from the state's 63 county boards of elections. The difference in personnel is enormous.

If you waited for the aggregate to arrive at the 63 county seats, you'd only need 63 people, but you couldn't call that information back to NES prior to 9:15 p.m.

We checked the largest county, Erie (1,136 precincts), who, along with Niagara (143 precincts) contracts National Time Sharing Data Service to tabulate their votes for the media. *A call to NTS revealed they didn't have any totals at all by 9:15 p.m.*

Only a combination of some 20 or more of the remaining counties could possibly have accounted for eight percent, but that just seems impossible on a statistical (if not human) level, unless, of course, NES has that elusive phone bank capable of handling 1,100 calls in about ten minutes.

Even if they had the phone bank capability, all the precincts in those counties needed totals read off the backs of the machines and phoned in just minutes after the polls closed. It would require the next three largest counties, Monroe (425), Onondaga (487) and Albany (295) to call NES (remember there are no computer hookups in fire stations or school houses), in the first few minutes after the polls closed, for the eight percent to be legitimately achieved.

Election supervisors we telephoned claim they don't rush to open the voting machines merely to satisify the media's demand for speed. First they put away their day gear and then they get to the vote counting procedures. Often people are still voting at 9 p.m.

The next day, Jim again used the Jerry Brown credentials when calling Naomi Bernstein, the press secretary for the Board of Elections in Manhattan.

He learned the police department picks up

the 5,300 canvass sheets (the forms in triplicate on which the votes are tallied as numbers are called off the backs of the voting machines at 9 p.m.), and delivers them to police precincts in the five boroughs. Police officers then total the numbers and send the results by computer to NES headquarters where Dennis Zire feeds them to AP and the networks. This is the "police feed" AP told Jim about.

One canvass sheet is delivered to One Police Plaza, one to the Board of Elections of each borough and the third is curbside-delivered to NES at One World Trade Center in Manhattan. From there the sheets are brought to the 13th floor and enter a secret world that no citizen can penetrate. We tried.

Jim was contacted by producers from the Geraldo Rivera show, *Now It Can Be Told,* who had read about *Votescam* in the Jonathan Vankin book, *Conspiracies , Coverups. & Crimes.*

They were interested in doing a show on vote fraud in America. Jim suggested they begin with a visit to NES, the legal government media monopoly (exempt from antitrust laws), that counts the votes on the 13th floor of the World Trade Center.

Jim told the show's investigative reporter, Gail Anderson: "I called Robert Flaherty and told him that I wanted to come over and see how his operation worked. He said that it was off limits to the press."

Anderson was taking notes during the cab ride to the World Trade Center.

"Then I added that I was working with Dan Bishoff, the national editor of the *Village Voice,* in developing a piece on vote fraud. I told Flaherty that I was on deadline and the story would print next week. He said, 'We'll see about that.'"

They got to the World Trade Center just minutes before Flaherty had the 13th floor closed off to the public. Once upstairs, Jim started taping outside the NES offices. Flaherty burst through the doors, apparently alerted by the guard downstairs.

"Turn off that camera!"

He refused to allow Jim and Anderson to view the operation where NES supposedly receives phone calls from the League of Women Voters in the precincts.

Jim had time to ask one question before Flaherty ran from the camera.

"Do the people who call in from the precinct indicate what precinct they're calling in from?"

Flaherty said "no, they didn't," and bolted behind closed doors.

On the cab ride back uptown, Gail said:

"If they don't indicate what precinct they're calling in from, somebody could be calling in bogus vote totals from a back room somewhere down the street and nobody would know the difference."

Within a week of that meeting *Now It Can Be Told* was cancelled.

Perhaps it was due to their ratings.

And that was that.

A story dated July 4, 1989 in the L.A. *Times*, quotes Craig C. Donsanto, Justice Department Attorney in charge of vote fraud prosecution:

"You have to have access and some degree of technical knowledge to penetrate an electronic tabulating system. All voting systems are capable of being corrupted," he told the *Times*. "Most of them have been or will be...simply because voting is the way we determine who gets power in this great country."

The story goes on to say that there have been no federal prosecutions for tampering with the computer vote counting programs, but Donsanto suggests that it might be because "federal investigators are more familiar with paper ballots or lever-operated machines."

What information Donsanto neglected to tell the *Times* reporter was that he himself had been sued by the Collier brothers for hindering federal prosecutors from ever looking into vote fraud.

The *Times* story also quotes Steve White, former Chief Assistant Attorney General in California:

"Election fraud is difficult to prosecute, because you need a co-conspirator who comes forward, or an election that is such an upset that people would look into it. A more likely scenario is that in a close election, you just change a few votes in a few states, and nobody would ever know."

The *Times* finishes with the frightening revelation that "some critics of computerized vote counting worry about the potential for 'trapdoors,' 'time bombs' and 'Trojan Horses.' A computer operator with the correct password could place a trapdoor, or a series of hidden vote counting instructions inside the system, according to *Election Watch Report.*

"Once into the system, the operator could program the computer to count votes for one candidate as votes for another. After the votes have been changed to swing the election, the trap door could be closed.

"A time bomb would have to be sprung by a computer operator on the scene, but a time bomb could be placed inside the tabulating system in advance. It could instruct the computer to add 500 dummy votes, while the perpetrator relaxed thousands of miles away."

As for the Trojan Horse concept — Howard J. Strauss, Princeton University computer scientist said: "Writing the 'source code' for one of these vote counting systems, a programmer could insert a 'Trojan Horse' that might not appear for years.

"Suppose I wanted to throw the 1992 presidential nomination to (Mario Cuomo, for example), I write the code so that every time the name comes up in the primaries, he receives a certain number of votes."

With the help of the above scenarios, we may have just described one of the methodologies used by computer wizard Sununu in New Hampshire to assure that the final results would agree with the exit polls.

As we had been unable to divine a paper trail on the exit polling operation, we called upon Ellis Rubin one more time. We hadn't seen him in ten years so we certainly couldn't forecast his reaction to being drawn once more into the breach.

We told him that we were on the trail of the smoking gun, and that we believed it was pointed at Voter Research and Surveys. No, we couldn't give him the details on how the gun was used, or how many political careers it had already terminated, but we could definitely smell the smoke.

We gave Rubin a copy of this book and told him that it should serve as a catalyst for a full public investigation of how the vote is counted.

On March 13, 1992 we met with Rubin in Miami and asked him to bring the issue of vote fraud once again to the proper authorities. He agreed. The following letter was drafted by Rubin and delivered to acting U. S. Attorney James McAdams in Miami, along with a copy of this book. Rubin requested that McAdams deliver them to United States Attorney General William Barr in Washington.

RUBIN, RUBIN & RUBIN
A PROFESSIONAL ASSOCIATION OF ATTORNEYS

ELLIS S. RUBIN
I. MARK RUBIN
GUY BENNETT RUBIN
ROBERT IVAN BARRAR, JR.
ERIC J. MILLER

OF COUNCIL

DANIEL R. AARONSON
JAMES S. BENJAMIN
ANDREW RICHARD lll

MIAMI
333 N.E. 23rd STREET
MIAMI, FLORIDA 33137
(305) 576-5600
(305) 576-3292 TELEFAX

FT. LAUDERDALE
100 N.E. 3rd AVENUE. SUITE 850
FT. LAUDERDALE, FLORIDA 3301
(305) 524-5600

March 24, 1992

William Barr
Attorney General of the United States
Main Justice Building
5111 Tenth and Constitution Avenue, N.W.
Washington, D.C. 20530

Dear General Barr:

Because I am mentioned throughout, the attached manuscript, VOTESCAM: THE STEALING OF AMERICA, was given to me by the authors for comment. I found the contents to be so explosive, current and important to every American voter that I requested and received permission to transmit it to you through the United States Attorney for the Southern District of Florida for immediate action.

The Presidential, Congressional, State and local elections of 1992 are almost upon us and, strange as it seems, no human eye will ever see or count most of the millions of votes cast due to electronic or computerized balloting. This manuscript exposes several examples of how votes were and can be manipulated.

Now, a new phenomenon has entered the picture. The exit poll, which never fails to call the final results within fractions of those tallies. By 7:01 p.m. election night, the networks and their mysterious exit polls tell us who won and by how much, ALTHOUGH NOT A SINGLE VOTE HAS BEEN COUNTED. This exit poll pool is called VOTER RESEARCH AND SURVEY (VRS). The public does not know how it works, they can't find out and, in fact, it is totally unaccountable to the public.

Along with VRS, the TV networks and wire services have put together and completely control the NEWS ELECTION SERVICES (NES). NES is the official vote counting apparatus of America. The VRS and NES numbers always jibe. How? Why?

And who are the shadowy vendors who come into the states and supposedly count the votes for the supervisor of elections and at great taxpayer expense? Since computers are involved in counting votes, anyone with access codes could punch into elections and change the results...and nobody would be the wiser. That also goes for the software involved.

Mr. Attorney General, I urge you to use this manuscript as background material and then tell the American public how you are going to sanitize every facet of how their votes are counted. More than that, I pray you will make our elections foolproof. With November rapidly approaching, time is of the essence. As I have said before: Computerized voting by punchcard thwarts the will of the people. A cancer is growing on our most precious franchise. It must be eradicated NOW.

Very truly yours,

RUBIN, RUBIN & RUBIN, P.A.
ELLIS S. RUBIN
For The Firm

ESR: ds/0052
Enclosure

U.S. DEPARTMENT OF JUSTICE
CRIMINAL DIVISION

Office of the Assistant Attorney General   Washington, D.C. 20530

Ellis R. Rubin, Esq.
Rubin, Rubin & Rubin
333 N.E. 23rd Street
Miami, Florida 33137-4926

Dear Mr, Rubin:

Your recent letter addressed to Attorney General William Barr and enclosing the manuscrpt of a document entitled "Votescam" prepared by Kenneth and James Collier has been referred to the Criminal Division.

This Division is very familiar with the Collier brothers and their claims that computerized voting equipment used throughout the United States to tabulate votes has been fraudulently manipulated as part of a national conspiracy to corrupt the outcome of elections. The information that we have received from these two complainants has failed to demonstrate any support for their thesis. For that reason, we do not consider that the matters referred to in the attachment to your letter warrant a criminal investigation by the Department of Justice.

I appreciate your sharing this manuscript with us.

Sincerely,
Robert S. Mueller, III
Assistant Attorney
General

By:
John C Keeney
Deputy Assistant Attorney
GeneralCriminal Division

May 20, 1992

Robert S. Mueller, III
Assistant Attorney General
U.S. Department of Justice
Criminal Division
Washington, D.C. 20530

Dear Mr. Mueller,

Your letter is signed by John C. Keeney and not by you. As an investigator I find that significant. You see, John C. Keeney is a name I know well. John C. Keeney's name runs the length of our investigation into vote fraud. It is John C. Keeney's name that appears on all documents protecting perpetrators. It is John C. Keeney's name we find on documents protecting Craig C. Donsanto. It is Donsanto and Keeney who are the stoppers-in-the-bottle of vote fraud prosecution in the Justice Department. So it is not surprising that we find John C. Keeney's signature on your letter.

After all, Mr. Mueller, we sent the *Votescam* manuscript to William Barr. We can now surmise that William Barr never saw it. Very probably, John C. Keeney intercepted the manuscript, and he alone made the decision to write to attorney Ellis Rubin, killing any hope of an honest investigation. We seriously doubt that even you saw the manuscript, but that John C. Keeney finagled it into his own possession.

You must understand that John C. Keeney knows

this story very well. He knows that Donsanto refused to see the *Votescam* videotape we shot in Miami, in which the League of Women Voters were punching holes in vote cards, and that hardly mattered because the computer operators were not counting votes. It was all preprogrammed weeks before the election. John C. Keeney knows that Elvera Radford, the Cincinnati election chief, quit her long-held post the day after we videotaped the LWV using tweezers that corrupted the vote cards. That tape was shown on television in Cincinnati but Donsanto, making a mockery of the position he holds, refused to see it.

John C. Keeney knows that the Printomatic device is used extensively to rig elections in this country. He allows that to happen. He knows that a network vote counting cartel can change the computer vote count in 60% of this nation without detection.

This nightmarish scenario can be accomplished from a master computer located on 34th street in New York City. But he refuses to share this frightening fact with the public. His letter states that the information he has "failed to demonstrate any support" for our thesis. Well, Mr. Mueller, we say the information he has proves exactly the opposite.

The information that Craig. C. Donsanto and John C. Keeney are protecting includes the names of a score of private companies that infiltrate American cities without public knowledge and count the vote on their private machines. The people who run these companies could be paid to rig any election from local, to state or federal, and John C. Keeney is protecting their identity. The public is kept unaware of who they are, who they represent and what they are paid.

Mr. Mueller, this country is in rotten shape. I have been on radio shows from coast to coast, and callers in dozens of cities testify as to how the computer in their town mysteriously "breaks down" when their honest candidate is winning. When the system returns on-line, the count is strangely reversed. The thieves won. It's a national epidemic. John C. Keeney's job in Justice has become making sure these facts are never open to public examination.

When the *Votescam* manuscript is published, you and the citizens of this country will be rightly incensed. This letter, of course, will be the book's final document. If there is any justice left in the Justice Department, the sequel to *Votescam* will include the indictment of John C. Keeney and Craig C. Donsanto.

Sincerely,

James M. Collier

17

THE LAST DISPATCH

Home News Wire

By: James and Kenneth Collier

NEW YORK (HNW) - It's amazing how the characters keep reappearing in the script. Like Gaeton Fonzi.

We thought Fonzi was just a simple scribe for a local magazine in Miami when he wrote his 1974 piece on *The Great Dade Election Rig*. However, Fonzi, it turns out, was also a firsthand reporter on the JFK assassination. When he was assigned to interview us on the vote fraud story, we got the top drawer, number-one investigator in America to report on our case.

Fonzi was also a member of the House Select Committee on Assassinations, which convened in 1975 to reopen the Kennedy case. In fact, Fonzi is probably the only man left in this country who hasn't written a book on JFK, when indeed, he is the best man around to piece this entire conspiracy together.

To begin with he knows, from reading our

reports in the *Home News,* that there was a
sniper's nest in Dallas that nobody ever talks
about. It has never appeared in any other
newspaper, and it has even escaped the
detection of Oliver Stone. Here is how we
discovered it.

Citizen's for Fraud-Free Elections, a group in
San Jose, California, called Ken in Washington in
l988. They wanted him to go out and investigate
their area for evidence of vote fraud, and they
promised to pay expenses once he got there.
Although that arrangement was against our rules
and we usually insisted on monies up front, a
hound cannot resist the pursuit, and so Ken
headed out across America one more time.

Once there, he appeared on a radio talk show
that covered the Bay area and drew a sizeable
audience. As fate would have it, one of those
listeners was the late and famous Mae Brussell,
the 66-year old Kennedy assassination buff who
had her own popular radio show out there.

If you read Jonathan Vankin's book,
"*Conspiracies, Coverups & Crimes: Political
manipulations and mind control in America,*"
by Paragon House Press (published in October
l991), you will have a better understanding of
this remarkable woman.

We too, appear in Vankins' book, which
profiles both the famous and infamous Hounds
of Hell who investigate conspiracy theories.
What makes the book highly unusual is that, for

the first time, it gives dignity to the citizens who look for answers in places where the mass media refuses to go.

Mae Brussel, according to Vankin, was the "best engaged mind" of all the theorists. She was brilliant as a researcher. The first, and probably the only person to cross-reference the 26 volumes of jumbled, non-indexed Warren Commission files.

Mae would go on the air, and what she said then is exactly what everyone is now discovering: the CIA, the FBI and the Mafia conspired to kill the President. She was subsequently vilified by the media as a "mad conspiracy theorist."

After listening to Ken's accounting of our *Votescam* investigation, she couldn't resist the urge to call him on the air. Mae told Ken that *the roots of vote fraud were to be found in Dallas* — that only there would we discover the truth behind the "front gunman theory."

Mae said that the media had done a trade-off immediately after the shooting in Dallas. The television networks and the major press agreed to go along with the Warren Commission, stifling any impulses to investigate the truth about a front gunman — in return for control of the vote count.

At this point, Ken needed immediate funds because the people who brought him to the coast refused to pay once the job was done. He was virtually stranded in Santa Cruz.

Unfortunately, at the time, Jim found himself in a familiar situation, working for no money on the *Home News*. MacKenzie was subsidizing the paper and his bank account was starting to run on empty.

Jim told MacKenzie the story about Mae Brussel and that Ken needed financial help in getting to Dallas. Considering that MacKenzie had just spent fifteen hundred dollars bailing Jim out of jail after State Attorney Janet Reno had him arrested for grand theft, he wasn't in the mood to dig deeper into his shallow pockets.

As Jim remembers it:

"To leave Ken stranded in Santa Cruz for a moment, let me explain how I happened to find myself in the Dade County Jail.

"It began when a wheeler-dealer, known on the street as 'The Big Shooter,' decided to take over the city of Opa-Locka by becoming its mayor." (Opa-Locka, you will remember from earlier in this book, is the city where the voting machine warehouse was located.)

"I got a telephone call one day at the paper telling me that The Big Shooter was printing his own ballots for the coming election. My source told me to go to his headquarters which was, I soon discovered, a printing plant.

"Inside the front door, under a campaign poster of The Big Shooter, smiling down benevolently, were several boxes of blank IBM computer ballots.

"I left the building to think the situation over

and telephoned MacKenzie. He told me to seize the evidence and deliver it to State Attorney Janet Reno. Minutes later, I drove my car up to the front of the print shop, left the engine running and ran into the shop. I grabbed the boxes and raced back to the car, just as an employee sprang out the door to give chase. I watched in my rear view mirror as he wrote my license number on his palm.

"At Reno's office, instead of being hailed as a hero, my old nemesis had me make a statement to one of her attorneys, who interrogated me as if I had just stolen someone's purse. However, knowing that ending up in court to present this evidence was my ultimate goal, I waived immunity from prosecution and gave a full accounting of my actions. Within a few days, MacKenzie was also called in to make a statement.

"Reno had a choice: she could either investigate my charges, or have me arrested. The latter was too sweet to resist.

"After MacKenzie bailed me out for that $1,500, I battled with Reno on the front pages of the *Home News,* predicting that she'd drop the charges – an act I taunted her *not* to do. But Reno took the prudent course. Rather than face me in court, the prosecutor told the judge at the hearing that he was dropping the case, and the Big Shooter went on to become Mayor of Opa-Locka."

Now, back to rescuing Ken from permanent residency in the San Francisco Bay. MacKenzie gave Jim $500 to fly Ken to Dallas and Miami.

In Dallas, Ken met his girlfriend, Lynnette, who flew in from Washington to help him search for whatever clues Mae Brussel said were waiting to be discovered.

They sat in that famous Dallas restaurant that rotates atop a skyscraper, and everytime the postage stamp-sized crime scene passed below they studied it with a hawk's view. They drew diagrams on the napkins, and somewhere between the soup and the coffee, they figured out that the front gunman had to have been near the railroad trestle in order to get a front shot to Kennedy's right temple.

Ken and Lynnette took a taxi to the scene known as the "Killing Zone," and headed directly to the corner of the grassy knoll where the concrete overpass meets the white picket fence.

As they walked, Ken told her about other anomalies in the Warren Report. For instance, the Kennedy Hounds had determined that no cordite smell was in the room where Oswald was to have fired the rifle. Cordite has an oily, burnt gunpowder odor that lingers in the air for hours after a rifle has been fired indoors.

He described the Ike Altgen's photo showing Oswald standing in the door of the Texas School Book Depository. Oswald had that same open-mouthed look of horror as when Jack Ruby shot him in the police station.

He was caught in that doorway by Altgen's lens at the exact moment Kennedy was shot. Thus, Oswald could not have been upstairs on the sixth floor pulling the trigger.

They walked up the grassy knoll to where the fence abuts the railroad bridge. At the moment of assassination, a train was slowly rolling by.

On that infamous day in 1963, 16 men were looking over the bridge railing as Kennedy was shot. So where could a gunman possibly hide? Then Ken and Lynnette literally stumbled into the evidence.

There, beneath cardboard boxes and old beer cans, was a hole in the ground. It was where the bridge and the knoll meet. Actually, it was a cistern, three by three-feet wide and five feet deep. It had a concrete water pipe at the bottom about eighteen inches wide. The water from the parking lot drained into the cistern.

Had they stumbled onto the sniper's nest used to hide the assassin when he shot the President from the front?

All a gunman in that sniper's nest had to do was to lift the metal catcher's mask-style grate, level his rifle on the top edge of the cement bunker, slide the gun under the bottom of the white fence, sight and shoot. The sniper's nest was set at exactly the proper angle to agree with the Zapruder film that showed the President was shot from the front right.

Then, the sniper could easily drop the rifle and inch himself down the 18-inch pipe, leading beneath the grassy knoll, to a six-foot sewer beneath the street that the President was riding over. Next he could simply walk down that pipe which exited at the Dallas police department.

(Ed. Years later, the son of a Dallas police officer told the American people that his father pulled the trigger on Kennedy, and that he had his deceased father's diary to prove it. Unfortunately, he gave the diary to the FBI and it disappeared.)

Before Ken and Lynnette left Dallas, they decided to check out the history of the bridge. Although the plans were classified under national security, they did find out that the bridge was a WPA project from the Great Depression era.

It was built by a young man with a legendary ambition to be President of the United States, Lyndon Baines Johnson – he was given the task of building that bridge in 1936, and he most certainly knew the existence of the cistern.

We had an ABC news crew from Dallas videotape the crime scene highlighting the cistern. We sold a copy to the producer of NOVA's 25th Anniversary of the JFK shooting that was shown on PBS. Although we were paid for the tape, the producer ran the standard Warren Commission version of events and never mentioned the newly found existence of a front sniper's nest.

At that time, Oliver Stone had not yet made the waters safe for conspiracy theorists with his revisionist film "*JFK*," and so Ms. Conover Hunt, the curator of the JFK Museum at the depository was the first to assure us:

"You'll be the enemy of all Dallas if you push that tape."

However, we were the first investigators to have video proof that a sniper could conceal himself in front of the motorcade, shoot the President and vanish into thin air. Our gratitude to Mae Brussel, who told us the networks were protecting the Warren Commission in return for control of the vote count.

After Vankin's book came out in 1991, we sent copies of the chapter on *Votescam* to people we were trying to educate, along with a copy of a November 7, 1988 cover story in *The New Yorker* by Texan Ronnie Dugger, a veteran JFK hound.

Dugger echoed our *Home News Wire* stories on *Votescam* printed years before in various publications around the country. The Hounds in pursuit of one story were beginning to cross paths with the Hounds of the other. JFK and *Votescam* were starting to meld edges. Just as the brilliant Mae Brussell had predicted there was, indeed, a causal link between the two.

With Vankin's book in hand, we called editor Jack Shafer of *City Paper* in Washington. In 1987, one of his writers, Jon Cohen, had printed a short piece on the *Votescam* investigation.

Although Cohen did an excellent job of reporting the root facts, he wrote that he didn't have time to investigate the charges.

We tried to convince Shafer that *Votescam* was a story with a future. He facetiously replied that "the Collier brothers think they have the unified field theory of conspiracies," and he refused to investigate any part of it.

For those of you who aren't familiar with that penultimate unified field theory of physics, it means: we have taken the JFK assassination and linked it with both Watergate and *Votescam* to show how nothing operates in a vacuum.

The theory is that when JFK was shot, the nation came under the control of the CIA and the Establishment media bosses. Richard Nixon was ambushed at the Watergate by the interests of media boss Katharine Graham, who was protecting her television license in Miami from charges of participating in an election rig.

Not until the JFK case is solved and the ties that bind the CIA to the media are exposed, will "all the poisons in the mud hatch out."

This is not the end.

###

EPILOGUE

18

KNOWLEDGE IS POWER

New York City
February 1, 1993

The war is escalating. More and more people call us during each election, asking us to check out their hometown voting procedures.

On election night last year we were interviewed on National Public Radio in Denver, Portland and in several other western cities. In New York, Jim went to the WBAI studios for a live interview. We were told that would have two hours that night, plenty of time to educate the New York audience to the perils of vote fraud. However, ex-New York *Times* reporter, David Burnham, who was also scheduled, refused to appear on the same show. He claimed that we were right wing radicals, and apparently feared his reputation would be smarmed if he shared air time with a Collier.

That was enough for the two sycophantic hosts to relegate us to a bleak studio office, where we shared tattered furniture with a mascot-cat. We listened to the first hour of Burnham dispensing his limited knowledge of the field. Indeed, Burnham had fallen out of the game years ago, soon after his Poindexter piece appeared in the *Times*. We heard that he was fired from the *Times* for exposing the top secret National Security Administration's investigation into computer fraud. Others say he just quit to become a freelancer. We never got the chance to ask him on the air.

When Burnham's hour was up it was our turn. We intended to tell New York listeners about WABC-TV's remarkable ability to perfectly predict 8 percent of the state vote in just 15 minutes after the polls closed on primary night.

We were pursuing that time-puzzle in the weeks before the WBAI show and discovered that it was Sequoia-Pacific, of Jamestown, New York, who had supplied the state counties with the lever-style voting machines. Normally, it is very difficult to rig lever machines, which left us pondering how WABC-TV could possibly get 1,100 precincts to call in vote totals in less than 15 minutes after the polls closed. When we telephoned Sequoia-Pacific they told us they also supplied the county election supervisors with the Primatomatic device; that double-piece of paper stuck in the back of the voting machine that gets cranked out like a gumball both in the morning and at night after the election. Those hidden pieces of paper have all the voting numbers supposedly imprinted on them by a roller-and-ink designed to keep the precinct workers from actually seeing-with-their-own-eyes the 0-0-0's in the morning and the final tallies at night.

Sequoia-Pacific refused to tell us which counties used the Printomatic but indicated there were more than the 8 percent needed to fulfill the WABC-News Election Services's predictions.

That presents the possibility that NES, which supplies WABC-TV with its predicted vote totals, can actually know the results from those Printomatic-counties several days before the election even takes place. Clearly the Printomatic is not used to protect the voters, it is used to hoodwink them. Indeed, the voters have lost their constitutional right to personally view those machine numbers. Any election supervisor who defends the use of the Printomatic should be closely watched.

But, we never got around to sharing that information on WBAI that night. Fueled by Burnham, the two hosts were determined to expose us as right wing radicals. They kept repeating that selling articles to the *Spotlight* was proof of it.

Our editor, Phyllis Vernick, was in the "green room" growing increasingly frustrated as she listened to Jim countering "conspiracy-theorist" attacks for the first 40-minutes of the hour.

"I couldn't stand it anymore," she said. "I suddenly found myself walking down that hall; I saw my hand reaching out and opening that studio door and I heard myself saying 'This is total garbage!.'"

She shocked the two amateur hosts into stunned silence for the entire length of her entrance speech; telling them how they were wasting precious air time with phoney posturing, snide comments, and since they had been given the *Votescam* book in the first place, it was pretty obvious by their limited questions that they hadn't done their homework. She then suggested to Jim they leave the two nerds and go get a corn beef sandwich.

On the way home Jim proposed marriage.

*   *   *   *   *   *   *

To be forewarned is to be forearmed. So we sent letters to New York Governor, Mario Cuomo, and to Jerry Brown, strongly suggesting the possibility they were entering contests they were unable to win. Worst yet, contests that might discourage them from ever running again. Governor Cuomo was repeatedly telephoned for a meeting. We then tried to approach him through his right-hand man, his son Andrew. We inundated both of them with materials on vote fraud. The refusals for meetings came through their front offices. Cuomo, however, did not run for the Presidency.

This man does not deserve to be a Supreme Court Justice. In "legalese" he has guilty knowledge of crimes that go to the birthright of the American public. Moreover, since it is our constitutional right to know every facet of how our vote is counted, and Governor Cuomo refused to defend (i.e. investigate) that right, it should prevent him from becoming a constitutional justice. However, just as in the Scalia case, this guilty knowledge just might translate into leverage; leverage that will guarantee a lifetime post on the court.

* * * * * * *.

As for Jerry Brown, his press secretary, Eli Mellor, telephoned us from California after reading the Vankin book. He felt that vote fraud would be a strong issue for Brown's campaign. Mellor spent weeks trying to convince Brown to meet with us. Finally, when Brown was in Boston, a short ride from New York City, Mellor called him and pushed hard for that meeting. Coincidentally or not, the next day he was fired. Nobody at Brown headquarters had any idea of his whereabouts. Today, in retrospect, Mellor probably smiles at his naivete in thinking Brown had the balls to expose vote fraud.

Picasso's goat he ain't.

* * * * * * *

Finally, we wrote H. Ross Perot. We even had his New York, New Jersey, Washington, D.C. and State of Virginia offices upset and indignant enough to fax him the following letter. We enforced their efforts with faxes and phone calls of our own. The little giant ignored all of us. His Richmond staff even contacted the local CBS television affiliate and demanded that a reporter see the letter. They hoped that he might be a stronger channel to Perot. A local reporter was rushed out at midnight to investigate.

According to the Richmond staff, the reporter seemed legitimately shocked at the letter's portent. He promised to call the Colliers in New York as soon as he returned to the station. He never did. For days we left messages for him, but he wouldn't return any of the calls, ours or from Perot's people. Perot also remained ominously silent. All this left his troops in New York, New Jersey, Washington and Virginia suspecting Perot's sincerity. It left us suspecting the ultimate game player just might use his guilty knowledge as a move on the political chess board.

After all, in politics, knowledge is power.

OPEN LETTER TO ROSS PEROT

by James M. Collier

June 10, 1992

Ross Perot
6606 LBJ Freeway
Suite 150
Dallas, Texas, 75240

Dear Mr. Perot,

I am an investigative reporter who has spent the past 22 years studying how the vote is counted in these United States. It is with that background that I can assure you the Presidency of this country; all you have to do is read the enclosed material and follow my instructions.

The 287-page manuscript you have there titled "VOTESCAM: The Stealing of America" is presently being circulated to all major publishers by my New York bulldog of an agent. I strongly suggest you read it first and when you finish you'll understand why an epilogue is definitely needed. That epilogue will consist of a chronicle of events that took place after we sent the manuscript to various people who could be helpful in exposing its contents to the American public.

With that predicate laid, I shall explain the

simple steps a billionaire may take to gain the crown. After all, others may have used this method before you, and if you are not aware of the current state-of-the-art in vote fraud this letter will surely be an eye-opener.

1.) You contact a shadowy group of computer firms that work the nation like a grid. These firms, without public knowledge or public bid, are paid millions of dollars to quietly go into cities on election night and count the vote. The elected Election Chief simply steps aside for these firms and allows them to entirely program and count-control the vote.

In Titusville, Florida, the Election Chief lives in a $750,000 house. She earns approximately $66,000 a year before taxes. Before she became Election Chief she was not a rich woman. She hired Fidlar and Chambers of Moline, Ill., and they do all the work for her. She just sits back and watches. The public knows none of this, of course, as the local papers refuse to print a word. F&D gets paid more than $100,000 per election and they use their own modems and programs. Interestingly, F&D controls most of the south and the midwest.

In California, a group called DFM creates the software and counts the vote for two-thirds or more of the state.

So, simply call F&D President Ralph Anderson up there in Moline, offer him something he can't refuse, and he can make you President...for two terms. Isn't that simple? You understand why the media is reluctant to expose this story. They get all that political advertising vigorish every couple of years, plus they control their local areas in so many other lucrative ways, why in the world would they want to kill the golden goose?

James Squires, your media chief, must look into this immediately. Just direct him to a source such as Fidlar and Chambers and you can save a fortune in advertising dollars.

2.) Wherever you find the Printomatic device used in the back of the lever style voting machines you can be pretty sure the elections are rigged for the highest bidder. You see, the Printomatic device is a piece of paper that is slipped over the vote counters so that those irritating (and often ethical) precinct workers can't see the numbers. A handle is cranked and a piece of paper slides out of a slot in the back of the machine, much like a gumball setup, and voila!…all the zeroes are printed there in the morning before the polls open. Over the years I've reported on how the precinct worker is weeded out so that only those who don't find this clever little gimmick an affront to democracy will get hired. Those who complain that the numbers are cranked out again at night, with no eyeball varification of what exactly went on in the back of those machines, have their poll-working careers cut short by the Election Chief. The local press gets its advertising vigorish and no story is ever printed alerting the public to this obvious disenfranchisement of the voters.

You just drop a few big bucks on those Election Chiefs around this country and you'll have that Washington patina in a flash. It's a national rite of the well-heeled and well-connected.

In the past 22 years I have been on radio shows from Miami to San Francisco. People have called me (referrals) to come into their town and check out their election systems. In Cincinnati we video taped the League of Women Voters using tweezers to alter the vote. That video was shown on channel 9 there in 1985 and the Election Chief quit the next day.

In Miami 1982, we video taped the LWV using officially-issued pencils to poke holes (unsupervised) in the vote card. We were dragged out of the counting room and threatened with arrest for that action.

Miami attorney, Ellis Rubin, recently sent our manuscript to the U.S. Attorney General and asked him to call for a public investigation. But this Justice Department remains so corrupt that last week it announced its latest refusal to act. As for the Miami tape — Pat Robertson bought it for $2,500. He even aired it on his show in 1987. David Burnham of the New York *Times* was on the same show and joined Robertson in decrying such deplorable acts. Burnham soon made his exit from the *Times* and Robertson ran for the Presidency.

Robertson didn't win, but he didn't crusade against vote fraud either. He did, however, buy

United Press International and he is now one of
the six members of the board of News Election
Services (NES). That means he is now a charter
member of the cartel that counts — and very
possibly controls — the American vote.

3.) How much do you know about NES? If
you know a lot, then you're in a wonderful
position to blackmail them. You see, NES was
created in 1964, just after JFK was killed, and
they have the exclusive franchise (from
Congress) to count the vote in every state.
Without a single actual vote being counted, they
proclaim the Presidency within minutes of the
polls closing. You must understand that the
networks don't really compete for vote totals
anymore. The LWV supplies them all from the
field and the pool uses the same numbers.
Those pretty boys, Rather, Brokaw and Jennings
get to sit there and pretend it's all earnest
competition.

Just in case you don't know what the hell I'm
talking about - NES is an AP, UPI, CBS, NBC,
ABC and CNN pool. It has a button it can push
up in a building on 34th St. in New York that
can literally change votes at will in every county
in America which counts the computer vote at a
central spot. Those counties make up about 60
percent of the nation. Their sister group Voter
Research and Survey (VRS) is the official exit
pollster. On election night, NES proclaims the
Presidency just minutes after the polls close,
while VRS proclaims the Presidency even before

the polls close. Both are 90% staffed by members of the League of Women Voters. Their numbers are always correct, before and after the polls close. Now that's state-of-the-art.

Down in Miami, the computer programmer for the elections division, ex-CIA man Joe Malone, is partners in an outside vote prognosticating business with the vote prognosticator for Spanish International Network-TV, John Lasseville. We're talking about 20 million Spanish-language voters nationwide. Joe Malone and John Lasseville know the vote totals before dawn on election day.

Lasseville is famous for going on the air at dawn and predicting exact final vote totals. He is always right on the money. The Cubans down in Miami get a big kick out of that. Imagine if Fidel had that luxury! Therefore:

5.) To win Dade County, simply contact Election Supervisor David Leahy and have a talk at Wolfies.

6.) The networks are understandably reluctant to expose their position of power; they can change those computer votes with a push of a button from New York.

Now, Mr. Perot, you are a computer man. Why not declare war on them all? You just get the access codes to those county computers and hack in yourself. You punch in numbers, and they'll punch in numbers and you'll counter. . . what a night! For the first time since 1964 the numbers will change on television. (They never change now, you know. They remain steady from closing gun until Rather crowns the king.)

Through Ted Turner's bureau chief in Washington, I contacted Ed Turner who runs the CNN network, and was told by E. T. himself that he would not touch this story under any circumstance. He's just one of the role models I can offer you in going for the gold.

7.) Anyway, call Bob Flaherty at News Election Services (NES) in New York. He heads the counting pool. Your options are either to pay a modest chunk of your billions, or just promise that you too will keep all this quiet if he'll push the right buttons. Chances are excellent that George Bush did it. Meditate a moment on how Ronnie actually got that landslide. Then, when you are President, make sure that the Justice Department (Craig C. DonSanto, attorney-in-charge of prosecuting vote fraud) continues to remain well protected, never having to bother with meddlesome vote-fraud investigations, and you are a free man. Pick your Attorney General well, of course. An honest Attorney General could cost you plenty.

Well, I hope I've been of some help to you. Surely, if you don't fight fire with fire you'll get burned. If by nature, your outrage has been sparked by this information, and if you can show true Presidential timber by calling for a full public investigation of the vote even before you're elected, then we will have helped each other.

Jerry Brown and Mario Cuomo were both contacted by us and both studiously refused to acknowledge this information. Coincidentally or not, Jerry Brown fired his media advisor Eli Mellor soon after Mellor read the Votescam chapter in Jonathan Vankin's book "Conspiracies, Crimes & Coverups" and became persistent in asking Brown to take steps.

This letter will appear in the final chapter of "VOTESCAM, The Stealing of America." We hope to include your reply.

Sincerely,

James M. Collier

P.S. Don't miss the chapter on Supreme Court Justice Antonin Scalia.

He was so responsive when the Republican National Committee asked his help in squashing a vote-fraud investigation, that he was given his position on the court.

Also, after you become President, don't forget to continue our great tradition of encouraging developing nations to adopt the computer method of vote counting, so that the United States will be able to control international elections from the White House. Forget India and Israel because they stubbornly insist on paper ballots, but controlling a host of other country's votes could cut the CIA budget in half while promoting democracy.

19

CAN'T YOU HEAR THE WHISTLE BLOWIN'?

*"You don't need a weather man to
know which way the wind blows."*
                                    - Bob Dylan

March Thirteen
Blizzard of '93
Manhattan

By James M. Collier

The storm rages outside. Hurricane winds.
Heavy snow. Freezing rain. I sit here, staring out
the window at the winter whiteout, thinking of
warmer times. Normally I can see the Statue of
Liberty down there in New York Harbor; giant

ships steaming up the Hudson, while at night, when the city glows, there is a wall of lights that is the World Trade Center.

Phyllis and I are still tanned from our recent honeymoon.

For two weeks we played in a tropical blue-green ocean and wondered how to handle the back page of this book. At first the petition you see was intended for Attorney General Zoe Baird. Unfortunately, she didn't pay her nanny taxes so we had to scratch her name and replace it with Kimba Wood. Then, the announcement came that Judge Wood had a nanny problem, too. It was turning into a bloody virus. So we called the printer and told him to delete Kimba Wood's name and just let it read "send this petition to the Attorney General."

However, there is a strange syndrome at work here. In fact, it's uncanny how that syndrome weaves a consistent path throughout this book. It's the journalistic equivalent of *coitus interruptus*. Just as we get to breathing heavily in anticipation of vote fraud being exposed, that apocalyptic orgasm keeps slipping away.

Remember how we were sure that we finally had the Dade County Elections Department cornered with overwhelming evidence of massive vote fraud back in 1974? That's when Rubin first confronted Assistant State Attorney Janet Reno with that blank-backed canvass sheet scam.

Rubin presented the bogus sheets to Reno in a closed door session and then emerged from her office to a battery of television cameras. But instead of proudly announcing an investigation, he repeated a Reno-concocted lie to the media:

"Ms. Reno told me to tell you that the statute of limitations has run out on the crime."

We don't know what words Reno used to intimidate him so completely, but whatever she said, it was enough to make Rubin bolt from the building as though the devil herself was on his tail.

But significantly, she admitted that a crime had, indeed, been committed. Why then didn't she investigate the Elections Department and clean out that nest of rats? Is it because such an inquiry would not have fit the agenda of the Miami *Herald*? After all, the Miami media which turned out in full force for the press conference, let the story hang after Rubin's desperate flight. They protected Reno and she went on to win five landslide victories as State Attorney. In turn, she protected the Elections Department from any criminal prosecution.

So imagine my surprise when I read a report by Jay Maeder in the New York *Daily News* that Janet Reno was nominated to become the next Attorney General of the United States.

"Do you want to hear something totally insane?" I asked Phyllis.

"Always," she smiled.

"It's come full-circle again…they're going to

make Janet Reno Attorney General!"

How mystical. How strange. The players never get off the stage. There was Janet...I mean, I worked with her mother and father 34-years ago. I was a cub reporter for the Miami *News*, while her father, Hank, was the legendary police reporter for the *Herald*. Hank taught me how to investigate a story as he and I shared the police beat on the nightside...and now there she was, waiting in the political wings, poised to make a grand entrance, gawky and smiling and pre-programmed to win.

"Ellis," I wailed into the phone, "What do you make of it?"

Rubin couldn't stop chuckling. "It's great," he said. "You'll sell a million books."

"Don't you think I should try to stop her before she gets there?"

"No," he said, laughing now. "Let her get all the way to Washington and then force her to look into how the vote is counted in this country. You may have her trapped. In any case, you'll be able to chase her for at least four years."

"Will you back me up if I do something?"

Rubin said he was in no mood to attack Reno. As a matter of fact, her departure opened the way for him to run for her vacated post as Dade County State Attorney. "My phone hasn't stopped ringing. People want me to run again."

But I needed him to make a federal case out of Reno's nomination.

And only Rubin had the clout with the press

to guarantee major coverage.

"Ellis, will you at least hold one last press conference?"

"No way. I'll corroborate if the press calls, but I'm not publicly going up against her."

Damn. *Coitus interruptus,* again.

Over the next two weeks the press did call him, asking about our charges. Rubin was true to his word: he told reporters that what Collier said was correct, but he didn't want to get involved. The press didn't pursue him any further, or Reno, either, for that matter.

It's interesting to speculate how Rubin could have changed the course of history if only he'd have stood up on his hind legs and brayed at the moon, but instead, he ducked by saying that Reno was investigating an indiscretion someone in his office had committed and he couldn't risk his career by angering her.

"I'm 67, Jim," he pleaded. "I don't need this."

The end of our twenty year relationship slipped quietly into the mud as I promised I wouldn't reveal the specifics of the investigation against him.

Phyllis thought that Votescam was a strong enough indictment against Reno to stop her nomination. She was sure that once the newspapers were informed, they would make it a major story.

"After all," she reasoned, "Look what they did with Nannygate. I think your evidence against

Janet Reno is a lot more important, don't you?"

I did, but twenty years worth of battle scars trying to get the press to inform the public about vote fraud made me less optimistic.

"Just call Jay Maeder at the *Daily News*," Phyllis urged. He was the reporter who did the story we read about Reno. "See if he'll investigate."

I did telephone Jay Maeder. He wanted the *Votescam* galleys brought over immediately.

Phyllis beamed. "The press said the next nominee will have to be purer than Caesar's wife. Just wait till they hear about Reno!"

Maeder had sounded enthusiastic over the phone, but when I handed him the galleys the next day he was noticeably subdued. I could sense that something was wrong. He didn't want to talk, or even ask a few pertinent questions; he demurred by saying the national desk would handle the story, but they never did. I called Maeder some weeks later, however, and found him friendly again. "I want to keep the book," he said. "Things could happen, you never know. I was out of the loop that made the decision not to do a story on Reno. The Washington bureau made that decision…but let me keep the book."

You never know.

We then called the *Wall Street Journal* in Washington and spoke to Joe Davidson. He was an astute reporter, asking a lot of good questions and requesting the galleys be sent to him that afternoon. The next day, before he even got the package, his voice turned cold on the phone.

"I've got lots of other stories to do," he said. "I don't know if I'll get to yours."

It appeared that someone was protecting Reno. Could that CIA media desk — that Mark Lane exposed — be working overtime? A healthy paranoia or fact?

Next we decided that Ted Koppel had one of the few honest images in television news. We spoke with his people at *Nightline* and made arrangements to meet one of their producers in Washington. The same arrangements were made with CNN's Larry King Show.

The next day Phyllis and I drove down I-95 to the nation's capitol. In just a few weeks this city would erupt with white and pink cherry blossoms, but on this day it was bleak, windy and harsh.

We parked in the public garage at the National Train Station, walked through the station's plush shopping mall, and up Capitol Hill to the Senate Office Buildings. Before we left New York we had arranged a meeting with the Judiciary Committee's majority counsel, Guy Moluk, who worked out of Senator Joseph Biden's office. It was his job to screen people who brought complaints against Janet Reno.

The meeting with Moluk was in the afternoon, so we spent the morning dropping off galleys to the press.

Our first stop was to Helen Thomas, the famous "mouth that roars" for UPI. The *grande dame* of Washington journalism works out of the White House Press Office. We left her the galleys, as she had requested, at her P.O. Box at UPI headquarters on 14th and I Street. The bureau chief of UPI also assigned the story to a reporter named Greg Henderson.

Henderson was confused over the telephone.

"I don't know why he gave me the story, I'm a Supreme Court reporter."

We suggested that his UPI boss thought our charges against Reno might be important enough to grab his interest. Henderson finally promised to read the material if and when it ever reached him. He made UPI's mail channels sound just a little slower than Pony Express.

Some days later he said that he "still hadn't gotten over to his mailbox." The day after that he wouldn't get on the phone.

Helen Thomas at least answered her phone but said she was "just too busy to handle it," then added, "I haven't even seen the galleys because I never go to my post office box at 14th Street anymore."

Nina Tottenberg of National Public Radio, who broke the Anita Hill, Clarence Thomas story, received material from us. However, without a pubic hair on a coke bottle, our story just didn't catch her attention. She never acknowledged it.

My new wife, who was an ardent feminist, was becoming more disillusioned by the minute. She had already torn up her NOW card in frustration after trying to convince their Washington office that vote fraud existed. Her view of reality was quickly being altered.

Associated Press assigned a Justice Department reporter, Carolyn Skorneck, to the story. We met her at the heavily fortified 10th and Constitution entrance of Justice. She took the material but evidenced little more than an air of boredom. The next day she indicated over the telephone that it was a non-story.

We were getting nowhere a lot faster than we hoped to arrive.

Back to two o'clock in Guy Moluk's office. He took notes on Reno's crimes:

1. Wouldn't investigate the canvass sheet forgeries.
2. Wouldn't investigate the blank-backed canvass sheets.
3. Wouldn't investigate the Printomatic scam.
4. Wouldn't investigate the League of Women Voters in 1982 punching holes in the vote.
5. Wouldn't investigate the 1982 video tape proof showing BMX counters were not running at the height of the election.

6. Wouldn't investigate the ballots that were being printed by the candidate for Opa Locka mayor in his own print shop — instead, she had me arrested for grand theft.

I assured Moluk that this was a hell of a lot more important than Nannygate; that it was imperative I testify against Reno at her confirmation hearings. He said to write Senator Biden a letter requesting permission but that he didn't think anyone was going to be allowed to testify.

To make sure that the Republicans had ammunition at the hearings, we had a meeting with counsel Jerry Petty in minority chairman Orrin Hatch's office. Jerry was a young man with a smile that promised a future for our cause. But it was to be the last time we ever spoke to him. He and Moluk both refused to get on the phone after those initial meetings

John Ebinger, producer for Ted Koppel's *Nightline* met us in the lobby of ABC-TV ready to grab the material and run. We feigned having only one copy of the FBI report in order to buy time while he was forced to make more. We wanted that time to convince him of the story's importance. So he impatiently took us upstairs to the city room while Phyllis made small talk and discovered who the genius was who choreographed Ted Koppel's hair.

When it was time to say good-bye, Ebinger hedged:

"If we decide to do nothing about this you won't write about giving us the material. A gentleman's agreement, alright?"

"Well…" It was a sticky moment.

"You mean," Phyllis asked smiling brightly, "so that you won't have what's referred to as "guilty knowledge" once this story breaks and you've done nothing about it?"

Ebinger couldn't believe she just said that.

"Well. yeah, I guess that's right," he swallowed.

"Sorry," she said, "but since I'm no gentleman, I'm afraid that I can't agree to that."

The next day Ebinger was openly hostile over the telephone.

"I showed it to people here," he said, then spat, "you haven't gotten this story recognized in a decade and they were not interested."

It was the old party line.

"Who have you shown it to? Did you show it to Tim O'Brien? He saw the video tape. Or Ed Fouhy of Arrowsmith?"

But it was no use. I threatened that we were definitely going to write that Koppel saw the material, but it was like trying to intimidate a man with an Uzi.

"Koppel didn't see it," he said.

"Then I'm going to write him that his staff is doing him a great disservice."

"Well, actually, he did see it."

"Which is it, John?"

"Look, nobody cares about your story," his voice rose. "Pedal it somewhere else."

He slammed the phone down.

We had one arrow left in our quiver and that was the Washington *Times* — the wannabe competitor of the Washington *Post.* Jerry Seeper is their top investigative reporter, and Seeper was also well aware of the *Votescam* charges. Back in 1986 we had given him a copy of the entire *Votescam* file. That year he sat in his downtown office in the National Press Building for three straight hours reading that file. He was fascinated. Then he turned out a major story and handed it over to the city desk where city editor John Wilson killed it.

This time Phyllis and I sat across from Seeper and reporter Mike Hedges in the basement cafeteria of the *Times*. Seeper told us that Wilson was no longer there. He assured us that he believed in the story and that now he and Hedges would have a clear shot at the editors.

We gave him the galleys and went to dinner feeling elated.

"I think we finally got a breakthrough," I told Phyllis as we sat in a little Italian restaurant in Georgetown.

She raised her wine glass. "Here's to the nick of time."

But within a week Seeper told us that the

editors wouldn't write a story about Reno.

Coitus rigor mortis.

It was now a Friday. Reno had been the Attorney General nominee for a week, but not a single disparaging word had been written by any of the national press.

The Larry King Show did call Rubin in Miami and heard that he would verify everything we said, but that he would not go on television. Their interest evaporated.

Evans and Novak mentioned in one syndicated column that there were some people in Miami trying to testify against Reno. *The Village Voice* reported the same. They both said that Reno's record showed that she was soft on prosecuting white-collar crime.

From there on, press silence.

Our next stop was the FBI.

The agent in charge of background investigations was James Mann. We drove to his headquarters at Tyson's Corners, a suburb of Washington located on the beltway.

We had requested a stenographer so that our statement could be signed into the FBI file we had been building for 23 years. But Mann and two assistants refused to allow us past the FBI anteroom.

Mann assured us that "nobody has ordered any investigation of Reno to this point."

"But she's supposed to be undergoing a

thorough background check, according to the media." Phyllis told him.

"I would know if something was going on, and *nothing* is."

We asked him to accept the *Votescam* galleys and to start an immediate inquiry into our charges of Reno's obstruction of justice. Mann, a six-footer with a healthy girth, took one look at the cover of *Votescam* and dropped it like a hot griddle.

"I don't want this," he protested.

I then insisted that he was in charge of investigations and that we wanted our charges against Reno investigated. I picked up the galleys from the anteroom coffee table — Mann's eyes still fixed on the full color CIA eagle on the cover — and I held it out to him.

"Where do you live?" he asked, his eyes magnified behind thick glasses.

"Before we give any information, we want to make a written statement...we want a stenographer. We want to sign it."

"You can't," he shook his head. "No steno."

"Then I don't have to answer your questions," I informed him. "I'll just leave this book and you can do the right thing."

"I want to know where you live," Mann demanded.

I showed him my Florida drivers license but told him "I live right here in Washington." I gave him a local address.

"Well, why can't you take this to the FBI in

Miami?" he persisted. It seems his purpose was to have us take the galleys to any other field office, he just didn't want to get involved. The Clinton administration hadn't asked for a background check on Reno and he wasn't happy about being pressured into one by us.

The address volley ball went back and forth until he eventually signed for the galleys.

The following Monday, ten days after Reno was nominated, the FBI started a limited investigation, but we were never contacted. Just the usual silence, oozing like an obscuring fog from the major media.

Our last stop was Pete Hamill, the streetwise columnist for the New York *Post*, the oldest newspaper in America. Hamill had just recently been named editor of the *Post* by the latest entrepreneur trying to buy the bankrupt tabloid.

"I was speaking to my man in Washington yesterday," Hamill said. "We were talking about Reno, get your stuff over here."

Well, a week later his assistant Anna, said Pete wasn't doing any stories until the paper was finally sold to someone, anyone, it was up to a judge.

The New York *Times* said that the original entrepreneur trying to bail out the *Post* was bankrupt himself and yet another suitor, a former Miami Beach city commissioner and real estate tycoon, was finally awarded the right to save the tabloid. The latest owner,

Abe Hirschfeld, gave Hamill until midnight to get off the property. Hirschfeld then announced that he wanted to fashion the paper after the Oprah Winfrey Show and that when he died he would become God. The staff went into apoplexy.

Always one to call a spade a spade, Hamill called Hirschfeld a nut and refused to leave. Supported by the entire staff, who hated Hirschfeld with a vengeance, Hamill continued to edit the paper without pay. It was the stuff that front pages are made of, and the *Post* sold every issue it printed denouncing the new owner. Hirschfeld obtained a contempt of court order against Hamill and ordered him off the property under threat of arrest.

As of this printing, Hamill has been hailed as a hero by almost all the media for his mutiny on that sinking ship. But a bankruptcy judge has sustained Hirschfeld's right to keep his rebellious paper, and the whole town is waiting for the next edition.

Meanwhile, the day that Reno was to testify before the Judiciary Committee, Phyllis and I went back to Washington in one last attempt to be heard. We had a meeting scheduled with Dave Hoppe, top aide to Senator Trent Lott, whom the Republicans had designated as the pointman to collect information for any possible attack on Reno.

The meeting was again scheduled for two o'clock so we spent the morning walking some thirty floors of the three Senate Office Buildings, handing out a 10-page press kit to all 100 Senate offices. It contained a Miami *News* article about Reno's refusal to investigate, FBI reports and a partial transcript of a two-hour radio program

I had done the radio interview by phone a few days earlier on WHO in Des Moines, Iowa. It was the Jan Mickelson Show. You may remember that we first did his morning talk show on WCKY in Cincinnati in 1985, the day after we video taped the League of Women Voters using tweezers to pluck out new votes in the computer ballot cards. Mickelson was one man who knew for sure that we were right about vote fraud in America because he witnessed the resignation of the Cincinnati elections supervisor, Elvera Radford, after we charged her with election rigging on his program.

"If I hadn't actually seen some of this stuff myself," he told his WHO listening audience, "I'd have given Collier a dial tone ten minutes ago."

Anyway, we were praying that even if the Judiciary Committee approved the Reno nomination, the entire Senate might have time to read our press kit and perhaps start some counter-debate. After all, we still had the customary seven days left before the final full-Senate vote and anything could happen.

Then, before the meeting at Dave Hoppe's office, we went to the Executive Office Building next to the White House and managed to receive a guarantee from President Clinton's press aide, Nancy Ward, that she would personally get our book and material to the President. An accompanying letter said in part:

"Mr. President, if the Committee has assured you that the FBI has found Janet Reno "clean" — then calculated ineptness has taken place or you were not told the truth."

The letter urged him to ask for the FBI files which were hidden under a national security lid. It would be less of an embarrassment, we urged, if he immediately dropped Reno, instead of trying to explain why he ignored the evidence against her until after our book came out.

Hoppe was late for our meeting so we watched the hearings on C-SPAN in his office. Joe Biden was being his unctuous, self-satisfied self, drooling over Reno and asking her Pablum-loaded questions. He told the television viewing audience that a radio show in New York was saying the Committee had failed to investigate charges against Reno and was keeping secrets under wraps. However, Biden assured everyone that was absolutely false. He said they had looked into every allegation against Reno, although, he admitted, some charges had been so outrageous that it had been downright embarrassing to investigate them.

"There has been no credible evidence related to the truly bizarre allegations that have come forward." he said.

He told viewers that any written allegations against Ms. Reno would be available to the public.

Of course, Senator Biden knew that people across the country wouldn't be flocking to Washington to read that testimony. Americans felt confident that their government was presenting them with all the vital facts. If there were no witnesses present to testify against Reno, why then, there must not be anything really damaging against her. Why should they think differently?

The papers later called the Committee questioning a "lovefest."

I couldn't stand Biden's grinning face, so I telephoned Nancy Ward at the White House press office.

"Did the President get the *Votescam* galleys?"

"Your material is being screened by someone first," she said.

"Who?"

"I can't tell you."

I pushed. "Who is it? This isn't Russia, Nancy, why can't I know what channels our book has to take to get to the President?"

Her voice was now exaggerated like a flashing neon sign.

"It's someone who has access to him." She drew out her sentence. "Some-one-who-sees-him-every-day…"

Later when I told Phyllis the conversation, she asked:

"Hillary??"

I never heard a word from the President.

By three o'clock Hoppe appeared. He had spent the afternoon with the Republicans. None of them, he told us, was willing to challenge the President.

"They haven't had any leadership since they lost the White House," he explained. "They don't know how to fight, they're a minority without a president."

Phyllis, who was new to this game, sincerely asked him all the right questions. Yes, Hoppe said, he knew that our charges were not frivolous. No, there was nothing more he could do but ask Trent again to speak to the senators.

I sat there silently staring out the window at the winter day. My brain had slowed to a dull drone and I suddenly felt exhausted. I'd been here too many times before.

I stood up and said to Hoppe, "I know a railroad train when I hear one."

A look of empathy, understanding and disgust somehow managed to merge in one quick flash across his face

"Yeah," he said. "I've heard a few whistles myself."

The next day, Wednesday, the Committee dropped the normal one week waiting period for the full senate vote and within 24-hours confirmed Reno 98-0.

One paper commented on "Janet Reno's dubious victory." Another dedicated an editorial to wondering if she would be her own person in Justice or the administrations' puppet. But whatever doubts they finally expressed; it was too little, too late.

Janet Reno is now Attorney General of the United States. We end this book with the following request of every reader. Don't wait for her to live up to the office. — force her to do the right thing.

The petition in the back of this book has the U.S. Attorney General's name on it and we want you to send it to Janet Reno.

If she investigates Justice Department attorneys Craig C. Donsanto and John C. Keeney for their part in vote fraud. . .

If she investigates how the vote is counted, not only in Dade County, but across America…

If she gets the national security seal taken off the 37 missing pages from our FOIA file; the pages which would prove the 1970-72 television elections were fixed and the canvass sheets forged. (That, of course, would cost Katharine Graham her WPLG television license…)

Only then can Janet Reno finally answer this book's allegations and redeem herself.

Well, that's finally that.

What have we learned since that first Dell Publishing contract we so naively obtained almost a quarter century ago?

We now understand why things have gone so

terribly wrong in this country. It is due to the corrupted vote. It is the stolen vote that perpetuates corrupt city, state and federal governments. When those corrupt power brokers in your town weed out that up-and-coming politician, they are looking for a person who is willing to "play ball".

Politics is "playing ball."

Suddenly you find property decisions going against nature; land and water needed for the perpetuation of life on our earth, suddenly disappear. A handful of developers get richer while the land, and the quality of life, gets poorer.

But those paid-off officials need judges to further their ambitions. Judges are either elected or they are appointed by elected officials. Judges make the final decisions on property. They also rule on probate; they can steal yours or your children's inheritance. Often, corrupt attorneys, working with corrupt judges, become the beneficiaries of your life's work, not your heirs.

In the same way, jobs evaporate, money inflates or deflates based on some political vote. You try to stop what you perceive as insanity by "voting the bastards out."

But when they get reelected, and reelected, the press tells you that it was your fault ..."you voted for them..."

You know that you didn't.

Who did?

April, 2000

As of this writing, Votescam is entering its third printing.

Since its publication eight years ago, the major bookstores have banned its display, it has been removed from the index of the Library of Congress, and falsely rumored to be out of print. What Votescam has *not* been is refuted, discredited, or for that matter, denied. In fact, it has been read by well over 30,000 people who continue to circulate the book by word of mouth. It is, without a doubt, one of the most dangerous and important books still in circulation in America.

As usual, the silence on the part of the accused is deafening. To ignore this book is their only line of defense, and an effective one at that, when coupled with a total Media blackout. For the record, there has also been no Federal investigation into the charges of vote fraud brought forth in Votescam, or into the evidence of vote fraud currently being compiled by citizens.

But after you read "Votescam," this will not surprise you.

My father, James Collier, and my uncle, Kenneth Collier, were America's lead investigators into vote fraud for twenty five years.

No longer. They have both died, leaving all of us with the legacy of this book, and the questions raised by their unfinished investigation.

Most Americans are at least partially aware of the myriad of ways our elections system is currently corrupted; from the obvious inequities of campaign financing, to jerrymandering, minority intimidation at the polls, absentee ballot fraud and the numerous twist and turns on the path where a ballot can be ambushed in secret. And certainly none of us are blind to the spectacle of bald-faced election-year lying, now standard strategy for the successful Establishment politician. It seems that nothing has rendered the competition for public office more meaningless than the candidates themselves.

The tawdry parade of an American election is fast becoming tiresome to most of us, with its worn-out floats, plastic candidates, and hollow patriotism. But we follow it anyway, because its the only parade in town which ends at the threshold of the voting booth.

The fact that we can do this one thing—cast a vote—is, for better or worse, what keeps this entire country from exploding into chaos. This single act defines our politics, whether we show up to do it or not, and many of us don't anymore. Just the fact that it is allowed, even encouraged, is enough to soothe us, assuage us, and convince us that indeed this is a Democracy. It also assures us that all mistakes made in Washington are really our own, and can be traced back to We the People. That keeps the brewing frustration and anger safely on the streets and in the homes, where the government wants it.

But of course, this is not a Democracy. And we know that, even if some of us only sense it intuitively. When we rest our eyes upon Washington, we all feel a little sick. We all feel the need to turn away. It's why so many of us don't vote anymore, even though they're begging us to. We might not know why, exactly, but we feel that it just doesn't matter whether we vote or not. And of course, this is true.

Let's take a lesson from Stalin who said, "Those who cast the vote decide nothing, those who count the vote decide everything."
Who counts your vote?

Democrat, Republican, Third Party, Green Party—it doesn't matter. Once the vote is cast, it is delivered, untraceable, into the hands of the faceless corporations running America's complex political machine. Whatever corruption takes place after that is better concealed than the voters themselves behind their curtains.

The questions that Votescam asks begin there.

Why was control of the national American vote abdicated by the Senate and secretly transferred to a little known private company? Why are American citizens denied key information on how their vote is counted? Is there an answer that might absolve of wrongdoing all who have played a part in this transfer of power? Or is Votescam's premise really true, and the entire electoral process in this country is no more than a charade, a tired script written and performed only by people with varying levels of criminal complicity?

We can assume that not every person involved in politics, especially at the lower levels, understands the extent to which our vote is corrupted. The mechanics of the electoral process differ from state to state and often appear to be deliberately confusing. Many of the people employed by the system are likely ignorant as to how it's *supposed* to work, let alone how it's manipulated, and by whom.

But, as Votescam illustrates, complicity can be found in unlikely places. The villains are not always lurking in the alley, often they're smiling at you from a respectable desk. Nor is complicity always sinister. It doesn't take a psychologist to understand how easy it is to motivate someone to rig a high-stake game, given the opportunity. Especially if they've convinced themselves it's in everyone's best interest. Particularly their own.

So, the significant question remains: Who knows what, and when did they know it? Who *exactly* , within the vast elections complex, are the culpable individuals? Who can explain what has been done to our system? Who must be brought to justice?

As Jim and Ken discovered, we can count on the Establishment Media to never, ever ask those questions.

That leaves it up to us, the tax paying citizens of America. Who among us will do it? Who is courageous enough? Who cares enough? Whose sense of justice is so deeply ingrained that they won't hesitate to stand up and demand honesty from their own government, their own people?

It's not so easy. We're tired, we're busy, and we're scared. We're afraid of our government. We feel powerless, and with good reason. But most of all, we don't want to be called crazy.

Jim and Ken weren't immune to any of this. They were scared, and they were vilified, and sometimes they lost hope. And sometimes they lost more than that.

In 1988 Ken was already nearly paralyzed with cancer. His wife had left him, taken their daughter, and moved to Australia to escape the trauma and danger of his political crusade. But the crusade had reaped no rewards. The vote fraud investigation had led him only deeper into Washington's dark labyrinth, a lonely, thankless journey, apparently leading nowhere.

He had already lost his family to his cause, and it looked like the cause was lost, too. Dozens of boxes filled his room. They were stuffed full of government files, bureaucratic memo's, court documents, newspaper articles—twenty years worth of investigation, desperation, and betrayal—all he and Jim had left.

Ken was deep in depression, and he knew he was dying. Often it was hard to tell if he was paralyzed by the disease or the despair. It was a deep, black pit.

Jim nursed him, swearing to him that it wasn't over. There was still one more move to make— the book, Votescam, had to be written. Jim stared deep into his brothers eyes and warned him, with no mercy, that unless he completed this one final task, he would die with nothing. He would never be vindicated in this life.

The investigation, the sacrifices, the past twenty years, would amount to a total loss, and the boys in the White House wouldn't even bother to laugh last.

Jim wanted to write the book. For him, the fight wasn't over, and Votescam was his only move. But he knew that without Ken's great talent, his fine literary mind, his poetry, Votescam would read like an FBI file. He also hoped that writing the book would fuel Ken's fire, lift him out of the pit, keep him alive. And it did.

Ken knew that Jim was right. There had to be a testament, the story of their investigation had to be told. He was no fool, he knew nobody with anything to lose would ever publish it. But he also knew that the power of a book, once unleashed, had a life of it's own. Whether

Votescam would become the catalyst of
revolution and change the course of history,
or fall through the cracks and disappear, was a
matter of destiny. Who reads the book, when,
and why, would inevitably decide its course. It
might sweep through the political world
immediately, like a sudden wild fire. Or it might
lie dormant for years, only to be taken up as a
sword by a new generation of furious,
disenfranchised Americans.

He could not control that game of chance,
he could only get it started. But first, they had
to sort through all of those boxes.

Ken died in 1990, leaving Jim with a 500
page rough draft of a story probably nobody
would ever believe, and without a partner for
the first time in over 40 years.

I was with Jim when he got the news. We
were sitting in a Chinese restaurant on the west
side of New York City. I was 14 years old, I
had never been to New York, and I was wide-
eyed, my nose pressed to the plate glass
window. I turned to Jim and was shocked to
see him sitting quietly and calm, as he usually
did, but with tears rolling down his face. He
never cried.

That was our first day in New York. We had
just pulled into town, after driving cross-country
from California for fifteen days. He had called
Ken to tell him we made it, but Ken was gone.

Votescam was born in a little apartment on the 37th floor of a skyscraper in Manhattan, with a view of the World Trade Center, the Harbor and the Statue of Liberty. Jim and my mother, Phylis, struggled to edit Ken's manuscript, working long hours into the night, writing, arguing, rewriting. In the end, the decision was made to write the whole story, including their personal lives, which Jim understood was a risk considering how radical he and Ken had been during those years. Their presence in the book drove the story forward and added a personal dimension that is not only entertaining, but warranted.

Jim was proud of the book. He and Phylis created Victoria House Press to publish it, and watched triumphantly as it was accepted into the major chain bookstores, all the newspaper and magazine stands in New York City, and Trovers bookstore in Washington D.C. where, along with Barnes and Noble in NYC's East Village, it was given a window display. Then, when word reached the higher levels of authority that Votescam was on the stands, Jim and Phylis watched as their book suddenly disappeared—off the shelf, out of the window. Gone.

Well, Jim hadn't come this far for nothing. Victoria House Press continued to make Votescam available, and America's alternative media advertised it. In that way, the word spread. For six years Jim manned the talk radio lines and navigated speaking tours across the country, sometimes meeting in the homes of working-class activists who had gathered in the traditional "grange" fashion to discuss what to do about their besieged democracy.

Votescam's readers have been for the most part educated, hard-working, blue and white-collar, patriotic Americans—angry members of a dwindling class of people who still believe in the Constitution, salute the flag, and haven't forgotten that eternal vigilance is the price of liberty. But working is the price of living, and they don't have much time left to start a revolution. They looked to Jim for that.

Jim decided to start the revolution where the story began. In 1998 he moved back to Miami, the home of his nemesis Janet Reno who had him arrested all those years before. Much to the excitement of local activists, he had resurrected the well-known newspaper the Miami News and planned to use it as a weapon against infamous Miami corruption. It's likely that this kind of bold attack right in the belly of the beast would have gotten him into more danger than he had been in yet. His two front page stories were devastating political timebombs, with a wealth of insider information.

But the newspaper never hit the stands. Jim fell suddenly ill, days before going to print. Unable to eat, rushed to the hospital, he was operated on and diagnosed with advanced, incurable, pancreatic cancer.

Jim was a blackbelt and a master chess player, he never backed down from a challenge. But this particular opponent was fast and furious, took all the low shots, and was always one move ahead. Jim couldn't beat it. After five months, he bowed out of the ring, and went to meet up again with Ken. And, as they said in Votescam, that was that.

Or so I thought.

Suddenly our phone was ringing, and continued to ring as the news of his death spread. I didn't know it, but to many people, Jim was more than just a knowledgeable investigator. He was a hero.

I hadn't expected to find myself comforting strangers over the telephone. I knew how difficult the years of investigation had been, and the vilification he had faced every step of the way, but I didn't know my father had been so respected for his work, how deeply he had impressed so many by endangering himself to expose the truth. It was never anything extraordinary for him. Like all dedicated activists, his sense of justice came naturally, he defended it without hesitation.

I was touched, and moved deeply by the phone calls. I had been mourning Jim as my father for so long, I had forgotten his other role in the world. In fact, I had been caring for Jim for all those months and I had forgotten the world altogether. But the world was about to make a come-back.

Two months after he died, our phone began to ring again, this time with anxious, ecstatic citizens searching for Jim, asking if he had seen the ABC Web-site. Apparently ABC had posted the results of the off-year election on their Homepage— the day before the election.

It was like that wild-fire Ken had dreamed of. The people were furious. Was the work of a whistle-blower? Talk-show telephones were ringing, the Internet was besieged with demands for an explanation. Finally, Sam Donaldson announced he would be presiding over a live chat that evening to discuss what ABC was already calling a definite mistake.

I was in the chat room that night as Donaldson explained that the page of posted results was a sample page, just to see how the vote results would look on their Website the next day. Got that?

The people were incredulous, and I immediately began inserting information about Votescam, but my comments were soon censored. I couldn't get one word on that screen. In short order, Donaldson directed the conversation neatly away from the matter at hand and onto the election in general.

Citizens who kept track of ABC's "test" results and compared them with the next day's "real" results, reported that ABC had called each race perfectly, over 90% of the time. Some of the numbers, of course, they had changed, for appearances.

And that was that.

Jim and Ken were not the first to discover an important fact, namely that Democracy in America works fine, as long as you don't challenge the status quo. American citizens are free to vote in an election, as long as they don't demand to know how their vote is counted, or whether it serves as anything beside demographics for the people who are already in power.

My father and uncle joined the long list of Americans who have encountered, in various forms, the entrenched nature of our power structure. The System, as we call it. This System is more than willing to persecute its own citizens if necessary, to kill them when there is no other choice, or when it simply needs to get the message across clearly: The People are not in control.

But let's be honest with ourselves, it has always been this way! Things aren't really getting worse, Democracy is not dead by any means. *It has simply never existed in this country.* The only thing that has existed is our right to demand it, to fight for it, to die for it, to protect the ideal. That we believe it is a guarantee is already our biggest mistake. We are raising a whole new generation of Americans who believe a lie. Will they know how to stand up for the truth when the time comes?

More than ever before, we are in the position to fulfill the real American dream—

not the consumer nightmare that we're being sold now, but the dream of a rich and free country of healthy and educated people living in peace, with each other and the land. People who elect their leaders thoughtfully, and remove them promptly when they fail them.

Simple? Yes. Impossible? Right now. But we can change that. First we need to be educated, then we need to continue asking questions and demanding answers. We absolutely cannot be afraid to expose the truth.

NEWS

REPUBLICAN NATIONAL COMMITTEE

Richard Richards
Chairman

RNC 82-100
FOR IMMEDIATE RELEASE CONTACT: JENNIFER
HILLINGS
OCTOBER 20, 1982   (202) 484-6550

RNC ANNOUNCES $5,000 REWARD PROGRAM TO
DETER VOTING FRAUD VIOLATIONS

Washington, D.C. — Republican National
Committee Chairman Richard Richards today
announced a program offering $5,000 rewards to
individuals who give information which leads to
the arrest, convictionand punishment of any
election official who violates state or federal laws
against voting fraud. "It has saddened us to learn
that vote fraud still exists in certain areas of this
country," Richards said in a letter to all 50
secretaries of state. "Since the right to vote is the
keystone of all other rights we cherish as

Americans, any dilution of the vote by fraud or error must be stopped."

Attached please find a copy of the letter.

Dwight D Eisenhower Republican Center: 310 First Street Southeast, Washington, D.C. 20003 (202) 484-6550

REPUBLICAN NATIONAL COMMITTEE

REWARD OFFER DRAFT

October 15, 1982

Dear Secretary of State:

As we approach this important general election, we wish to recognize the excellent work of the hundreds of thousands of American Citizens who will serve their fellow citizens as election officials. We recognize they must serve long hours, often for nominal pay, and often in cramped work places. In the vast majority of cases, American election workers do a fine job of quickly and accurately obtaining the vote and reporting the totals to their fellow citizens. However, it has saddened us in the last few years to learn that vote fraud still exists in certain areas of this country. Fraud serves to undermine the most precious right of Americans — the right to vote. Since the right to vote is the keystone of all other rights we cherish as Americans, any dilution of the vote by fraud or error must be stopped. We know that your office will make every effort to see that every lawful vote is counted accurately, and that violations of the law are quickly stopped and offenses are prosecuted.

In order to help in such efforts, the Republican National Committee has decided to post a reward of $5,000 to any citizen who gives information that leads to the arrest, conviction and punishment of any election official who violates state or federal laws against vote fraud. We have established telephone numbers that will be manned by attorneys who will assist in putting them in touch with the proper State and Federal officials who will proceed with such complaint.

We ask you to cooperate with us by informing us of a contact person in your state that might be used in the event such an occurrence happens in your state. Please contact Mark Braden or Catherine Gensior at 202/484-6638

Very truly yours,

Richard Richards

RR: jd
cc: State Chairman
CLA Members

United State Court of Appeals

FOR THE DISTRICT OF COLUMBIA CIRCUIT

_____

No. 84-5884   September Term, 1985

Kenneth F. Collier,   C.A. No. 84-03570
James M. Collier
Appellant

vs.

United States of America, et al.

BEFORE: Wright, Ginsburg and Scalia, Circuit
Judges

O R DE R

Upon consideration of appellees' Motion for
Summary Affirmance and the opposition thereto.
It is

ORDERED by the court that the motion is denied.
The district court's peremptory dismissal of this
case on the same day the complaint was accepted
for filing issued prior to this court's decision in
Sills v. Bureau of Prisons, 761 F. 2d 792 (D.C.

Cir.1985) Summary affirmance of the dismissal, as Sills clarifies, received the "fullest consideration necessary to a just determination." 781 F.2 at 794. It is FURTHER ORDERED by the court that the district court's dismissal is reversed and the case is remanded to that court for further proceedings consistent with this court's opinion in Sills. It is FURTHER ORDERED that the requests to treat the parties'submissions on the Motion for Summary Affirmance as briefs on appeal are dismissed as moot.

The Clerk is directed to withhold issuance of the mandate herein until seven days after disposition of any timely petition for rehearing. See Local Rule 14.

PETITION TO THE SUPREME COURT OF THE UNITED STATES

<u>WHY THE WRIT SHOULD BE GRANTED</u>
CONDENSED: Where Petitioners have been victimized by a jurist who obtained jurisdiction <u>sua sponte</u> to rule in a case wherein a long-term colleague is a material witness due process demands that such a ruling should be vacated.

Your Petitioners recognize the extreme seriousness of actually accusing a judge of the Superior Court of the District of Columbia of willful and deliberate political case-fixing, but when the following facts are considered, no other conclusion can be drawn. A lengthy investigation of Judge HENRY F. GREENE'S behavior in this matter was conducted by his peers and superiors on that Court, including three Chief Judges thereon whose cooperation with Your Petitioners was voluntarily granted in the wake of the several facially-anomalous actions committed by Judge GREENE in his so-far successful derailing of a "non-frivolous" $20 million damage suit against the Republican National Committee. "Non-frivolous" in that <u>two</u> judges on that Court have <u>denied</u> summary judgment to the RNC's attorneys on identical pleadings, (plus one lengthy hearing), in the litigation proceeding the events described below. "Non frivolous" in that several Court-ordered depositions were granted to Your Petitioners in their preparation for the jury trial which RNC attorneys sought to avoid at any cost.

1. The first "facially-anomalous" action committed by Judge GREENE was the manner in which he used self-help to obtain pre-trial jurisdiction of the case. The Chief Judge's investigation confirms that Judge GREENE personally picked up the telephone and called the pre-trial assignment office just a few minutes before Your Petitioners (acting pro se) were scheduled for a long-awaited and hard-won pretrial conference. With this phone call Judge GREENE ordered the assignment clerk to send the "next available" case to his chambers. Significantly, Judge GREENE was not the official pretrial judge, but was conducting a trial in another division, which he recessed to enable him to reach out for this case. In light of what ensued, Your Petitioners took the extraordinary step of bringing suit against Judge GREENE and the RNC attorney who worked hand-in-glove with him to run two "non-frivolous" (as above) pro se litigants out of Court. The following are three key sentences from the Complaint of that suit...

THAT this is an action sounded in tortious conduct amounting to civil conspiracy in which the defendants had a meeting of the minds and cooperated together for the same object which they mutually sought to be accomplished, namely the unlawful misuse of Henry Greene's employment as a Superior Court judge to deny Plaintiffs due process in a United States court in the District of Columbia, (<u>Superior Court Case 10935084)</u> both <u>on</u> and <u>off</u> the bench.

THAT in furtherance of said civil conspiracy, Defendants committed unlawful acts to calculatedly and deliberately and knowingly defraud Plaintiffs from being treated in Superior Court in an impartial, non-prejudicial manner as related to being assigned a judge for a <u>pre-trial conference</u>, and conspirator GREENE misused his position of implied authority to deliberately telephone the Civil Assignment office at the precise hour (1/6/85) when Plaintiffs' $20 million lawsuit was <u>already assigned to be heard by Judge W. Thompson, (a duly-appointed judge of the PRE-TRIAL DIVISION)</u> but which phone call "suddenly" WRONGFULLY caused motions clerk SANFORD COLEMAN to <u>switch</u> Plaintiffs from the proper and normal routine assignment of a judge in the <u>pre-trial division</u> to HENRY GREENE, <u>a trial judge in Civil II</u>

THAT in deliberately reaching out from his busy schedule as a trial judge to <u>snare a highly political and controversial multi-million dollar suit to place under his EAGER jurisdiction,</u> GREENE conspired with CARR as judge-and-attorney for the Republican National Committee (Defendant in the suit) to silence and ignore Plaintiffs vigorous objections that GREENE had no right whatsoever to overturn a <u>previous ruling denying defendants a summary judgment, acting without permission or due process to "hear" a motion for reconsideration which had been framed solely for reconsidertion by the judge who had denied the original motion,</u> but instead conspired with CARR to reopen the entire case, to fabricate "Supreme Court" opinions on the record, and to dismiss the case out of hand. Certainly, your Petitioners objected to the jurisdiction of Judge GREENE and did so during the off-the-record meeting in his chambers during which Judge GREENE revealed that he had been a colleague for 13 years in the Justice Department with the key (adverse) material witness listed on the plaintiffs' pretrial form. Then, when the RNC attorney asked Judge GREENE to "reconsider" the <u>denial</u> of summary judgment rendered by a co-equal Superior Court Judge just three weeks earlier, Petitioners objected once again, but were silenced on threat of arrest and told to "be" at a hearing three days hence at which time the entire case would be re-argued in <u>de novo</u> proceedings. Thus, using coercion in the form of guaranteed dismissal if Your Petitioners failed to appear at the hastily arranged hearing, Judge GREENE set the stage for his granting a summary judgment, thus obviating the necessity for his former colleague/friend (above) to testify in a highly public jury trial featuring the videotaped votefraud evidence which that former colleague/friend had refused to screen when it had been presented to him at the Justice Department in connection with the REWARD OFFER.

At the fatal hearing itself, which was purported to be a "motion to reconsider" on the part of the RNC, no testimony was taken, no evidence whatsover was introduced by the RNC, nothing to justify holding such a motion hearing on the dispositive issues of the case.

The only purpose in holding a <u>de novo</u> hearing at that stage of the litigation was to provide a courtroom context for Judge GREENE to suddenly "reverse" the law of the case as previously determined by two previous Superior Court judges. The record shows that Your Petitioners objected to being forced to participate in the hearing. With the Court's indulgence, your Petitioners extract a portion of that hearing below:

MR. COLLIER: Judge Nunzio did, in fact, sit and hear lengthy argument on both sides, oral argument, and when it was over, he stated that he would throw out the punitive damages and he would allow us to continue to press our claim in court so that we could have a jury determine what is reasonable or not reasonable for the public to assume when they read a reward offer put out by the party in power.

THE COURT: Well, Mr. Collier, let me just say I resolved that issue when I resolved to hear the motion for reconsideration. I told you and Mr. Carr in chambers that it seemed to me appropriate for Judge Nunzio to hear the motion for reconsideration, and that's the way it usually works, but I also told you that Judge Nunzio was in a situation where he was in a different assignment now and, indeed he has retired, but the effective date isn't clear, and I wasn't sure how the civil division of this court and the administrators of that division would want to handle this matter. I called the assignment commissioner — they asked me to handle it, and I indicated to counsel that I would. So, for purposes of this motion to reconsider I am, in essence, sitting as Judge Nunzio and reconsidering what he did in that case. So, the fact — *stare decisis* does not apply to reconsideration of this matter.

Now, if Judge Nunzio articulated some things in his denial of the motion for summary judgment that you think are relevant, I would certainly like to be informed about those things, because I was not there. So, if he articulated some reason as to why he thought there were material factual issues that remained in dispute in this case, and what those issues are, please address those.

MR. COLLIER: Judge Nunzio, by his very decision, stated to us — looked right in my eye and said. "It's not all over. You can still pursue it," or words to that effect. He had come to his decision —

THE COURT: But did he say what factual issues, what material factual issues he viewed as remaining in dispute in this case?

This type of colloquy continued throughout a five hour hearing, during which time the issues under examination were boiled down to what Judge GREENE referred to as "the crux of the matter." To wit:

THE COURT: Now tell me what's the evidence?

MR. COLLIER: I submit that the statements made by Richard Richards in his deposition are exactly what Your Honor is referring to, and that where the complaint in this case states that the — that the Defendants had no authority to make this promise, during our participation.

THE COURT: Okay. Well, I guess that gets to the crux of the matter.

MR. COLLIER: He agreed he had no authority to make the promise, and he signed the letter.

THE COURT: I think that — okay. I think that gets to the crux of this matter, Mr. Collier. It is my view, as a matter of law, that no reasonable person could interpret the language "Who will proceed with such complaint" following "federal officials" as anything other than predictive, that no reasonable person could construe that language as a guarantee by the Republican National Committee as to what federal officials would do and —and I guess that really is the crux of the matter.

MR. COLLIER: May I address myself to that?

THE COURT: And I say that as a — as a predicate to my restating the same question. Now, if — if we view that language as a guarantee, as you tend to view it and think it should be viewed, then I grant you that under the language of Bennett versus Kiggins, one could conclude that at least the reward offer and that portion of the reward offer which constitutes an alleged promise was made by the promiser with knowledge that the events would not occur. As you've indicated, Mr. Richards indicated in his deposition that nobody ever intended to guarantee what federal officials would do, but, it seems to me that the word — and I — I — I — in preparation for this, I was looking in a dictionary of English usage last night, and the word "will" of course, used as a verb, has several connotations. Sometimes it has connotations that amount to a guarantee but, in other contexts, it has only a predictive

connotation, that is, that it will rain today. If I tell you it will rain tonight or it will snow tonight, the word "will" is being used with a predictive connotation, because there's no way that I can guarantee that it will rain or that it will snow tonight.

Your Petitioners were appalled that Judge GREENE was so obviously contemptuous of us as <u>pro se</u> litigants that he would simply and cavalierly refer to his home dictionary as being the sole source from which he drew the conclusion "as a matter of law" that the word "will" under dispute had no guarantory meaning. Significantly, Judge GREENE conceded that here are "several" ways of interpreting that word, thereby conceding that the language was clearly facially ambiguous.

Your Petitioners were cognizant of the background of Judge GREENE related in his prior 13 year employment as an attorney in the Justice Department, due to Judge GREENE's remarks in chambers (as above) and further recognized that if we were to later claim bias and prejudice on the part of the trial judge we would have to confront him on the record and ask for his recusal due to his past lengthy association with the above-mentioned "material witness" whose

tenure at the DOJ mirrored Judge GREENE's.
The following comprised his reply:

**THE COURT: Your request is denied, Mr.
Collier, and you may have a seat.**

MR. COLLIER: All right.

**THE COURT: Your request for recusal is
denied.**

CONCLUSION

When the District of Columbia Court of Appeals affirmed the Court's summary judgment, it provided in its rationale the very reason (and legal citation) why the decision of Judge GREENE should be reversed. As the below-quoted paragraph from the D.C.C.A. shows, a "<u>facially ambiguous</u>" phrase should <u>not</u> be interpreted by the Court "as a matter of law." The REWARD OFFER agreement itself placed an obligation on the RNC to "<u>put Claimants in touch with the proper state and federal officials who will proceed with such complaint.</u>" The evidence in this case shows that Your Petitioners relied on that phrase when they embarked upon their videotaping mission. <u>(COLLIER Affidavit, PARA: 1-12)</u> That phrase (the inducement clause) should be interpreted by a jury to determine whether or not a "reasonable person" would have relied upon it as a "promise."

DISTRICT OF COLUMBIA
COURT OF APPEALS

We turn first to a key argument of appellants on appeal, that the trial court erred in its interpretation of the reward offer as affording no guaranty to those responding to the offer that enforcement action would in fact be taken by state and federal officials to whom possible voter fraud information was provided.

An interpretation of an integrated agreement in a document is facially ambiguous. <u>1010 Potomac Assoc. v. Grocery Manufacturers of America, Inc.</u> 485 A, 2d 199, 205 (D.C. 1984).

Clearly, Your Petitioners have earned the right to a jury trial to resolve the issues in dispute in this lawsuit, and therefore pray for reversal of the lower Court's arbitrary, capricious and prejudicial extinguishment of our claim.

RESPECTFULLY SUBMITTED.
DATED 23 June 1987
KENNETH COLLIER
JAMES COLLIER

Ed. NOTE: THE COURT DECLINED TO REVIEW THE CASE AND NO WRIT OF CERT. WAS ISSUED.

INDEX

ACKNOWLEDGEMENTS

Lynette Yount offered us refuge in the Washington winter of our discontent; Chuck Gross is the fourth brother and business partner who made sure we survived the rigors of the road; Larry Pizzi taught us that a slave can crumble a mountain with a pickaxe; Phyllis Vernick, already our friend, agreed to become our editor. This book started out as an elephant. If it now flies it is because of her vision.

The U.S. Constitution specifies that only the United States Senate may count the vote for President of the United States. Why the Senate gave up that power, and to whom they gave it will be the subject of our next book.